Romantic vs. Screwball Comedy

STUDIES IN FILM GENRES
edited by
ANTHONY SLIDE

1. *Romantic vs. Screwball Comedy: Charting the Difference*, by Wes D. Gehring, 2002

Romantic vs. Screwball Comedy

Charting the Difference

Wes D. Gehring

Studies in Film Genres

The Scarecrow Press, Inc.
Lanham, Maryland • Toronto • Plymouth, UK
2008

SCARECROW PRESS, INC.

Published in the United States of America
by Scarecrow Press, Inc.
A wholly owned subsidiary of
The Rowman & Littlefield Publishing Group, Inc.
4501 Forbes Boulevard, Suite 200, Lanham, Maryland 20706
www.scarecrowpress.com

Estover Road
Plymouth PL6 7PY
United Kingdom

British Cataloging in Publication Information Available

Library of Congress Cataloging-in-Publication Data

Gehring, Wes D.
Romantic vs. screwball comedy : charting the difference / Wes D. Gehring.
p. cm. — (Studies in film genres)
Includes bibliographical references and index.
ISBN-10: 0-8108-4424-9 (alk. paper)
ISBN-13: 978-0-8108-4424-7 (alk. paper)
1. Screwball comedy films—United States—History and criticism. 2. Comedy films—United States—History and criticism. 3. Love in motion pictures. I. Title: Romantic versus screwball comedy. II. Title. III. Series.

PN1995.9.C55 G428 2002
791.43'617—dc21

2002006524

™ The paper used in this publication meets the minimum requirements of American National Standard for Information Sciences—Permanence of Paper for Printed Library Materials, ANSI/NISO Z39.48-1992.
Manufactured in the United States of America.

To Sarah & Emily
(with Em being the catalyst)

BRINGING UP BABY

or

Save That Professor

Hepburn awakened Grant from
A prehistoric past to the
Present tense . . . present and tense.

Her love was a question of
Mind over matter; she didn't
"Mind" and he didn't matter.

But in a dark Connecticut
Forest they both lose their
Way and find each other.

Sometimes the middle of
Nowhere can lead to the
Most beautiful of places.

—*Wes Gehring*

CONTENTS

Illustrations ix
Foreword by *Steve Bell* xiii
Preface xv

CHAPTER ONE Introduction 1

CHAPTER TWO Screwball Comedy 29

CHAPTER THREE Romantic Comedy 67

CHAPTER FOUR Cary Grant and Katharine Hepburn 97

CHAPTER FIVE Screwball and Romantic Comedy in the Modern Era: Since 1960 145

CHAPTER SIX Epilogue 185

Selected Filmography 191
Selected Annotated Bibliography 209
Index 215
About the Author 222

ILLUSTRATIONS

Frontispiece:
While *It Happened One Night* (1934, with Clark Gable and Claudette Colbert) is often credited with being the start of screwball comedy, it plays more as a romantic comedy. xii

1. Comedy Combatants Carole Lombard and John Barrymore in *Twentieth Century* (1934). 7
2. That key *Thin Man* (1934) couple, William Powell and Myrna Loy. 13
3. The "Forgotten Man" and title character (William Powell) of *My Man Godfrey* (1936), with Carole Lombard and Franklin Pangborn (center). 16
4. *Topper* (1937), with Cary Grant (center), Constance Bennett, and Roland Young, gave the screwball world a new catalyst for comedy. 17
5. Claudette Colbert's long-legged girl in *The Palm Beach Story* (1942, with Joel McCrea). 37
6. A *Thin Man*–like scenario goes screwball in *The Ex-Mrs. Bradford* (1936, with William Powell and Jean Arthur). 51
7. The hat routine from *The Awful Truth*, with Cary Grant, Irene Dunne, and screwball comedy's favorite pooch—Mr. Smith (Asta). 55

8. Leo McCarey (left) on the set of *The Awful Truth* with Irene Dunne and Alex D'Arcy. 58

9. Rooftop romance in *Hands across the Table* (1935, with Carole Lombard and Fred MacMurray). 70

10. A pivotal romantic comedy *Love Affair* (1939, with Irene Dunne and Charles Boyer). 77

11. A calmer moment in *Adam's Rib* (1949, with Spencer Tracy and Katharine Hepburn). 81

12. Clark Gable and Claudette Colbert on the verge of the hitchhiking scene in *It Happened One Night.* 82

13. A stressful moment from *The Shop around the Corner* (1940, with Margaret Sullavan and pen pal Jimmy Stewart). 90

14. Thawing the ice goddess (Katharine Hepburn) of *The Philadelphia Story* (1940), with Cary Grant (left) and Jimmy Stewart. 99

15. Leo McCarey (right), a student of all kinds of comedy, is pictured on the set of his *Ruggles of Red Gap* (1935), with actor Charles Laughton (left) and crackerbarrel humorist Irvin S. Cobb (center). 102

16. George Cukor (left) on the set of *Holiday* (1938), with (from right to left) Cary Grant, Doris Nolan, Henry Kolker, Lew Ayres, and Katharine Hepburn. 106

17. Cary Grant and screwball comedy's most underrated actress (Irene Dunne) in *The Awful Truth* (1937). 109

18. Romantic comedy thrives on differences, as demonstrated by this scene from *The Bachelor and the Bobby-Soxer* (1947, with Cary Grant and Myrna Loy playing bookends to Shirley Temple). 113

19. Screwball comedy's toy factor in *Holiday*, with Cary Grant and Katharine Hepburn. 122

20. Netting her man, Katharine Hepburn's gift for physical comedy is showcased in this scene from *Bringing Up Baby* (1938, with Cary Grant). 125

21. Spencer Tracy and Katharine Hepburn can only avoid romance so long in *Without Love* (1945). 131

22. The most unlikely of romantic comedy couples—Katharine Hepburn and Humphrey Bogart in *The African Queen* (1951). 136

23. Barbara Stanwyck gets comic revenge by convincing poor Henry Fonda she has had an army of lovers in *The Lady Eve* (1941). 149

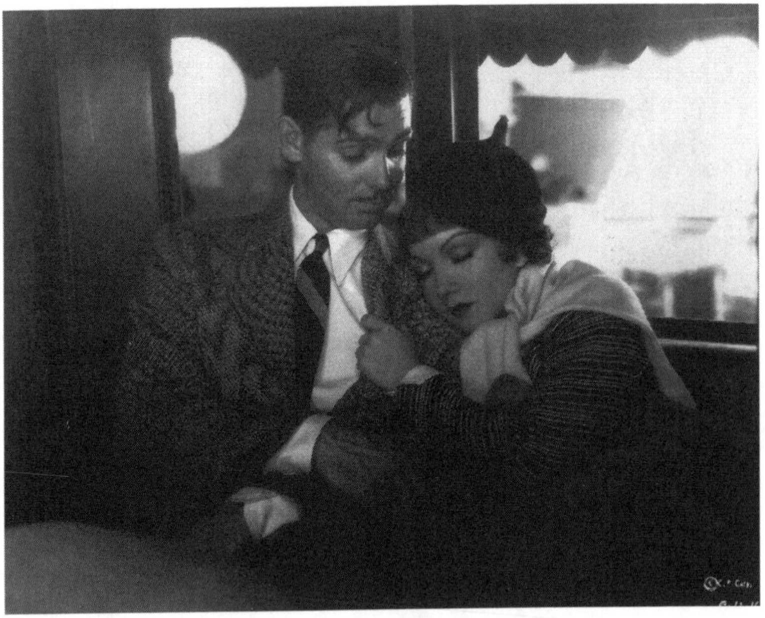

While It Happened One Night *(1934, with Clark Gable and Claudette Colbert) is often credited with being the start of screwball comedy, it plays more as a romantic comedy*

FOREWORD

I intended to be with you on our honeymoon, Hildy, honest I did.

—Cary Grant to Rosalind Russell
in *His Girl Friday* (1940)

Wes Gehring is a prolific writer. His product is a learned, informative, and delightful series of books on American film comedy. For this admirer, the essence of a Wes Gehring book is "context." Comedic performers like Cary Grant, Irene Dunne, and a host of other comedy leads were a part of my cultural milieu while growing up in the same rural Iowa where Wes spent his formative years. Yet, until reading his books, I had no idea how intertwined comedy has been with cultural, political, and economic history.

This book, with its insightful focus on the basic differences of screwball and romantic comedy, continues the tradition. But I must confess I was not prepared for the intellectual leap. Screwball and romantic comedy a vehicle for social commentary? The thought would never have crossed my mind.

Yet, here it is, all set out for us in a style and format worthy of scholars and accessible to those of us for whom film comedy is more entertainment, even escape, than a vehicle for serious study. Much about comedy may be in the eye of the beholder. But this study helps us to put the perceptions of the beholder in context.

As Wes points out, screwball comedy in particular was a hot topic of its day, often accused of having "gone too far" with its antics.

Yet the public responded. And once you have read this illuminating volume the door is open to a new level of illumination.

In the years of the Great Depression, the world itself seemed zany, and its inhabitants seemed impotent to do anything about it. Thus, the wacky antihero stepped centerstage, providing both a metaphor and a solace for audiences whose daily lives were almost too much to bear. And, more often than not, this antihero was the male of the species, who in real life was too often unable in those years to "bring home the bread."

But this is not a book about sociology, political science, or economics. It is a book about film genres, specifically the differences between basic screwball and romantic comedy. It is a book that reflects the devotion of the author to the art form and its subtleties. As a former journalist who has spent a lifetime observing the human condition, I find myself always being drawn into Wes's comedic research and the genres under consideration.

In his dedication to the study of what the unsuspecting might consider trivial, he opens our minds and makes us all a little wiser, and hopefully more perceptive, about the role of popular culture in the life of a nation like ours.

That is no small contribution. Not when you consider the dominant role of popular culture in today's world, a world with its own unique set of challenges.

Steve Bell
Ball State University and
former anchor of *Good Morning America*

PREFACE

Stand still, Godfrey. It'll all be over in a minute.

—Carole Lombard to William Powell
as their wedding ceremony begins in
My Man Godfrey (1936)

Always fascinated by American film comedy, I especially zeroed in on the screwball variety in graduate school. From a dissertation that celebrated one of its architects (Leo McCarey) to a 1986 text on the genre, screwball comedy has and remains an ongoing fascination. The book in hand, however, attempts to address a longtime weakness in defining this comedy type—the propensity of film fans and scholars alike to lump everything with laughter and love under a "screwball comedy" umbrella, while also making that phrase interchangeable with "romantic comedy."

The following pages demonstrate how screwball and romantic comedy are two distinct genres. The first chapter is a short historical overview setting the period perimeters for the book (1930s to the present) and highlighting pivotal social and artistic changes that impacted the genres. These changes range from the effect of the Depression to a major development in American humor: the rise of the comic antihero. These elements and more created both the farcical screwball world and the somewhat more reality-based romantic comedy.

The second chapter examines a watershed collection of screwball comedy films to chart the genre's basic components. Chapter 3 studies a comparable inventory of romantic comedies to better sketch this genre's fundamental configuration, as well as contrasting it with the screwball standard.

Chapter 4 traces the two genres through the seminal careers of Cary Grant and Katharine Hepburn—both of whom helped define and redefine screwball and romantic comedy. The fifth chapter examines the two genres since 1960—the beginning of cinema's modern era. The closing epilogue is a brief summing up, as well as a reiteration of the need for a dual-focus text to better understand both *screwball* and *romantic* comedy. The appendix material includes an annotated bibliography and a two-part filmography.

This study was immeasurably enriched by several important research archives. The most pivotal involved the New York Public Library System, especially the Billy Rose Theatre Collection at Lincoln Center, as well as the main branch at Fifth Avenue and Forty-second Street. I was also greatly assisted by the archives at both the Margaret Herrick Library of the Academy of Motion Picture Arts and Sciences and the Doeheny Library at the University of Southern California. Closer to home, Ball State University's Bracken Library (Muncie, Indiana) was a great aid. Having written sixteen film comedy texts prior to this one, I was also able to draw from a large private collection of movie research material and stills.

The preparation of the book was greatly facilitated by several professional colleagues. My department chairman, "Dr. Joe" Misiewicz, assisted with securing both release time for me and financial aid. I appreciate the ongoing support of Ball State University Provost Warren C. Vander Hill, as well as Scott R. Olson, BSU Dean of the College of Communication, Information, and Media. Janet Warrner, my local copyeditor, was forever available and insightful. The computer preparation of the manuscript merits a thank you to Jean Thurman. Friend and teaching colleague Conrad Lane was invaluable for both brainstorming sessions and manuscript proofing.

For me, as for most people, appreciation ultimately comes down to the love and support of family. Thus, I am blessed to have an ongoing rooting section including parents and children. Plus, Emily was full of pivotal romantic and screwball comedy suggestions, having pushed for this project long before I had a contract. Thank you one and all.

CHAPTER ONE
INTRODUCTION

New American romantic film comedy and screwball comedy are sister genres of comic courtship, both born of the mid-1930s Depression. Unfortunately, critics and historians have frequently used the phrases "screwball comedy" and "romantic comedy" interchangeably through the years. To clear up the confusion, this dual-focus text will examine both varieties.

There are five key differences between these two comedy genres. First, the screwball variety places its emphasis on "funny," while the more traditional romantic comedy accents "love." Put another way, the screwball genre represents America's distinctive take on farce—accenting broad physical comedy and ludicrous events. A prime example would be the inspired misadventures of Cary Grant and Katharine Hepburn in *Bringing Up Baby* (1938) as they scour the Connecticut countryside for a misplaced brontosaurus bone and a tame leopard. It was not unusual for some period critics to even pronounce the nuttiness of the genre as having gone too far in movies now considered screwball classics. For instance, Eileen Creelman's *New York Sun* review of Preston Sturges's *Palm Beach Story* (1942) declared the "proceedings became too daffy even for farce."[1]

In contrast, romantic comedy is more reality-based, with little or no slapstick. An unforgettable example would be the Budapest bittersweet relationship between coworkers Jimmy Stewart and Margaret Sullavan in Ernst Lubitsch's *The Shop around the Corner* (1940), which served as the basis for the later *You've Got Mail* (1998).

Neither Stewart nor Sullavan initially realizes they are lonely hearts pen pals. The charm lies in the fact that this could be anyone anywhere. The *Brooklyn Daily Eagle* credited Lubitsch's film with having "full-blown people" for characters, while the *New York Herald Tribune* called the story a "realistically human narrative of the everyday events . . . in everyday lives."[2]

What about romantic comedy's occasional tendency to go "Cinderella" on the viewer, as with the close of *Pretty Woman* (1990), where a Fortune 500 type (Richard Gere) ultimately falls in love with Julia Roberts's Hollywood Boulevard hooker? The answer lies in a story that attempts to keep at least one foot in reality until that point. But had this been a screwball comedy, the ludicrous quotient would have been markedly higher from film frame one. For instance, when someone likens the *My Man Godfrey* (1936) scavenger hunt gathering to an asylum, the rich but ineffective father (Eugene Pallette) agrees: "All you need is an empty room and the right kind of people."

Second, and consistent with farce's anything goes atmosphere, screwball comedy spoofs the romantic process; love comes across as hardly more significant than a board game. The dominating screwball heroine is often assisted by the fact that only she knows a courtship is occurring; witness the kooky persistence of Barbra Streisand in *What's Up, Doc?* (1972), a loose remake of *Bringing Up Baby*. More often than not, the screwball comedy male must suffer through a ritualistic humiliation at the hands of the zany heroine and/or the plot itself. Love often seems displaced in favor of dark comedy. Conversely, romantic comedy tends to forever keep love front and center. Indeed, the romantic genre frequently embraces sentimental and/or melodramatic story developments completely alien to screwball comedy. An example is the tearful plot twist of *Love Affair* (1939) and its two remakes—*An Affair to Remember* (1957) and *Love Affair* (1994). In all three versions crippling injuries from an accident almost sabotage romance. Thus, while pain and suffering (emotional and/or physical) are a real threat in romantic comedy, both components are either conspicuously lacking in the screwball landscape or not to be taken seriously. Coupled with screwball's *Nothing Sacred* (1937) attitude, to recycle a celebrated title from this type, one might say the genre only gets serious about satire.

A third way in which screwball and romantic comedy differ is in basic character development. Most obviously, the former genre is dripping with eccentrics, starting with the archetype zany heroine, Carole Lombard in *My Man Godfrey,* and the aforementioned complementary crazy supporting cast. Romantic comedy often showcases a decidedly less controlling, more serious heroine, such as Greta Garbo's "comrade" in *Ninotchka* (1939), or an Audrey Hepburn who flirts with suicide at the start of *Sabrina* (1954). Consistent with this, supporting characters in the romantic genre also tend to be more funny than flakey.

A fourth contrast between the two genres involves the dating ritual itself. In the screwball category, the eccentric heroine frequently finds herself in a triangle with the sought-after male and his life-smothering fiancée. This includes such central examples as *Bringing Up Baby* (1938) and *Arthur* (1981). The heroine's mission is to free the male from a rigid woman. This is not to say romantic comedy cannot have a third party, but conflict for this genre is more apt to occur over character differences, rather than over another character. Coupled with this is romantic comedy's tendency to have a more traditional interaction of the sexes—the male often takes an active part in making the final happy ending work. For instance, at the close of the original *Love Affair*, it is Charles Boyer who searches out Irene Dunne when it becomes clear her injury-related concerns (she does not want pity) will not allow her to make the first move.

A final difference between the two genres is in plot pacing. Screwball comedy escalates near the close, as the title of one pioneering example of the title suggests: *Theodora Goes Wild* (1936, with Irene Dunne as Theodora). Contrastingly, romantic comedy slows to a turtle's pace at the close, as the audience agonizes over whether the couple will ultimately get together, such as Tom Hanks drawn out orchestration of love at the end of *You've Got Mail* or Billy Crystal finally reconnecting with Meg Ryan at the conclusion of *When Harry Met Sally . . .* (1989).

These five factors and more will be further examined in succeeding chapters. But in the remaining pages of this chapter a short historical overview presents the basic period perimeters for the book (1930s to the present) and highlights significant social and artistic changes that impacted these two genres.

Depression-Era Developments

The birth of screwball comedy and the revitalization of romantic comedy were predicated upon several developments taking place in early 1930s America. First, the two genres were tied to a period of transition in American humor that had gained great momentum by the late 1920s. The dominant comedy character had been the capable crackerbarrel type of a Will Rogers; it now became an antihero best exemplified by *The New Yorker* writing of Robert Benchley and James Thurber, or by the film short subjects of Leo McCarey's Laurel and Hardy. While both screwball and romantic comedy traded upon this antihero development, the former genre more fully embraced it, á la the ritualistic humiliation of the male. The screwball approach dressed up the surroundings and added beautiful people, but this was more a reflection of the need to mass-market feature films than a substantive difference. The screwball outcome was essentially the same: an eccentrically comic battle of the sexes, with the male generally losing.

There is no easy way to explain why the transition from capable to incompetent comic hero took place. Yet if an explanation were attempted, it would probably focus on an issue of relevance that will be frequently repeated in this chapter—the Depression. In a world that seemed more irrational every day during the early 1930s, the antihero was fated to be forever thwarted. His frustration is the result of his attempt to create order—as did his nineteenth-century counterparts—but now in a world where order is impossible. And the relevance factor has only increased during the passage of time, since the commonsense platitudes of any updated crackerbarrel philosopher are inadequate in today's nonstop crisis world.

A second, long-lasting 1930s factor, with a more obvious period connection, is the proclivity of screwball and sometimes romantic comedy to embrace the Depression-era fascination with the upper classes. Movie audience escapism is hardly limited to any one period. But 1930s viewers were so taken with these la-de-da film backdrops that period Wall Street analysts sometimes called the movies "Depression proof." More to the point, plotlines for these two genres sometimes have couples coming from different classes, such as the watershed film for both genres, director Frank Capra's *It Happened One Night* (1934). In this movie a blue-collar reporter (Clark Gable) and a runaway heiress (Claudette Colbert) battle but eventually fall in love. The beauty of this romance is that it becomes a metaphor for "any kind of reconciliation—between the classes, the genders, the generations; between Depression anxiety and happy-go-lucky optimism."[3] Thus, like much great art, this movie reflects a given period yet defines itself through universals that embrace many ages.

Film theorist and later director Andrew Bergman has termed the mid-1930s attempt of screwball comedy (and for our purposes, romantic comedy) to pull all things together—"implosive."[4] It is an apt expression, for one might define the first years of the Depression as *explosive* in two ways. First, in the early 1930s the extreme political left was actually encouraging class warfare. Second, this volatile period was paralleled in cinema by such anarchistic edgy personality comedians as the Marx Brothers and W. C. Fields. Indeed, the Marx's *Duck Soup* (1933), under the masterful direction of Leo McCarey, showcases both satirically violent politics and dark comedy in an inspired story where Groucho is the leader of a country!

To further briefly pursue this political Depression analogy, the more class conciliatory screwball and romantic comedies came along at a time when President Franklin Delano Roosevelt's new administration was attempting to orchestrate its own version of "implosive" politics in all walks of American life. Not surprisingly, some Marxist period critics ludicrously suggested Hollywood's then new love affair with come-together romantic comedy was the result of a White House directive. (Screwball comedy further softened possible class differences by frequently portraying the idle rich as entertainingly odd.)

A third 1930s development that impacted both genres was Hollywood's implementation of a censorship code. The 1934 enforcement of the Motion Picture Production Code was an outgrowth of public controversy over the period's violent gangster films and the sexual innuendo in the movies of Mae West and others, like Jean Harlow and Norma Shearer. The industry's self-regulation, under heavy pressure from the Catholic Church's powerful Legion of Decency censorship organization, would seem to have stimulated development of both a new romantic comedy and screwball comedy. American censorship has always been more concerned with sexuality than with violence. So it hardly seems a coincidence that a genre (screwball) sometimes defined as "the sex comedy without sex" (equally applicable to a new romantic comedy) should blossom the same year the code appeared. Fittingly, while Hollywood is now decades past any censorship code, explicit sexuality is still not a basic component in either of these genres.

A fourth period factor was the film industry's embracing of sound technology. Whereas silent comedy keyed upon the solo hero status of pantheon personality comedians like Charlie Chaplin, Buster Keaton, and Harold Lloyd, talking pictures were geared toward the verbal interaction of doubled heroes, such as the romantic or screwball couple. Even the early sound personality comedian films had a multiple hero interaction tendency. That is, the 1930s was the heyday of comedy *teams*, from the celebrated Marx Brothers and Laurel and Hardy to the now less well-known period favorites like Wheeler and Woolsey and the Ritz Brothers. Thus, romantic and screwball couples were in good verbal comedy company.

A fifth 1930s development that influenced these two genres is an extension of the manic comedy of teams like the Marx and Ritz

Comedy Combatants Carole Lombard and John Barrymore in Twentieth Century *(1934).*

Brothers. A defining trait of the screwball and new romantic comedy couples was having them act more like broad comedians. They were sophisticates gone silly. A pioneering example of this sexy but clowning duo was the zany slapstick interactions of John Barrymore and Carole Lombard in director Howard Hawks's benchmark screwball comedy *Twentieth Century* (in pivotal 1934). Hawks would later describe this innovation as having the romantic leads "make damn fools of themselves."[5] Armies of critics have since acquiesced on this *attractive stars play slapstick* point. But a case could be made for shifting the credit from Barrymore and Lombard to the *It Happened One Night* duo of Gable and Colbert, whose broad comic playing opened in theatres two months ahead of *Twentieth Century.*

Period critics were not unaware of the parallels between these clowning sophisticates and cinema's personality comedians. For instance, the *Los Angeles Times* review of *Twentieth Century* noted,

"Howard Hawks' direction is admirable, maintaining an element of surprise as it has not been maintained since the last Marx Brothers' nonsense."[6] Hawks is a good example because he created comedy with clowns in mind. For instance, to assist Cary Grant's absent-minded professor characterization in *Bringing Up Baby*, he had the actor play him like a Harold Lloyd innocent. And when Grant goes into a bentover loping walk opposite Rosalind Russell in *His Girl Friday* (1940), one cannot help thinking Hawks had suggested Groucho as a model.

One need not, however, limit case studies of 1930 nuttiness to film comedians. In 1934 America was captivated by the crazy behavior of major league baseball's world champion St. Louis Cardinals, aka the "Gas House Gang." The team's success was largely the result of pitching brothers "Dizzy" and "Daffy" Dean, with Dizzy being the principal source of Cardinal eccentricity. The zany antics of Dizzy were not, moreover, limited to the sports page. On April 15, 1935, he made the cover of *Time* magazine, with the accompanying article noting,

> it was clear that with Shirley Temple, Father Coughlin, the Dionne Quintuplets and Mrs. Roosevelt, Jerome Herman Dean was definitely one of that small company of super-celebrities whose names, faces and occupations are familiar to every literate U.S. citizen and whose antics, gracious or absurd, become the legend of their time.[7]

While there was hardly a preponderance of baseball references in screwball and romantic comedy literature, they occasionally occurred. For example, *Variety*'s review of *My Man Godfrey* (1936) observed:

> Lombard has played screwball dames before, but none so screwy as this one. From start to finish, with no letdowns or lapses into quiet sanity, she needs only a [baseball] rosin bag to be a female Rube Waddell [a Dizzy Dean-type, turn-of-the-century pitcher].[8]

Moreover, the mere "game playing" of screwball comedy stars sometimes even encouraged comparisons with famous baseball players not normally associated with eccentricity. For instance, the *New York Times* saluted John Barrymore's wildly ingenious *Midnight* (1939) performance by calling him "the [Lou] Gehrig of eye-brow batting."[9]

Still, *screwball* comedy probably drew its name from the term's entertainingly unorthodox use in the national pastime. Prior to the term's application in 1930s film criticism, "screwball" had been used in baseball to describe both an oddball player and "any pitched ball that moves in an unusual or unexpected way."[10] Obviously, these characteristics also describe performers in screwball comedy films, from oddball Carole Lombard to the unusual or unexpected movement of Katharine Hepburn in *Bringing Up Baby* (1938). As with the crazy period antics in baseball, screwball comedy uses nutty behavior as a prism through which to view a topsy-turvy period in American history.

A sixth and final Depression-era factor that impacted both romantic and screwball comedy is best examined as a combined development of the previous two highlighted components, which addressed both the coming of sound and the tendency of sophisticated stars to act like clowns. First, moving beyond the doubled hero (or couple) focus encouraged by the sound revolution, talking pictures were also the catalyst for an army of wordsmiths to descend upon Hollywood. Journalists, playwrights, novelists, humorists, and every other kind of writer found at least a temporary California home as the film capital panicked over the sudden importance of words. All this talent helped usher in a golden age of dialogue comedy, both sophisticated and screwball. And sometimes these transplanted writers fed on their journalistic past. Former newspaperman Ben Hecht's script for *Nothing Sacred* included this opinion of reporters: "The hand of God reaching down into the mire couldn't elevate one of 'em to the depths of degradation."

This heyday of witty screenplays was capped off by the early 1940s films of writer/director Preston Sturges. A former Broadway playwright who came West during the Hollywood transition to sound, he parlayed a successful 1930s scriptwriting career into a precedent-setting move to the director's chair. Now able to megaphone his own screenplays, no one wrote more witty dialogue, such as the following observations from his screwball *Palm Beach Story*: "Chivalry is not only dead, it's decomposing" and "Men don't get smarter as they grow older; they just lose their hair."

Romantic comedy lines can be equally inventive, such as the comment to Garbo's hungover title character in *Ninotchka* (courtesy of scripters Charles Brackett, Billy Wilder, and Walter Reisch), "Yes, I know exactly how you feel, my dear. The morning after always does look grim if you happen to be wearing last night's dress." But romantic comedy dialogue can also have the added bewitchment (at least for romantic audiences) of capturing the charmingly ephemeral joy of love. For instance, just prior to passing out, a Ninotchka equally flush with love says:

> Comrades! People of the world! The revolution is on the march! . . . Civilization will crumble. But not yet! Please—wait. What's the hurry? Give us our moment. Let's be happy! We're happy, aren't we, Leon?

Witty and/or poignant dialogue is at the heart of romantic comedy, but screwball's farce component necessitates a balance between funny lines and visual comedy. This is a direct outgrowth of the fact that many 1930s directors received their cinematic start in silent pictures. With regard to the subject at hand, this especially applies to McCarey and Hawks. Indeed, McCarey's lifelong filmmaking motto was "Do it visually." Thus, the sight gag (from a facial expression to a fall) was a natural component in the screwball comedy arsenal.

Though this visual component is fleshed out further in forthcoming chapters, it bears noting that the Laurel and Hardy factor looms large in screwball tradition. A succinct explanation for this is the team's ties to both McCarey and the then groundbreaking antihero revolution. Without going to individual examples at this point, gifted period director George Stevens nicely summarized the duo's impact on the genre:

> The Laurel and Hardy concept moved over into other films considerably, with Cary Grant, Roz Russell, and Irene Dunne doing the

> late take and even the double take. That had comeout of the personalities of Laurel and Hardy, and the people that worked with them.[11]

Stevens is an excellent source here, since he started his film career under McCarey as the cameraman on many of the early Laurel and Hardy short subjects.

All this is not to say that visual shtick is totally absent from romantic comedy. But it is not central to the genre, as is the case with the screwball slant. Moreover, even at its best, romantic comedy slapstick often seems out of place and/or forced. For instance, Grant's funny face shove of Hepburn at the start of *The Philadelphia Story* (1940) creates a slapstick promise the movie never again delivers on. More problematic still is Stevens's own Laurel and Hardy conclusion to his otherwise near perfect romantic comedy *Woman of the Year* (1942). This sophisticated love story, the first teaming of Hepburn and Spencer Tracy, excels at the verbal exchange, such as the memorable scene of Hepburn trying to understand her first baseball game. Consequently, her physical comedy humiliation in the kitchen close to *Woman of the Year* is now uniformly seen as the picture's only false note.

Pivotal Depression Pictures

Besides the six Depression developments examined in this chapter's previous section, screwball and romantic comedy were also impacted by five significant films from the 1930s. The key starting point is Capra's watershed *It Happened One Night*. Long cited, with *Twentieth Century*, as the 1934 starting point of screwball comedy, it might be time to reassess that view. *Twentieth Century* had more of what would now typically be considered screwball tendencies in the years to come, including the escaped meandering of one certified crazy (who bankrolls John Barrymore's play with nonexistent money) and an ongoing comic battle royal between Barrymore and Lombard.

It Happened One Night fits much more comfortably under the five-point romantic comedy umbrella sketched out at the beginning of this chapter, especially with regard to an accent on reality and love over pure eccentricity. (Please see chapter 3 for additional reasons why the romantic camp is a more logical choice for *It Happened One Night.*) This text will not take the blasphemous path of pulling the film from the screwball pantheon because its phenomenal critical and commercial success undoubtedly put a new emphasis on what would become *both* screwball and a revitalized romantic comedy.

More importantly, it should be underlined that Capra's 1930s and 1940s films after *It Happened One Night* are populist rather than screwball comedies (a common mislabeling). Genre critic Jim Leach notes,

> Capra's vision is not really screwball at all . . . whereas the only positive strategy in screwball comedy is to accept the all-pervasive craziness, the populist comedy argues that what society regards as crazy (Mr. Deeds'attempt to give away his fortune) is really a manifestation of the normal human values with which society has lost touch.[12]

Moreover, while Deeds must face a sanity hearing, a true screwball comedy would not progress at all if eccentric behavior (the genre norm) were subject to the courtroom. The inherent naturalness of kookiness to the genre is best articulated by the matter-of-fact fashion in which John D. Hackensacker III (Rudy Vallee) tells his *Palm Beach Story* sister (Mary Astor): "You know Maude [Astor], someone meeting you for the first time, not knowing you were cracked, might get the wrong impression."

Paradoxically, another case for taking Capra out of the screwball equation is that several films from the genre actually parody the director's work, especially *Deeds.* For example, the opening of *Nothing Sacred* is a comic sendup of the populist small-town beginning of *Deeds.* And Ralph Bellamy's failed attempt to read his romantic poetry to a distracted Irene Dunne in *The Awful Truth*—as well as to sing it to her in *Lady in a Jam* (1942)—parodies the recitation by Gary Cooper (the ultimate populist hero and title character) to Jean Arthur in *Deeds.*

That key Thin Man *(1934) couple, William Powell and Myrna Loy.*

Pivotal 1934 also produced W. S. Van Dyke's adaptation of Dashiell Hammett's comedic murder mystery *The Thin Man*, which impacted both screwball and romantic comedy. The central character, Nick Charles (William Powell), is more capable than the usual screwball comedy male, but he does have some antiheroic traits. That is, he is not of the Sherlock Holmes mold, a hero who can deduce six dozen things about a suspect merely from his footprints. Charles can be frustrated. He is more vulnerable, more human, and decidedly funnier than the classical detective, from his ongoing comic inebriation to shooting balloons off the Christmas tree with a toy air rifle, attributes that make him a first cousin to the screwball male.

Charles's sophisticated charm and ultimately take-charge manner, however, best pencil him in more as a candidate for the romantic comedy male. Moreover, the bemused restraint of Powell's lovely costar, Myrna Loy, quickly nominates her for inclusion in romantic rather than screwball comedy, too. Whereas a screwball heroine is most likely manipulating the male and/or plotting his ritualistic humiliation, Loy's character is, as described by a period critic, more likely "wondering what her husband's [Powell] next move will be."[13] Consequently, *The Thin Man*'s greatest legacy, with regard to both romantic and screwball comedy, is best captured in the couple's companionable relationship, as described by *Variety*'s 1934 reviewer as, "Their very pleasant manner of loving each other and showing it."[14]

If one truly wanted a formula for a screwball *Thin Man*, the answer would be provided by *The Ex-Mrs. Bradford* (1936). Powell made this comic murder mystery on a short sabbatical from his home studio (MGM). Produced at RKO to capitalize on the success of *The Thin Man*, the key difference was that costar Jean Arthur was written as a free-spirited, disruptive eccentric, miles away from Loy's restrained Nora Charles character. Screwball heroines tend to dominate, which is what the ex-Mrs. Bradford does, fittingly, as the title character. Arthur biographer John Oller appropriately labeled the movie a "screwball murder mystery."[15]

Interestingly enough, the third highlighted film in this section is the 1936 William Powell picture that followed *The Ex-Mrs. Bradford*—*My Man Godfrey*. What is forgotten today is the period significance of the picture. More than any of its predecessors, including the zany *Twentieth Century*, *My Man Godfrey* offered a whole house full of screwballs. Thus, for many period critics, *Godfrey* represented a more obvious starting point for the genre. For instance, Kate Cameron's 1938 *New York Daily News* review of *Bringing Up Baby* placed it in the tradition of "the whole crazy variety of screen comedies that began with 'My Man Godfrey.'"[16] Moreover, the greatest film critic of the 1930s, the *New Republic*'s Otis Ferguson, credited the movie with being the first to rate the screwball label—"With 'My Man Godfrey' in the middle of 1936, the discovery of the word screwball . . . helped build the thesis of an absolutely new style in comedy."[17]

Part of the picture's special status would seem to have a connection to the huge critical and commercial success of the Marx Brothers's comeback film, *A Night at the Opera* (1935), which opened less than a year before *Godfrey*. The Marxes's previous outing, the aforementioned *Duck Soup*, had been too provocative for the times, failing with both the public and the critics. Repackaged and homogenized at MGM, there was still enough inspired silliness in *A Night at the Opera* for the Marxes to be quickly recannonized as the kings of crazy. Premiering in late 1935, *Opera*'s popularity had it playing in many markets well into 1936. More than ever before, manic movies seemed to be the wave of the future. Consequently, the late summer launching of the screwy *Godfrey* undoubtedly benefited from this surreal lead-in.

Still, the *Opera-Godfrey* connection went beyond convenient timing. Both movies were coscripted by the same man, the sometime playwright Morrie Ryskind. The winner of a Pulitzer Prize (with George S. Kaufman and Ira Gershwin) for the stage musical *Of Thee I Sing* (1931–1932), Ryskind had already had a major hand in helping to guide the Marxes's early screen work. He scripted their first two pictures, *The Coconuts* and *Animal Crackers* (1929, 1930), adapting them from stage plays he had coauthored with Kaufman. After the Gregory LaCava–directed *Godfrey*, he would return to the team yet again with the screen adaptation of *Room Service* (1938).

Granted, the common consensus is that the Marxes were a comedy force of nature, with no one behind the camera ever putting an auteur stamp upon them, with the possible exception of McCarey's

The "Forgotten Man" and title character (William Powell) of My Man Godfrey *(1936), with Carole Lombard and Franklin Pangborn (Center).*

Duck Soup. So while we might debate at length just how much influence Ryskind had on the team, there can be little doubt that his insider status with them was an excellent starting point for the penning of a screwball classic.

Ironically, as with Ryskind's Marx Brothers work, the writer's creative status on *Godfrey* is sometimes questioned, given LaCava's gifted propensity for improvisation. There is no denying that Ryskind's last-minute script tweaking and encouragement of cast collaborations made him a decided plus on *Godfrey*. But an equally telling fact is that Ryskind coscripted LaCava's two best films, *Godfrey* (with Eric Hatch) and *Stage Door* (1937, with Anthony Veiller), and both screenplays were nominated for Academy Awards.

Regardless of one's take on the Ryskind connection, *Godfrey* is the most Marx Brothers–like screwball comedy of the 1930s. As the period reviewer for *Variety* put it, the film's focus family has definite "psychopathic ward tendencies."[18]

The fourth focus film is the screwball fantasy *Topper* (1937). To knock off a beautiful young couple (Cary Grant and Constance Bennett) and have them return as "ectoplasmic screwballs" was a then unprecedented plot twist.[19] *New York Post* critic Archer Winsten went so far as to call it the "Great Experiment"—the "most unusual picture of the year."[20] *New York Daily News* reviewer Dorothy Masters credited Grant and Bennett as being "two such ghosts as have never before been seen."[21]

Drawn from the comic novel by the now neglected humorist Thorne Smith, *Topper* was merely a new twist on the farce nature of screwball comedy—a truly ludicrous situation generously sprinkled with slapstick. And in an age (the 1930s) forever scrambling for a fresh

Topper *(1937), with Cary Grant (center), Constance Bennett, and Roland Young, gave the screwball world a new catalyst for comedy.*

screwball catalyst, fantasy proved the perfect answer: what better excuse for eccentricity than visitation by the most free-*spirited* of couples.

Topper also provided a new slant upon the vanquishing of male rigidity, which is the goal of all good screwball comedies. Normally, the rigidity cure is applied to the film's leading man. But in *Topper* Grant and Bennett must perform a good deed to guarantee their safe entry into heaven. The project they decide upon is loosening up the most rigid of milquetoast males—their banker Topper (Roland Young). By introducing an antiheroic supporting player, *Topper* broadened the comic scope of screwball comedy. It also brought the genre back to its antiheroic literary roots. Interestingly, later critics would describe the alter egos of Thurber and Benchley and other antiheroic pioneers as the "little man." Maybe they were influenced by period reviews of *Topper*, because that was how Roland Young's character was often described.[22]

This section's final focus film is McCarey's *Love Affair*, the era's most important romantic comedy. It is difficult to significantly underline the importance of this movie to the genre, especially with it having been out of circulation until recently. Yet with this picture McCarey created a hauntingly bittersweet mix of romantic humor and pathos.

Unlike some watershed works, which are neglected upon their initial release, *Love Affair* arguably garnered the best reviews of any movie mentioned in this text. *New York World-Telegram* critic William Boehnel's take on the picture was typical of its glowing marks: "I found it the most absorbing and delightful entertainment of its kind that I have seen in a long time—a beautifully acted and directed offering full of taste and distinction."[23] Reviewers seemed to risk running out of superlatives. For instance, another period critic called it "a picture of such exquisite beauty that it is a joy to the beholder. It is a tender, poignant film, sentimental without being gooey, funny but not goofy [screwball]."[24] Peppered throughout these raves was an ongoing appreciation of a comic artist too little known today. For example, the *New York Times*'s Frank S. Nugent observed, "Leo McCarey, who directs so well it is almost anti-social of him not to direct more often, has created another extraordinarily fine film in 'Love Affair.'"[25]

The innovation that McCarey brought to romantic comedy, which *Variety* called "daring," was his ability to mix an amusing love story with a serious subject—the aforementioned crippling accident Irene Dunne suffers on the way to her Empire State Building rendezvous with Charles Boyer.[26] What made McCarey's pivotal *Love Affair* all the more definitive for romantic comedy was that the director had made one of the archetype screwball comedies (*The Awful Truth*, 1937) two years earlier—for which he had won his first Oscar. The contrasts between these two high-profile pictures and the genres they represent (for review, see the opening pages of this chapter) greatly simplify the confusion between screwball and romantic comedy.

Post-Depression Developments of Both Genres

By World War II screwball comedy had become almost passé. The only real holdout of the war years was screwball latecomer Preston Sturges, who represented a summing up of the genre. His *Lady Eve* (1941) and *The Palm Beach Story* (1942) are almost flawless examples of the antiheroic world of screwball film, combining fast, witty dialogue with the genre's slapstick nature. In *The Miracle of Morgan's Creek* (1944), Sturges successfully blends a war backdrop and screwball comedy, largely through the genius of focusing on an antiheroic "4-Fer" (someone not subject to the military draft for physical or mental reasons), perfectly cast with diminutive Eddie Bracken.

Ironically, the most provocative screwball comedies during the war years were the failures. For instance, McCarey's *Once Upon a Honeymoon* (1942) tried to combine European war themes with romance. But the whole film comes to a halt when Cary Grant and Ginger Rogers find themselves in a concentration camp, hardly a suitable subject for nonpolitical screwball comedy. Lubitsch's *To Be or Not to Be* (1942) also addressed the war directly, following the misadventures of a troupe of Polish actors during the Nazi occupation of that country. Jack Benny is outstanding as the nearly cuckolded antiheroic husband who leads the group; Lombard provides excellent support as the romantically dizzy wife. But, as with McCarey's *Once Upon a Honeymoon*, the film is frequently punctuated with concentration camp–like issues. And though Lubitsch's film is far superior, it is superior on a black comedy level; it does not work as a screwball comedy.

As if in recognition of the waning days of screwball's first heyday, the 1940s seemed to register an upswing in romantic comedy titles, even prior to our entry into World War II. A major player in this romantic movement was Katharine Hepburn, starting with her critical and commercial smash *The Philadelphia Story* (1940), in which she had originally starred on Broadway. The war years were also the beginning of Hepburn's romantic comedy teamings with Spencer Tracy, starting with *Woman of the Year* and *Without Love* (1945). Despite these successes, it was another George Stevens film (after *Woman of the Year*) that rates the brass ring for best wartime romantic comedy—*The More the Merrier* (1943). Set in then overcrowded Washington, D.C., it finds Charles Coburn orchestrating a romance between Jean Arthur and Joel McCrea as they all attempt to share one apartment.

Coburn would win an Oscar for his crafty matchmaker performance (a part Cary Grant would play in the 1966 remake, *Walk, Don't Run*), while the movie's popularity spawned an army of copycat productions. But at least one of these D.C. housing shortage follow-ups, *Standing Room Only* (1944), was an outstanding contribution to the genre in its own right. Starring Fred MacMurray and Paulette Goddard as a businessman and his assistant in the capital to obtain a government contract, they must double as servants to have a place to stay. Naturally, love wins out.

In the postwar era (1946–1960) screwball comedy was still often tied to a 1930s talent pool. The two most successful outings were collaborations between Howard Hawks and Cary Grant, *I Was a Male War Bride* (1949, with Ann Sheridan) and *Monkey Business*

(1952, with Ginger Rogers and Marilyn Monroe). The former picture took a topical situation, the red tape involved in getting the brides of American servicemen into the country, and gave it a screwball twist—Grant is a foreign groom trying to accompany his WAC wife (Sheridan) back to the United State. The story jettisons the genre's standard romantic triangle but otherwise maintains the basics, such as Grant's ritualistic—in drag—humiliation.

Monkey Business might be called a delayed sequel to *Bringing Up Baby*. Once again Grant is an absentminded professor, but this time his preoccupation is discovering a youth serum. Comically, one of his lab monkeys concocts a rejuvenation serum first, though for much of the movie Grant assumes he has made the breakthrough. Regardless, this special elixir becomes a new catalyst for becoming screwball, just as *Topper* had jumpstarted the genre with ghosts. Grant and Rogers are married, with Monroe as his favorite playmate when he is under the influence. But given it is the more conservative 1950s, Grant finds new happiness in his old marriage.

The decade also saw several mediocre screwball remakes: *The Lady Eve* resurfaced as *The Birds and the Bees* (1956) and a new *My Man Godfrey* opened in 1957. With the 1950s being the last hurrah of the studio musical, as well as an era in search of proven properties (to compete with television), several screwball classics were remade as musicals. For example, *The Awful Truth* was musically reborn as *Let's Do It Again* (1953). But as with the straight remakes, there was little magic taking place.

Of more period interest was Billy Wilder's inspired salute to screwball comedy in the otherwise darkly comic gangster parody *Some Like It Hot* (1959). Named this country's greatest movie comedy by the American Film Institute (2000), much of the picture showcases a dead-on impersonation of an antiheroic Cary Grant by a never funnier Tony Curtis. *Hot* was the most comically layered American comedy since Preston Sturges's prime. Indeed, Curtis's Grant-like character also has elements of Sturges's spoof of John D. Rockefeller in *The Palm Beach Story*.

Romantic comedies during the postwar period were more prevalent than the screwball variety, but there were many ties to the past here, too. Aging male stars from the 1930s dominated the genre in the 1950s, with only one, Clark Gable, sometimes spoofing his years. He was at his late career best opposite Doris Day in *Teacher's Pet* (1958). Wilder's *Sabrina* (1954) makes casting against type work when tycoon Humphrey Bogart successfully romances Audrey Hepburn in a bona fide period classic. Wilder returns to similar ground in his 1957 salute to Lubitsch, *Love in the Afternoon*, with Hepburn again romantically teamed with a much older leading man (Gary Cooper). There would also be two more Tracy-Hepburn teamings during the decade—*Pat and Mike* (1952) and the *Desk Set* (1957), not to mention her offbeat love story with Bogart, *The African Queen* (1951).

The decade's busiest male veteran, however, was Cary Grant. Starring opposite a myriad of actresses, Grant dominated late 1950s romantic comedy as he had once done late 1930s screwball comedy. Highlights would include his reteaming with director McCarey for the celebrated *An Affair to Remember* (1957, opposite Deborah Kerr), and reunion films with both Ingrid Bergman (*Indiscreet*, 1958) and Sophia Loren (*Houseboat*, 1958). No one aged better than Grant. Indeed, one might apply a critic's description of *An Affair to Remember*—as one of those rare "twilight masterpieces"—to much of Grant's late career oeuvre.[27]

There is no easy answer as to why the 1950s seemed predisposed to older male leads, besides the ongoing box-office clout of the aforementioned actors. But maybe having an aging caretaker president (Dwight D. Eisenhower) in the White House contributed to that mind-set. Interestingly enough, period critics sometimes drew parallels between Gable and Eisenhower. For instance, the *Saturday Review* critique of *Teacher's Pet* felt "Mr. Gable looks and sounds a little too much like President Eisenhower," while *The New Yorker*'s review of Gable's *It Started In Naples* (1960) observed, "The picture gains an adventatious interest from the fact that Clark Gable often sounds exactly like President Eisenhower."[28]

Regardless of one's take on this older man scenario, the modern era (since 1960) would soon dictate major alterations for both romantic and screwball comedy. The first significant post-1960s screwball comedy might suggest, however, that little had changed. Hawks has created yet another entertaining variation upon his archetype *Bringing Up Baby*—*Man's Favorite Sport?* (1964). Originally written for Cary Grant, Rock Hudson plays a professor-like expert on sports fishing comically victimized by the enthusiastically zany Paula Prentiss in her best role.

Fittingly, this 1960s screwball comedy lead-in also involves Hawks, since the decade's explosion of interest in classic cinema (á la film societies and the emergence of university film programs) often involved his groundbreaking contributions to the genre. A direct outgrowth of this more scholarly phenomenon was behind the watershed *What's Up, Doc?*. Its director, Peter Bogdanovich, came out of a criticism/academic background and had authored several texts, including *The Cinema of Howard Hawks* (1962). *Doc* was his celebrated reworking of *Baby*, and Bogdanovich screened Hawks's picture for his own cast before shooting started. The resultant critical and commercial success of *Doc*, coupled with screwball's already increased visibility, helped fan a further revival of interest in the genre.

By the early 1980s a mini-screwball renaissance was occurring. There was Neil Simon's homage to the genre, *Seems Like Old Times* (1980, with Goldie Hawn and Chevy Chase), the tour de silly by Dudley Moore in writer/director Steve Gordon's laugh-fest *Arthur* (1980, with John Gielgud in Oscar-winning support), and writer/director Blake Edward's stylish *Victor/Victoria* (1982, with Julie Andrews masquerading as a man and James Garner oh so confused). Also included was the reworking of Preston Sturges's *Unfaithfully Yours* (1983, with Dudley Moore), classic antiheroic indecision in *Micki & Maude* (1984, again with Moore), and Steve Martin in brilliant physical comedy form as Lily Tomlin's soul invades his body in *All of Me* (1984).

There were more, but these were the highlights, with the impish, "Cuddly Dudley" Moore surfacing as an economy-sized Cary Grant for this late twentieth-century revival of the genre. While the screwball numbers declined in the 1990s, there was no denying its return. Examples range from the traditional eccentricity of *House Sitter* (1992, with Hawn and Martin) to the revisionist slants of *My Best Friend's Wedding* (1997) and *Forces of Nature* (1999)—where screwball heroines Julia Roberts and Sandra Bullock do *not* break up weddings.

Romantic comedy in the modern era also had begun to have a younger look, save for that ageless Cary Grant. In films such as *That Touch of Mink* (1962, opposite Doris Day) he continued to be a top box-office draw. Grant's longevity notwithstanding (he would retire after *Walk Don't Run*), Doris Day was the centerpiece of 1960s romantic comedy, starring opposite a bevy of male leads during the decade. Most famous for her teamings with Rock Hudson (beginning with *Pillow Talk*, 1959), she also had multiple movies with James Garner (such as *The Thrill of It All*, 1963) and Rod Taylor (including *The Glass-Bottom Boat*, 1966).

Of Day's leading men, Garner would have a longevity all his own, culminating with an Oscar nomination for *Murphy's Romance* (1985, opposite a much younger Sally Fields). But generally speaking, the initial modern era film actors have been less likely than their earlier counterparts to key upon a romantic comedy career. Thus, one-time heartthrobs like Robert Redford and Warren Beatty have had years pass between legitimate romantic comedies. With regard to Beatty, one goes from *Heaven Can Wait* (1978) to his remake of *Love Affair* (1994). With Redford the wait is even longer, stretching from Neil Simon's *Barefoot in the Park* (1967, opposite Jane Fonda) to *Legal Eagles* (1986, with Debra Winger).

Love stories in other films by these actors have taken a backseat to different dominating genres, such as Redford's fascination with a Capra-like populism in *The Electric Horseman* (1979) and *The Horse Whisperer* (1998), or Beatty's interest in the gangster genre—*Bonnie and Clyde* (1967) and *Bugsy* (1991). As Redford and Beatty pursued other cinematic interests, Woody Allen was working toward the funniest of bittersweet romantic comedies—the much-honored *Annie Hall* (1977). But as with Redford and Beatty, there are competing genre distractions. For many viewers, including this author, Allen's dominating personality comedian persona automatically places anything he does in the clown genre. Yet, when romantic comedy would begin its own mini-renaissance late in the 1980s, Allen's influence would be ever present.

More specifically, Rob Reiner's Allen-ish *When Harry Met Sally . . .* (1989) kicked off a wave of quality romantic comedies that continues unabated to this very day. Everyone, including Reiner, has acknowledged the general influence of Allen's antiheroic oeuvre in this inspired picture, about two New Yorkers attempting not to spoil a friendship with love. Having another former stand-up comedian (Billy Crystal) as the male lead no doubt further cemented the Allen connection.

Harry screenwriter Nora Ephron then parlayed her success into scripting and directing another romantic comedy blockbuster, *Sleepless in Seattle* (1993), with repeated allusions to *An Affair to Remember* and its romantic meeting place—the top of the Empire State Building. Ephron's later follow-up with her two *Sleepless* stars (Tom Hanks and Meg Ryan) was yet another critical and commercial hit—*You've Got Mail.*

While Ephron's behind-the-scenes work has been pivotal to this romantic comedy revival, Garry Marshall's *Pretty Woman*, following *Harry* by a year, was also a catalyst for the genre's comeback. Plus, the picture's huge critical and commercial success made Julia Roberts an influential romantic comedy player, though she was equally at home in such later screwball comedy outings as *Notting Hill* and *Runaway Bride* (both 1999).

Other quality additions to the field would include Reiner's *An American President* (1995, with Michael Douglas), writer/director James L. Brooks's *As Good As It Gets* (1997, with Oscar winners Jack Nicholson and Helen Hunt), and Nancy Meyer's fantasy *What Women Want* (2000; Mel Gibson "hears" women's thoughts). These and other recent pictures suggest romantic comedy's revival will continue well into the future.

The following chapters attempt to more thoroughly examine the primary components of romantic comedy, as well as contrast the genre with its closest variation—screwball comedy.

Notes

1. Eileen Creelman, "Another Preston Sturges Comedy, 'The Palm Beach Story,'" *New York Sun,* December 11, 1942.

2. Herbert Cohn, *The Shop around the Corner* review, *Brooklyn Daily Eagle,* January 26, 1940, p. 11; "Interior of a Budapest Shop Reflects American Influence," *New York Herald Tribune,* January 21, 1940, p. 3.

3. Elizabeth Kendall, *The Runaway Bride: Hollywood Romantic Comedy of the 1930s* (New York: Doubleday, 1991), p. 54.

4. Andrew Bergman, *We're in the Money: Depression America and its Films* (New York: Harper & Row, 1972), p. 134.

5. Todd McCarthy, *Howard Hawks: The Grey Fox of Hollywood* (New York: Grove Press, 1997), p. 197.

6. Philip K. Scheuer, "Barrymore Has Acting Holiday," *Los Angeles Times,* May 1934.

7. "Me 'n Paul" (cover story), *Time,* April 15, 1935, p. 52.

8. *My Man Godfrey* review, *Variety,* September 23, 1936, p. 16.

9. Frank S. Nugent, *Midnight* review, *New York Times,* April 6, 1939, p. 31.

10. Harold Wentworth and Stuart Flexner, eds., *The Pocket Dictionary of American Slang* (New York: Pocket Books, 1967), p. 287.

11. Patrick McGilligan, *Film Crazy: Interviews with Hollywood Legends* (New York: St. Martin's Press, 2000), p. 80.

12. Jim Leach, "The Screwball Comedy," in *Film Genre: Theory and Criticism,* ed. Barry K. Grant (Metuchen, N.J.: Scarecrow Press, 1977), pp. 82–83.

13. Mordaunt Hall, *The Thin Man* review, *New York Times,* June 30, 1934, p. 18.

14. *The Thin Man* review, *Variety,* July 3, 1934.

15. John Oller, *Jean Arthur: The Actress Nobody Knew* (New York: Limelight Editions, 1999), p. 93.

16. Kate Cameron, "Babies, Just Babies, On Music Hall Screen," *New York Daily News*, March 4, 1938, p. 46.

17. Otis Ferguson, "While We Were Laughing" (1940), in *The Film Criticism of Otis Ferguson*, ed. Robert Wilson (Philadelphia: Temple University Press, 1971), p. 24.

18. *My Man Godfrey* review, *Variety*, September 23, 1936.

19. *Topper* review, *New York Times*, August 20, 1937, p. 21.

20. Archer Winsten, "Fantastic Occurrence Celebrated at Capitol," *New York Post*, August 20, 1937.

21. Dorothy Masters, "'Topper' Riot of Ghosts at the Capitol," *New York Daily News*, August 20, 1937, p. 44.

22. For example, see Eileen Creelman, "Two Young Ghosts Make Merry in a Thorne Smith Comedy, 'Topper,'" *New York Sun*, August 20, 1937.

23. William Boehnel, "'Love Affair' Seen as Outstanding Film," *New York World-Telegram*, March 17, 1939, p. 23.

24. Kate Cameron, "Exquisite Romance on Music Hall Screen," *New York Daily News*, March 17, 1939, p. 48.

25. Frank S. Nugent, *Love Affair* review, *New York Times*, March 17, 1939, p. 25.

26. *Love Affair* review, *Variety*, March 15, 1939.

27. George Morris, "ENCORE: 'An Affair to Remember,'" *Take One*, July 15, 1979, p. 14.

28. Hollis Alpert, *Teacher's Pet* review, *Saturday Review*, March 22, 1958, p. 41; Brendan Gill, *It Started in Naples* review, *The New Yorker*, September 17, 1960, p. 170.

CHAPTER TWO

SCREWBALL COMEDY

Things are just the same as they always were only you're the same as you were too. So I guess things will never be the same again.

—Screwball logic from Irene Dunne
in *The Awful Truth* (1937)

To clarify the nature and role of screwball comedy, the films of the genre can be examined for five key characteristics of the aforementioned comic antihero: abundant leisure time, childlike nature, basic male frustration (especially in relationship to women), a general propensity for physical comedy, and a proclivity for parody and satire.

More than any other genre, including romantic comedy, the screwball variety focuses on the leisure life, often in "high-society" style. A period critique of the fantasy screwball comedy *I Married a Witch* (1942) tellingly describes the condition with the phrase "caviar comedy," while insightful modern critic/historian Richard Schickel would simply observe "screwballism was purely a disease of the wealthy."[1] The titles of two other celebrated examples of the genre further express this ambience quite effectively: Mitchell Leisen's *Easy Living* (1937) and George Cukor's *Holiday* (1938).

A 1938 *New York Times* article, "Laughter at So Much per Tickle," even examined how the high-society comedy eventually led to higher production costs:

> The current vogue of goofy [screwball] comedies necessitates more elaborate sets than those used for the ancient laughmakers. The old-fashioned gag comedies could be played in front of any kind of scenery, but the characters in the modern mad cycle are invariably millionaires, and their antics must be chronicled in settings befitting their wealth.[2]

From wealth to high-society decadence, the beautiful people of *My Man Godfrey* (1936) can find no more meaningful activity than a scavenger hunt at the city dump; the whole focus of the characters in *Topper* (1937) is to learn how to spend leisure time with the correct amount of frivolity. Flash forward to the modern (since 1960) era's *Arthur* (1981) and one has the ultimate study in frivolity. Dudley Moore's Arthur Bach is a potential billionaire who divides his time between beautiful women, racing cars, and verbal sparring with his independent man servant Hobson (John Gielgud).

If a character does flirt with a profession in a screwball comedy, it is usually in a field middle America does not view as serious or "real" employment. For instance, Melvyn Douglas's character in *Theodora Goes Wild* (1936) is a painter. In fact, Douglas's self-centered traditionalist film father uses this to put pressure on him when requesting a favor, "You owe at least that much to me, especially after your choice of professions."

Pivotal screwball comedy director Leo McCarey does not even attempt to establish an occupational cover for Cary Grant in *The Awful Truth*, a situation basically repeated in *My Favorite Wife* (1940), from a McCarey story (with Bella and Samuel Spewack), which McCarey produced. That this was a conscious effort by McCarey—lack of concern over establishing a profession—is best illustrated by the director's response to the difficulty Grant has in playing a scene in *The Awful Truth*, when the actor's character offers to assist his estranged wife monetarily:

> When Cary came to that scene he stopped and laughed. "Where am I supposed to have gotten any money?" he asked. "I never work . . . you never show me doing any sort of a job." My reply was that the audience would not be interested in how he got the money, but merely in the efforts of the two young people to straighten out their married life.[3]

The genre's favorite example of a profession nebulous to many Americans is the absentminded professor, a type fully realized by the irreplaceable Cary Grant in Howard Hawks's *Bringing Up Baby* (1938). When Grant's academic is not socializing with rich patrons of the arts to obtain contributions to his museum, he is busy assembling the giant skeleton of a brontosaurus. The tools of his socializing "trade" include nine irons and cocktail attire.

Hawks had a penchant for professors, creating many such characters in the screwball milieu. After *Bringing Up Baby*, there were the seven little professors of *Ball of Fire* (1941), headed by Gary Cooper's Professor Potts; the film also doubled as a live-action parody of Walt Disney's huge critical and commercial smash *Snow White and the Seven Dwarfs* (1938).

In 1952 Hawks brought Grant back as yet another absentminded professor in *Monkey Business*—an often inspired variation upon the actor's *Bringing Up Baby* character. Though this is the definitive professorial trilogy for the genre, screwball comedy managed to offer up several other academic variations, such as Preston Sturges's *The Lady Eve* (1941, with Henry Fonda as the ultimate milquetoast professorlike ophiologist).

Fittingly, however, the most entertaining screwball professor of the modern era had a Hawksian connection, Peter Bogdanovich's loose reworking of *Bringing Up Baby*—*What's Up, Doc?* (1972). Ryan O'Neal stars as yet another stiff academic comically derailed yet redeemed by a screwball heroine.

The beauty of the professorial phenomenon in screwball comedy is that it goes a long way toward explaining why the genre works in terms of comedy theory. This necessitates drawing from the writing of the Nobel Prize–winning philosopher Henri Bergson (1859–1941), who is a central figure in any popular culture discussion of comedy. Bergson's theory of comic superiority, based in "mechanical inelasticity," can best be related to the screwball genre by examining the effects on character development of its two primary components: (1) "absentmindedness," and (2) "inversion" or "topsy-turvydom"—where character roles are switched.

First, the main thrust of comic rigidity comes about by way of absentmindedness, a state Bergson ranks as nearly "the fountainhead of the comic," where there is a "growing callousness to social life. Any individual is comic who automatically goes his own way without troubling himself about getting into touch with the rest of his fellow-beings."[4] Bergson notes that this rigidity is most apt to occur among career professionals, a narrowness that he labels as the "professional comic," and exemplifies with the teacher who has concern only for his own subject.[5]

This Bergsonian composite character articulates beautifully the state of most screwball comedy males. Bergson has all but said the absentminded professor, a central figure in screwball comedy, is equally central to his theory of superiority. Moreover, even when Bergson refers to a nonteacher model of absentminded rigidity, there are frequently eccentric professor roots. For example, he discusses the classic rigidity of Don Quixote, a figure also dealt with in the comedy superiority theory of Bergson contemporary George Meredith.[6] But just how does the windmill-attacking rigidity of Quixote connect with the absentminded professor, beyond a mutual tunnel vision approach to the world? The answer lies in the evolution of Quixote's comic rigidity—a self-administered academic straitjacket normally associated with the absentminded professor:

> he [Quixote] made away many acres of arable land to buy him books of that kind [on knighthood], and therefore he brought to his house as many as ever he could get . . . the poor gentleman

> grew distracted [with difficult passages], and was breaking his brains day and night, to understand and unbowel their sense, an endless labour. . . . In resolution, he plunged himself so deeply in his reading of these books, as he spent many times in the lecture of them whole days and nights; and in the end, through his little sleep and much reading, he dried up his brains in such sort as he lost wholly his judgement.[7]

This dovetails perfectly into screwball comedy's tendency to focus on the professionally rigid male, often a professor or someone professorial in his actions, and on the heroine's attempt to perform the "corrective" act of bringing him back to some degree of normalcy. (Interestingly enough, *the* unrealized joint film project of screwball comedy's greatest director and actor, Hawks and Grant, was the making of *Don Quixote*.)

Bergson's second comedy theory component, "inversion" or "topsyturvydom," seems equally tailormade for screwball comedy, as defined through the absentminded professor. That is, the traditional role of the teacher in our society is to act as an authority figure, with other characters often falling into the *supporting* category of surrogate student. Yet, this genre reverses that by having the absentminded professor be dominated by the screwball heroine.

On occasion the genre's heroine even plays a student. During screwball's golden age (1930s) this is best showcased in George Stevens's *Vivacious Lady* (1938), where Jimmy Stewart the professor suddenly finds Ginger Rogers as one of his college charges. She surfaces again in Billy Wilder's sexually provocative *The Major and the Minor* (1942), an excellent but rare reworking of the theme during World War II. Ray Milland is a military prep school instructor revitalized by Rogers . . . masquerading as a schoolgirl. Though it was Wilder's American directing debut, he was hardly a stranger to the genre; he had coscripted (with Charles Brackett) the often neglected screwball classic *Midnight* (1939) and the densely professor-populated *Ball of Fire*.

The most entertaining screwball heroine-as-student, however, occurred during the modern era. Barbra Streisand's star turn as the brilliantly eccentric Judy Maxwell in *What's Up, Doc?* is integral to the picture, since her constant change of majors enables her to be amusingly knowledgeable in a variety of scenes. Moreover, she wins a major research grant for her love interest, Professor Howard Bannister (Ryan O'Neal), by proving his chief rival (Kenneth Mars in yet another turn as a comic German) has plagiarized his entry.

If one applies "topsyturvydom" more generally to screwball comedy, it comically explains the attraction of a genre that turns the American courtship system on its ear. That is, the woman leads the charge while the male holds back in the manner of the stereotyped weaker sex. Even the rare appearance of a strong male does not change this situation. In *My Man Godfrey*, William Powell as a butler seems more than capable, but once he serves future wife (and former real-life spouse) Carole Lombard breakfast that first morning, she more correctly predicts *their* future: "You're my responsibility now. See you in church." More than anything else, this is also the phenomenon that separates screwball comedy from romantic comedy, since the latter genre is more traditionally likely to have the man ultimately take charge.

A final corollary to Bergson's professorial "absentmindedness" and "topsyturvydom" embraces "automatism"—"what is essentially laughable is what is done automatically."[8] This is best demonstrated in *Bringing Up Baby* whenever George the dog enters the picture. Since it is assumed that he has buried the rare brontosaurus bone of Cary Grant's Professor David Huxley, whenever he wanders into the film frame David and his companion (Katharine Hepburn) immediately drop what they are doing and proceed to start following the dog—forever hopeful they will discover the lost bone. The comedy is compounded further in *Baby* when another couple, Aunt Elizabeth (May Robinson) and Major Horace Applegate (Charles Ruggles), also starts joining in . . . even though they have no clue as to why they are running.

Comic "automatism" took another slant when Peter Bogdanovich updated *Baby* in *What's Up, Doc?*. The comedy catalyst for automatic behavior this time around was several sets of identical luggage owned by various cast members, with contents ranging from Professor Bannister's research rocks to secret government documents to a valuable collection of diamond jewelry. Consequently, whenever one of these bags appears, there is a hum of activity by an army of surveillance types—comic spies, jewel thieves, gangsters, and government agents.

The second antiheroic component in screwball comedy, after the abundant leisure time associated with being a professor, is an adult who is childlike. Traditionally, one associates the childlike with comedy, but the association has a special focus here. Whereas the capable crackerbarrel figures were caretakers for a nation, the screwball comedy male is often in a situation where he quite literally is being taken care of, from the fiftyish Egbert (Charles Ruggles) getting a haircut under the supervision of his wife in *Ruggles of Red Gap* (1935) to the middle-aged Douglas of *Theodora Goes Wild* taking orders from his father.

The childlike males, in the apparent antiheroic tradition of James Thurber, often have a dog—an obvious corollary of childhood. Thurber wrote about the dog because he felt it was the one animal that had been domesticated so long that it had taken on most human frustrations. A dual focus of frustration, male and canine, plays an important part in several screwball comedies, including such pivotal examples as *The Awful Truth*, *Theodora Goes Wild*, and *Bringing Up Baby*, a film that also incidentally adds a leopard. In Neil Simon's script for *Seems Like Old Times* (1980), the frustrations of the husband are mirrored repeatedly in his wife's (Goldie Hawn) pack of dogs. This final example is especially important because *Seems Like Old Times* is a conscious celebration of the screwball genre, from storyline parallels such as the use of dogs to the inclusion of stills from earlier screwball films in its own theater release posters. This male-canine dual focus is best illustrated by McCarey's *The Awful Truth*, where Grant and the dog Mr. Smith (the same dog that appears as Asta in the screwball-related *Thin Man* series) show a great propensity for similar slapstick frustration. For example, each (at different times) performs a monumental pratfall from a precariously balanced chair—all while investigating the activities of Irene Dunne.

The dog sometimes represents a surrogate child for a screwball comedy couple who "play house" when one partner, usually the male, is not adult enough for a real marriage. A custody fight over Mr. Smith at the divorce proceedings in *The Awful Truth* allows McCarey to extend his parody of divorce without the real pathos a human child would have given the scene. Since a dog is used, any sexuality between the couple is not undermined by a "family" situation. (In *Bringing Up Baby* having a pet represent a surrogate child is addressed much more baldly, for "Baby" in the title is actually a tame leopard.)

In *Theodora Goes Wild* Douglas tries to use the image of child and dog as a defense against real housekeeping, the responsibility of marriage. Near the end of the film, when the unmarried Dunne returns to her small town as an infamous sex novelist, she is holding a friend's baby. Given the X-rated reputation of her work, everyone assumes the child to be hers. Douglas, there finally to declare his love, is taken aback at the sight of the baby. In every ensuing scene Douglas cradles his dog Jake just as Dunne does the baby, the contrast in bundles underscoring the "I'm just a boy playing at being a husband" nature of the male's role.

In addition, the dog can represent a metaphor for the petlike existence to which the screwball comedy child/man is frequently reduced by the genre's female. This is best exemplified by Preston Sturges's 1942 *Palm Beach Story*, in which Princess's (Mary Astor) latest male satellite is named Toto (Sig Arno). No doubt playing upon the celebrated dog Toto from *The Wizard of Oz* (the film version starring Judy Garland just having appeared in 1939), Sig Arno could not have played a more obedient pooch to Mary Astor's Princess. Moreover, since Arno's Toto could not speak English (no one knew or tried to decipher his comically obscure tongue), he was in the same situation as any barking-at-the-heels neglected pooch.

Claudette Colbert's long-legged girl in The Palm Beach Story *(1942, with Joel McCrea).*

The male also reveals his childishness in several other ways. Traditionally the screwball characteristic is associated with the female in the genre, but the male, too, may have a screwball tendency. While the heroine is either pleasantly potty to begin with or merely assumes that comic role to better control the situation, the male is just as likely to become a screwball as a result of female shenanigans. Examples can be found in Grant's classic breakdown in *Bringing Up Baby* and the Stanwyck-engineered comic crackup of Fonda in *The Lady Eve*. Such incidents have a close affinity to the frustration and resultant tantrums of childhood. In *Bluebeard's Eighth Wife* (1938) Claudette Colbert's antics actually result in the institutionalization of her victim/husband Gary Cooper. It is a refreshingly dark comedy take on an aspect of screwball comedy not normally addressed during the 1930s.

The settings for this genre often accent the childlike in the male. In *Holiday* (1938) Cary Grant, Katharine Hepburn, and her movie brother (Lew Ayres) spend much of their time in the family mansion's only intimate and comfortable setting—the childhood playroom. This setting is full of toys: a stuffed giraffe named Leopold, a Punch-and-Judy show, a sailboat, dolls, a globe, drums, and miniature furniture. The "adult" trio actually play there, with Ayres banging away at his old drum set and Hepburn and Grant doing acrobatics. The playroom setting further exemplifies the childlike quality of the characters because it is the one place where all positive members of the film can interact in the natural, uninhabited manner of children. A term McCarey often used seems applicable here: spontaneity. Screwball players are nothing if not spontaneous.

In *Holiday* this natural trait of childhood is underlined by the fact that Hepburn and Ayres, the only members of a crusty old money family worth saving, tend to limit their spontaneous behavior to the playroom. In the world of screwball comedy, such actions are triggered by an association with the freedom of childhood. Fittingly, for a genre so often inhabited by professors, the ongoing spontaneity of Hepburn's romantic interest (Grant) in *Holiday* is linked to his surrogate parents (Edward Everett Horton and Jean Dixon) . . . who play two delightfully free-spirited professors.

The toyshop mise-en-scène occurs throughout the genre, from the previous examples to Robert Benchley's playroom "office" in *Take a Letter, Darling* (1942). The Benchley situation is especially entertaining, both because he so comically obsesses on the games and toys and they have no discernable connection with his in-film position as Rosalind Russell's advertising agency business partner. Thus, it is a pure example of the genre's childlike male in game-playing action.

More recently, Dudley Moore's toy-strewn bedroom in *Arthur* (1981) also exemplifies the condition, as well as the playthings with which Moore gifts his servant/friend John Gielgud. (The periodic use of the tune "Santa Claus Is Coming to Town" further reinforces

Arthur's toyshop mise-en-scène.) But the best example occurs at the close of *My Favorite Wife*. The frustrated Cary Grant is still faced with a which-wife-should-I-choose problem. (The film had opened with Grant marrying Gail Patrick shortly before the surprise return of first wife Irene Dunne—missing for the past seven years in the South Pacific.) Grant finds himself in a child's bed stored in the attic, surrounded by toys. He is obviously on the verge of making his decision in Dunne's favor but he is too frazzled by this point to know how to express it. Moreover, at bedtime Dunne does not hurt her cause any by attractively and yet forcefully assigning separate rooms—she to the *master* bedroom, he to the attic.

The effect of Grant's trek upstairs is that of a small boy sent to his room without supper. It is heightened by the nursery surroundings of the attic and the little bed in which he must sleep. The setting is a scaled-down version of the children's bedrooms in McCarey's celebrated Laurel and Hardy short subject *Brats* (1930), in which the duo play double roles as fathers and little boys.

Grant gets ready for bed with toys literally hanging from the low ceiling. As he crawls into the squeaky bed, knocking things down, the viewer's eyes focus on two specific toys—a doll beside the bed and a toy cannon just underneath. (Without being overly metaphorical, this reduction of male to toy cannon, subservient to the female on high, nicely describes *My Favorite Wife* and numerous other screwball comedies.) As if to accent the childlike focus while revealing Grant's thoughts, the doll falls and says "mama." With this suggestion, he does, in fact, get up and go to "mama's" room.

After Grant has made the long trek down to Dunne's room, she reinforces the earlier suggestion of the supperless child by asking in the most motherly of ways, "Are you hungry?" Needless to say, the true answer is something of a yes and a no; but Grant replies in the most appropriate of little boy styles that he cannot sleep. There are no "nice mattresses" in the attic as there are here—referring to the spare bed in Dunne's room. She coyly says that, then, he can sleep on the unoccupied one. After his face has sufficiently lit up, like a little boy's at Christmas, she tells him he would be most welcome to take the mattress upstairs.

The crestfallen child then takes the mattress out of the room but McCarey's camera remains with Dunne. Grant returns in seconds complaining that the mattress does not fit, adding quietly in befuddlement, "I'm stuck. This could go till doomsday. I'm stuck but I don't care what people think." After this pointed regression, we once again see the two in their separate beds.

Grant must somehow express to Dunne that she truly is "my favorite wife." But because of his long puzzlement over the decision and this complete childhood regression, which itself could be seen as the actualization of a little boy ego that refuses to admit a mistake, Grant seems to be literally struck dumb—unable even to communicate with normal speech patterns.

When you note this verbal incapacity of Grant's, you also remember that "'Do it visually'" was McCarey's byword. Grant, therefore, can be expected to perform some very comically symbolic act to resurrect the marriage. Moreover, whatever symbol is chosen to represent the uniqueness of this day should be commensurate with a red-letter day in childhood. Grant is obviously operating with the mind of a child, and it is only natural that he should communicate as such. (A key point to keep in mind, however, is the earlier suggestion by Grant that he take an ocean cruise alone to help him choose his favorite wife—a cruise that would last until Christmas.)

After individual shots of Grant and Dunne in their separate beds, the camera remains on Dunne. The viewer then hears Grant's attic bed collapse, another crash, the squeal of the attic door, and finally jingle bells. Grant then bursts in dressed as Santa Claus and cries "Merry Christmas!" Since Christmas is probably the most anxiously awaited moment of childhood, Grant's happiness over this apparent reconciliation proves to be a most effective communication, as well as suggesting the aforementioned possible reconciliation date. Just as in childhood, Grant plays his game by dressing up as someone else and imagining it to be a different time. And, despite the fact that "goodnight" is then written across the screen, ending the film with Grant's Santa Claus entry maintains the asexual nature of the child (and the comic antihero).

The concept of the child-husband and mother-wife are essential factors in the husband-wife reconciliation at the close of several McCarey films. Throughout these films, the males have assumed somewhat asexual roles. As with McCarey's Laurel and Hardy films, extramarital activities in screwball films are not condoned, though their rejection does not match the physical degree of rejection of feminine advances shown by Laurel in *We Faw Dawn* (1928) in which a flirt gets too familiar with his Adam's apple. The antihero of McCarey's features is more apt to be in a state of intense confusion and frustration.

This husband-wife reconciliation thus takes on rather significant consequences in several McCarey films. In *The Awful Truth*, *My Favorite Wife*, and to a certain extent, *Six of a Kind*, the child-husband attempts to have himself tucked in by the mother-wife, or be enabled to slip into bed with "mother." It occurs at the film's close, and is symbolic of the new world—the new marriage—that traditionally ends comedy, for at this point the McCarey child-man is finally allowed the suggestion of sexual adulthood. But for the viewer, he remains forever the child.

In *Too Many Husbands* (1940), Jean Arthur finds she must decide between two husbands, after husband number one returns from having been lost in the Atlantic, thus reversing the sudden romantic comedy triangle of *My Favorite Wife*. Here the male species of the screwball genre displays still another example of his childlike nature. The two husbands in question (Fred MacMurray and Melvyn Douglas) compete, schoolboy style, in "events" like chair jumping, spelling, and playing sick for the interest of their joint wife. Jean Arthur will later admonish that "You two men act like children!" but she really enjoys the interest. Frequently she slips into the role of mother, checking for brushed teeth and tucking the two into bed.

A charming modern-era variation upon the child-husband of McCarey's *My Favorite Wife* occurs in Blake Edwards's *Micki &*

Maude (1984), where diminutive leading man Dudley Moore also finds himself with two wives. But the inventive new twist for *Micki & Maude* is that both wives (Ann Reinking and Amy Irving) are keepers. Consequently, Moore has a more legitimate reason for being indecisive than Grant, whose second wife is the beautiful but witchy Gail Patrick.

Micki & Maude is also more of a comically twisted modern tale, since child-man Moore enters into the second relationship while his first wife (Reinking) is very much around. (In Grant's case, first wife Dunne had been reported missing at sea.) Regardless, it seems most fitting that Edwards has created a new variation upon *My Favorite Wife*, since McCarey was his early comedy mentor.

Sometimes screwball comedy's signature childishness is at immediate risk when the antiheroic male is threatened with a romantic union that promises to usurp his fun-loving nature. Though a norm in the genre since 1938's *Bringing Up Baby*, this plot twist has been even more prevalent during the modern era. For example, in *Arthur* Dudley Moore's title character is the ultimate fun-loving little boy. But all this is to change after Moore's marriage, arranged by his wealthy family, to a proper daughter of high society. He risks becoming fossilized in his future father-in-law's big business. Moore's screwball comedy deliverance is made possible, as is often the case with the genre, by the arrival of a free-thinking heroine (Liza Minnelli).

Steve Martin finds himself in a similar situation in the equally inspired *All of Me* (1984). Martin, a jazz musician at heart, is caught in a rigid relationship, as well as an equally numbing day job with his fiancée's wealthy father. In a fantasy turn as provocatively entertaining as *Topper* (1937), Martin is romantically rescued by the spirit of an eccentric (Lily Tomlin) . . . who, for a time, occupies one-half of his body. The film put a punning spin on the expression "getting under one's skin."

Of course, *the* screwball *fantasy* most associated with childlike behavior is Hawks's postwar revisionist *Monkey Business*, where a youth serum periodically returns Cary Grant's professor to childhood. The definitive scene along these lines occurs when the rejuvenated Grant teams up with some real children as they pretend to be Indians on the war path. Nominal Chief Grant, complete with Indian war paint on his face, comically assists his underaged band in almost burning a negative character at the stake. Being a childlike screwball comedy male had never been quite so liberating. And one might ultimately call the movie both a salute to childhood and "monkey business."

A third commonality between the worlds of the antihero and the screwball comedy male is that both focus on frustration. The antihero is always thwarted by women, a situation also generally evident in the screwball genre, from Cary Grant's domination by Irene Dunne in *The Awful Truth* to Ryan O'Neal's derailment by Barbra Streisand in *What's Up, Doc?*.

The inevitability of the woman's victory is nicely summarized by Streisand at the close of the latter picture. She accepts O'Neal's romantic surrender with the apt observation, "You can't fight a tidal wave." This *mother* nature metaphor still applies for the genre. For instance, the title of the revisionist screwball comedy *Forces of Nature* (1999) doubles as a description of its zany heroine (Sandra Bullock).

The genre is all about the ritualistic humiliation of the male. And though this is usually precipitated by a woman, there can be other causes. For instance, when the youth serum wears off in *Monkey Business*, Grant must face the consequences of his nutty under-the-influence behavior, not to mention a butch haircut and loud clothing. Or, in *I Was a Male War Bride* (1949), Grant has to masquerade as a woman to be able to board a troop ship back to the United States. With a new wife in the American military, the movie Great Britain retitled *You Can't Sleep Here* chronicled the paperwork absurdity of a nontraditional Army marriage.

Having noted these exceptions, however, it is safe to state that the primary source of screwball ritualistic humiliation is the heroine. Writer/director Preston Sturges best articulated the tendency toward female ascendancy in the genre with the title *The Lady Eve*, which also features a cartoon serpent in the delightful opening and closing credits. Not surprisingly, the Lady Eve (Barbara Stanwyck) wraps the sweet boob of a man-child (Henry Fonda) around her little finger during two different courtships, after appropriately starting things off by hitting him with an apple. So great is her mastery of this simple male that Stanwyck even convinces Fonda she is two different women. (Not quite a year later, Greta Garbo will persuade Melvyn Douglas of the same thing in the aptly titled George Cukor film *Two-Faced Woman*, 1941. While the film revives nicely today, the 1940s audience was not ready for Garbo as a screwball heroine.)

The Adam and Eve story is sometimes suggested in the screwball film at a nearly subliminal level, as in *Theodora Goes Wild.* Theodora (Irene Dunne) is a small-town girl who has written a successful novel about a big city girl, *The Sinner*, using the pen name of Caroline Adams. Her hometown is straight out of Lysistrata, with female domination underscored by a name that suggests a female garden: Lynnfield. Dunne, who will go on to prove herself the most daring and daffy of this female tribe, ends up courting and besting the man (Melvyn Douglas) in several Garden of Eden encounters, from picking berries to catching fish. Even when Douglas momentarily flees, his note explains he has gone "to tend other gardens." His eventual fall, however, has been foreshadowed by the painting he was working on when they first met: *Eve and the Serpent.*

Eve is also the name of Claudette Colbert's delightfully manipulating character in *Midnight,* and Irene Dunne brought her own brand of comic manipulation to a character nicknamed Eve in *My Favorite Wife.* (Dunne's shipwrecked island companion, Randolph Scott, is, naturally, Adam, though a supporting player thinks he resembles Johnny Weissmuller—Tarzan.)

As the genre entered the 1940s, the image of the screwball heroine as a power broker Eve-type became progressively stronger—culminating in Sturges's *The Lady Eve* and *The Palm Beach Story.* Sturges, as if somehow aware of *The Palm Beach Story*'s historical placement at the close of the initial screwball movement, even provides this Eve character with a gold digger's summation, or bill of grievances. Joel McCrea has just discovered that a stranger called the "weiner king" has given wife Claudette Colbert enough money to pay all their numerous bills. When he asks whether sex entered into it, she replies:

> Oh, but of course it did, darling. I don't think he would have given it to me if I had . . . little short legs like an alligator. Sex always has something to do with it, dear. From the time you're about so big and wondering why your girlfriend's fathers are starting to get so arch all of a sudden. Nothing wrong. Just an overture to the opera that's coming . . . but from then on you get it [the sexual come-on look] from cops, taxi dancers, bellboys, delicatessen dealers . . . the "how about this evening, babe?"

Put more succinctly, Colbert later observed, "You have no idea what a long-legged girl can do without doing anything."

In Hawks's much later screwball comedy, the modern-era *Man's Favorite Sport?* (1964), a then contemporary visit to Eden is more than suggested. Film critic Molly Haskell notes, the director "gives us Rock Hudson and Paula Prentiss as primordial man and woman, Adam and Eve in the lush, hazardous Eden of a hunting and fishing resort."[9]

Haskell also wisely notes that it is "an Adam and Eve saddled with a bitter, comical heritage of sexual distrust, bravado, and fear, archetypes that are infinitely closer to the American experience."[10] This observation could be applied to most antiheroic/screwball comedy—the why behind the significance of the Adam and Eve metaphor to the genre. She goes on to examine the "sexual allegory" of the film—how Hudson has written the book on fishing but has never actually sunk hook into water—he is a "how to" sexual author who is really a cowardly virgin.[11] Other examples include the *Bringing Up Baby* bone, which Cary Grant says, "belongs in the tail," or the later missing "intercostal clavicle"—which film comedy theorist Stanley Cavell also refers to as a "sexual allegory."[12]

Bogdanovich's variation on *Baby*—*What's Up, Doc?*—is even more bold about its sexual allegory. "Professor" O'Neal, who mixes musicology and geology, is constantly concerned about endangering or losing "his rocks."

The best sexual allegory in the genre, however, which also plays nicely upon the interrelatedness of antiheroic and screwball comedy, occurs in *The Lady Eve* when the question is posed, "Are snakes really necessary?" which immediately brings to mind the title and text of the 1929 antihero classic by James Thurber and E. B. White—*Is Sex Necessary? Or, Why You Feel the Way You Do.* The book anticipates the timid, virginal characteristics of many antiheroic/screwball males, particularly Henry Fonda's professorial role in *The Lady Eve.*

The domination by the female sometimes takes a more extreme course: reversal of sex roles. Such a switch occurs often in the genre, as in works by McCarey, Hawks, Sturges, George Stevens, and Mitchell Leisen. And with the increased 1940s visibility of women in society (due to the war), there was more opportunity for screwball comedies like Leisen's neglected *Take a Letter, Darling* (1942), which finds Rosalind Russell as a chief executive and Fred MacMurray as her private secretary.

The most extreme example of sex role reversal in the genre occurred under Hal Roach's direction in *Turnabout* (1940), from Thorne Smith's 1931 novel of the same name. A husband and wife, John Hubbard and Carole Landis, exchange bodies, thanks to a genie-like bust named Mr. Ram. Unlike onlookers in similar "exchanges" in the genre, the other characters in *Turnabout* are well aware that everything is not right with Hubbard and Landis. Although the exchange unfortunately lasts so long that its humor evaporates, the film remains *the* example of the screwball "turnabout."

An inspired modern-era take on screwball comedy confusion over sexual roles occurs in Blake Edwards's stylish *Victor/Victoria* (1982), which is set in 1930s Paris. Julie Andrews masquerades as a male cabaret performer who is a female impersonator. A visiting Chicago gangster (James Garner) falls hard for her/him and suffers a near comic meltdown trying to reevaluate his sexuality. (Alex Karras is especially entertaining as the tough guy bodyguard who comes out of the closet.)

Edwards later attempted a closer variation upon *Turnabout* called *Switch* (1991). Though not a perfect screwball comedy fit (a male chauvinist wakes up in the body of Ellen Barkin), it does provide a modern-era slant upon what might be the ultimate male frustration/nightmare—suddenly being a woman. And befitting of a comedy director (Edwards) weaned upon McCarey's visual legacy, Barkin's physical comedy performance is often truly inventive.

Frustration continues for the dominated male as he attempts, like the comedy figures of the past, to follow a rational lifestyle, but it is an irrational world now, and he finds it nearly impossible. The female, just as irrational as the modern humor we date from the twentieth century, is somehow capable of getting through because she makes no rational demands. Appropriately enough, one of the first screwball comedies is called *Twentieth Century* (1934), although in this film the male enjoys a surprising victory.

Accompanying this transition in American humor from competence to frustration is a further innovation. Women are given a major part, something American humor had previously largely neglected. The nineteenth-century crackerbarrel world had little place for women. The focus was too much on interests then labeled "male," from New England humor based in politics and business, as with Thomas Chandler Haliburton's Sam Slick character, to the emphasis in the comedy of the Old Southwest on raising hell, best exemplified by Johnson J. Hooper's world of Simon Suggs.

There had been earlier female comedy types, the vast majority seemingly products of New England humor, such as Frances M. Whitcher's Widow Bedott or B. P. Shillaber's Mrs. Partington, also a widow. These female characters tended to be rather screwball themselves. But since they existed in the world of the capable Yankee, their irrational characteristics, their malapropisms and long-winded chatter, were shown to be liabilities in what was seen as a rational world. They survived merely because their late husbands, presumably Yankees, had provided nicely for them.

Later, with the antihero *New Yorker* writers and with screwball comedy, a premium was set on female eccentricities, the logic no doubt being that the best defense against an illogical world is an illogical nature. The key example of the female eccentric in *The New Yorker* group is found in Thurber's *My Life and Hard Times*, especially in the personality of his grandmother:

> Who . . . lived the latter years of her life in the horrible suspicion that electricity was dripping invisibly all over the house. It leaked . . . out of empty sockets if the wall switch had been left on. She would go around screwing in bulbs, and if they lighted up she would hastily and fearfully turn off the wall switch . . . happy in the satisfaction that she had stopped not only a costly but dangerous leak.[13]

Yet, as eccentric as Grandma Thurber may be, she makes decisions and then gets on with living. The male attempts to make sense of situations, both with women and the world, and goes nearly crazy in the process. He cannot proceed without understanding, and there is no understanding.

A more direct screwball comedy related articulation of the illogical mind of a woman and all its power occurs in Eric Hatch's 1935 novel *My Man Godfrey*, which was adapted to the screen the following year. The central male and otherwise capable title character has a weakness: "Feminine logic—that whirligig lovely thing called the feminine mind—had always bewildered Godfrey. Now it out-and-out startled him."[14]

Screwball film comedy developed the female eccentrics of antihero fiction and soon produced such celebrated mad hatters as Carole Lombard in *My Man Godfrey* (though she showcased her special craziness in numerous other outings) and Katharine Hepburn in *Bringing Up Baby*. In contrast, the genre's most underrated heroine, Irene Dunne, skillfully shifts into kookiness as the need arises.

Because the illogical screwball heroine is better prepared than the male for an illogical world, she frequently meets new challenges in a radically different manner from her counterpart. For example, whereas Cary Grant is just this side of a nervous breakdown trying to decide which wife to choose in *My Favorite Wife*, Jean Arthur relishes a similar comic dilemma in *Too Many Husbands*. Arthur's near constant enjoyment of having two husbands competing for her is aptly captured in her evolving dialogue from three different points in the movie: "This is awful [having two husbands] but I love it." "Let's wait another day; I shouldn't be hasty about this [choosing just one]." "It [a doubled courtship] was wonderful while it lasted."

There can also be a darker side to this female dominance. The classic age of this genre anticipates the more sinister woman-as-predator film noir movies of the 1940s. One might even call screwball comedy an upbeat flipside of noir—in both cases it is a frequently irrational world with women hunting vulnerable men (though one merely desires a husband while the other desires his money). Screwball comedy regulars Fred MacMurray and Barbara Stanwyck even star in an early archetype of the genre—*Double Indemnity* (1944), with sometime screwball comedy writer/director Billy Wilder coscripting and directing. Moreover, while screwball heroines do not murder people (though zany Lombard claims she did in *True Confession*), murder is not alien to the genre. For example, madcap merriment joins murder in such genre works as *The Ex-Mrs. Bradford* (1936), *True Confessions* (1937), *Mad Miss Manton* (1938), and *Topper Returns* (1941).

The late 1930s influx of fantasy into screwball comedy also reinforced the frequent tendency toward female dominance in the genre. Pivotal films, such as *Topper* (1937, which triggered the movement), *Topper Takes a Trip* (1939), *Turnabout* (1940), *Topper Returns* (1941), and *I Married a Witch* (1942)—all of which are drawn from the work of novelist Thorne Smith—frequently favor the female lead via her supernatural powers. Even *Turnabout*, which is more about comic fantasy victims (the misadventures of a husband

and wife who exchange bodies), ends with a decidedly pro-woman screwball twist. While female star Carole Landis howls with laughter, it is revealed that, though genielike Mr. Ram has returned the husband and wife to their correct bodies, the baby Landis has been carrying did not leave Papa's body. But this surprising final plot twist was anything but hidden in the film's print ad campaign, where *the stork* gives an overview of the plot, closing with "And who's to get Baby? Makes my face red!"[15] Thus, husband John Hubbard is soon to make medical history, and screwball comedy registers another "turnabout."

The female's domination of the screwball male also exists on a more self-conscious level. Stanley Cavell has written of his fascination with *The Lady Eve*'s "daring declaration" of its "awareness of itself, of its existence as a film."[16] The "daring declaration" he has in mind is what might be called the Barbara Stanwyck–directed scene of the handsome but awkward, naive Henry Fonda first entering the ship's dining room/nightclub. The viewer watches the reflected image of Fonda in Stanwyck's makeup mirror as she narrates to the point of providing dialogue and direction for both the antihero and the many coquettes interested in the fortune from his family's brewery ("Pike's Pale, the Ale that Won for Yale").

Cavell's observation "that the woman [Stanwyck] is some kind of stand-in for the role of director fits our understanding that the man [Fonda], the sucker, is a stand-in for the role of the audience."[17] Cavell's realization of the Stanwyck-as-director, film-within-a-film nature of this scene is insightful. But, while he relates this incident to the generally self-conscious nature of the genre, he misses the opportunity to add two other observations: here is another strong screwball comedy heroine (what he would call a Hollywood comedy of remarriage heroine) and such woman-as-director scenes occur in other films of the genre.

Excellent variations occur in both *My Favorite Wife* and *The Ex-Mrs. Bradford.* The funniest and most traditional example presents Irene Dunne's in-film manipulation of Cary Grant in *My Favorite*

Wife, when she "directs" the reenactment of his marriage proposal to his second wife (Gail Patrick). While Stanwyck's "direction" of Fonda might be labeled omnipotent narration because the antihero male is unaware of her, Dunne's assumption of the director's role follows more customary lines.

She discusses Grant's motivations and his lines, defining his physical movement in an imaginary set of her own design. She also portrays her version of the second wife, a delightful parody somewhere between the stereotype of the icy, self-centered socialite that Gail Patrick played so well (see also her Cornelia Bullock in *My Man Godfrey*) and the comically bored attitude of a Gabor sister discussing her collection of husbands. And, as in *The Lady Eve*, the female "director" has the male jumping through hoops.

The heroine as director of a film-within-a-film scene goes beyond the merely metaphorical in *The Ex-Mrs. Bradford.* In this *Thin*

A Thin Man*–like scenario goes screwball in* The Ex-Mrs. Bradford *(1936, with William Powell and Jean Arthur).*

Man–like film (though a more vulnerable William Powell is now teamed with Jean Arthur), Arthur orchestrates a movie-closing marriage to Powell using a minister who has already been filmed going through the ceremony (with more apparent direction from Arthur). Powell and Arthur face a truly "cinematic" minister on a screen within the movie, while the viewer becomes witness to probably the best example of screwball heroine as film director.

Despite this growth of the female role, there are occasionally pre–World War II screwball comedies in which the male apparently is in a more commanding position, like wheeler-dealer Cary Grant of *His Girl Friday* (1940) or suave and cerebral William Powell of *My Man Godfrey*. But this commanding position is only apparent; there are four qualifiers.

The most obvious qualifier is that if a screwball comedy allows one male more than average power, it creates additional female-dominated males. The genre maintains a balance that never allows maleness much total power. The Grant figure of *His Girl Friday* is more than balanced by a host of frustrated milquetoast antiheroes, especially Rosalind Russell's comic "yes-man" fiancé Ralph Bellamy, an insurance man living with his mother (Bellamy being the period's favorite romantic also-ran), and such engaging characterizations as Billy Gilbert's Silas F. Pinkus, a much buffeted-about messenger. (Gilbert's other credits already included two-reeler frustrations at the hands of *the* antihero "couple," Laurel and Hardy, and as the voice of cartoon character Sneezy in Walt Disney's *Snow White and the Seven Dwarfs*, 1938.)

In *My Man Godfrey* the key milquetoast qualifiers to Powell are the female-dominated Bullock father (Eugene Pallette, who specialized in this type of role—see *The Lady Eve*) and his wife's art "protégé" (Mischa Auer, whose characterization of family pet Carlo and his ape imitations rated a nomination for Best Supporting Actor Oscar in 1936).

The second balance to any depiction of male strength is that the focal male initially is shown in a lowly or weak situation. The wealthy Powell is first seen as a tramp, a "forgotten man," at the city dump, and later as the Bullock butler, which makes him Lombard's servant. Grant's newspaper editor character is overpowered by Russell, verbally and physically, at the opening of *His Girl Friday*. By initially leaving Grant, she defeats him in professional as well as private life, having formerly been both his wife and his reporter. Throughout the rest of the film he must play catch-up. (Russell's delightfully overwhelming reporter in *His Girl Friday* draws heavily on a similar role she had in *Four's a Crowd*, 1938, a fact that has seemingly gone unnoticed.)

A third explanation for any male strength is that on the rare occasion when he seems to win, it is only a Pyrrhic victory. For example, at the close of *My Man Godfrey* Lombard masterminds a marriage with Powell (more "direction" by the female), something he has been avoiding during the whole film, and one's last impression of the two records that inevitable transfer of power from male to female. The *New York Times* even put it more strongly, claiming Powell's Godfrey never had a chance against

> the forthright emotional processes of that bovine divinity (or vice versa) Irene [Lombard], who is somewhat surer than death or taxes. Godfrey, when we leave him, is being led to the slaughter and it's enough to bring tears to the eyes of an Eli.[18]

Lombard has, quite literally, made Powell "my man Godfrey."

A final qualifier encourages the viewer to reexamine the screwball comedy in question for role reversal. For instance, a revisionist "reading" of *His Girl Friday* might suggest Grant is playing the genre's traditional eccentric female in order to save Rosalind Russell from the comic rigidity of marrying a boring "stiff" (Ralph Bellamy).

The fourth antiheroic component in screwball comedy (after professorial leisure time, childlike nature, and male frustration) is a propensity for physical comedy. This visual shtick is a product of four factors. First, the genre's farcical foundation is geared toward broad comedy. In *The Awful Truth* Irene Dunne is visited by three love interests in quick succession. The first two (Cary Grant and Alexander

D'Arcy) end up selecting the same bedroom hiding place. Once Grant discovers he has company in paradise, an off-screen donnybrook soon follows, which comically parallels the arrival of lover number three (Ralph Bellamy) and his mother. The slapstick conclusion finds Grant chasing D'Arcy out of the apartment and down the hall. (Prior to their sprint past a shocked Bellamy and company, the Grant-D'Arcy fight is showcased via comic off-screen sound effects—another regular component of McCarey's Laurel and Hardy films.)

Variations on this romantic hide-and-seek are common for the genre, be it Streisand avoiding O'Neal's fiancée (Madeline Kahn) in *What's Up, Doc?*, or Goldie Hawn's constant concealing of a past lover (Chevy Chase) from her husband (Charles Grodin) in *Seems Like Old Times*. And Blake Edwards orchestrates the sexy slapstick of bedroom farce to high art in *Victor/Victoria*.

A second reason for screwball comedy's physical comedy tendencies is that the genre was born (1934) just after the heyday of silent comedy. Indeed, pivotal director Leo McCarey, a great fan of Chaplin, helped redefine silent comedy by way of his teaming and molding of Laurel and Hardy. And for the remainder of his career he frequently applied those visual skills to his feature films, especially when they were screwball comedies.

In McCarey's *The Awful Truth*, for example, he showcases his signature scenes of escalating destructiveness and/or absurdity. Thus, when Irene Dunne decides to win Cary Grant back, she first crashes a private party and pretends to be his screwball sister. She then orchestrates a series of misadventures with their car while the radio blares away. But instead of adjusting the car radio knob, Dunne pulls it off and mischievously tosses it. And when they are stopped by the police and exit said car, she pulls the emergency brake—guaranteeing the vehicle will crash. This necessitates that Dunne and Grant each ride on the motorcycle handlebars of the two policemen . . . and so it goes.

What makes such comic nonsense doubly entertaining are two additional McCarey touches—a starting point in believability (Dunne wanting Grant back) and Grant's dignified composure while Dunne wreaks havoc around him. Once again, this is straight from the world McCarey created for Laurel and Hardy—where comedy antagonists exercise serious self-control while taking turns with their tit-for-tat violence as the commonplace becomes chaos.

McCarey could, moreover, take the most basic of Laurel and Hardy visual shtick, such as their comic propensity to accidentally switch derbies, and turn it toward farcical ends. For instance, when Grant is about to leave Dunne's *Awful Truth* apartment (with Alexander D'Arcy already hiding in her bedroom), the dog brings him D'Arcy's derby, instead of his own. Besides being every bit as funny as Stan and Ollie in mismatched hats, this time around it resonates with the promise of the slapstick farce about to follow. Indeed, *Time* magazine would praisingly label this the scene of "shriekingly circumstantial derby hats."[19]

The hat routine from The Awful Truth, *with Cary Grant, Irene Dunne, and screwball comedy's favorite pooch—Mr. Smith (Asta).*

Significantly, *The Awful Truth* was a major critical and commercial success that became a must-see picture for film lovers everywhere. *New York Daily News* reviewer Wanda Hale best captured this enthusiasm when she wrote, "About every person in New York who goes to the Music Hall [theatre] this . . . week will report that 'The Awful Truth' 'IS THE FUNNIEST PICTURE I EVER SAW.'"[20] Fittingly, the *New York Time*'s rave review added,

> McCarey . . . shocks us with a comedy in which speech is subsidiary . . . [and] the final result is a picture liberally strewn with authentic audience laughs which appear to be just as unashamedly abdominal as they were in the days of [silent comedy star] Fatty Arbuckle.[21]

Hawks, screwball comedy's other pivotal director (besides McCarey) during the genre's heyday, was equally known for his physical comedy. Though not as innovative as McCarey, his visual style had possibly a greater ongoing impact on the genre because of the longevity of his screwball career. As with McCarey, Hawks started as a silent director. And through the years he peppered his work with a compendium of classic visual shtick from an earlier era.

Bringing Up Baby, for example, has numerous Laurel and Hardy gags, such as characters stepping into allegedly shallow water, only to comically disappear from sight. Moreover, Hawks based Cary Grant's character on silent comedy star Harold Lloyd, yet also gave him Buster Keaton traits, such as a mock strangling of leading lady Hepburn when she exasperates him yet again.

In Hawks's *I Was a Male War Bride* he more ambitiously footnotes Keaton by shooting a variation of a scene from the silent star's *Sherlock Junior* (1924). In the original, Keaton is being given a ride on the handlebars of a policeman's motorcycle. But the cop soon falls off, after hitting a bump, and Keaton's title character is left unaware he is riding solo on the handlebars. The comedy that follows is then predicated on a series of miraculous near misses. Hawks reworks this scenario in *War Bride*, with Grant riding in a motorcycle sidecar oblivious to the absence of a driver.

The Hawks-Keaton physical comedy connection also has another parallel. Hawksian slapstick often works on a cerebral level, as is the case with Keaton. Thus, when Grant's brontosaurus skeleton collapses (the ultimate pratfall) to close *Bringing Up Baby*, it is funny for intellectual reasons—the symbolic collapse of the professor's rigidity.

In contrast, McCarey's visual comedy often plays on a more emotional level, which was also typical of his hero (Chaplin). For instance, at the conclusion of *The Awful Truth*, the mechanical male clock figure (Cary Grant) shows decidedly human (sexual) emotions when it deviates from its normal path to join a female figure. (The scene is reminiscent of Chaplin becoming a mechanical figure in a giant clockfacelike setting during *The Circus*, 1928.)

A third explanation for the genre's physical comedy's tendencies is tied to the phenomenal pantomime skills and ongoing influence of Cary Grant. Though these gifts and more are examined at length in chapter 4, it bears noting that he was screwball comedy's most indispensable performer. Even Hawks was moved to say, "It's pretty hard to think of anybody but Cary Grant in that type of stuff [screwball comedy]. He was so far the best that there isn't anybody to be compared to him."[22] While the screwball vision of McCarey and Hawks is largely visual, it is best realized when Grant stars in their productions—which he did a whopping seven times.

It is an often ignored fact that as a boy Grant began his entertainment career as an acrobatic comic in the music halls and variety theaters of England, where he was born. Grant spent most of his teen years with Robert Pender's celebrated collection of knockabout boy comedians and their completely visual routines. It was one of Britain's top acts and toured continuously, eventually bringing Grant to the United States in the 1920s. This background mirrors the Karno music hall tours and training of cinema's greatest visual/physical comedian, Charlie Chaplin, a special favorite of Grant's. (Moreover, Grant's first wife was Chaplin's

Leo McCarey (left) on the set of The Awful Truth *with Irene Dunne and Alex D'Arcy.*

former leading lady from *City Lights*, 1931, Virginia Cherrill, who played the blind girl.)

Grant, who has revealed that the high point of a frequently unhappy childhood was attending silent film comedy (from the pioneering John Bunny to Charlie Chaplin), observed of his experience with the Pender troupe:

> I grew to appreciate the fine art of pantomime. No dialogue was used in our act and each day, on a bare stage, we learned . . . how to convey a mood or meaning without words . . . how best immediately and precisely to effect an emotional response—a laugh or, sometimes, a tear.[23]

Longtime Grant friend and associate Don Barclay, having noticed Grant take some unnecessary falls in the mud for a film (presumably *I Was a Male War Bride*), said, "It would seem that these bits of slapstick were Grant's favorite requirement for a cinema role."[24] In many ways, the revisionist screwball comedy *Male Bride* is best examined as *the* Cary Grant tour de force of visual comedy, from this book's already highlighted examples to the inspired scene where he attempts to sleep the night away in a chair. Pete Martin, the *Saturday Evening Post*'s legendary movie biographer, would credit Grant at that time with having lifted silent comedy basics to a "high plane."[25]

A fourth and final reason for screwball comedy's slapstick ways is the 1940's meteorlike impact of writer/director Preston Sturges on the genre. He made several classic screwball comedies at the close of the genre's initial movement (early 1940s), including *The Lady Eve*, *The Palm Beach Story*, and *The Miracle of Morgan's Creek* (1944).

Coming at a time when the genre was winding down, these major critical and commercial hits were perceived as both a screwball summing up, as well as stretching the genre's basics to the comic maximum. The passage of time has only confirmed these verdicts. And not surprisingly, physical comedy is central to Sturges's work. Indeed, at the height of this auteur's career, *New York Times* critic Bosley Crowther fittingly entitled an article on Sturges "When Satire and Slapstick Meet."[26] And shortly after this (1945), film critic and scriptwriter Frank Nugent penned a *Variety* essay on Sturges titled "Genius with a Slapstick."[27]

The latter piece includes Sturges's own laws of what govern film box office, with the final axiom being, "a pratfall is better than anything."[28] Appropriately, Sturges's laws were initially composed in 1934—a year now considered the starting point of screwball comedy—in Sturges's early Hollywood days as a scriptwriter. Though he could write witty dialogue like few others, his use of slapstick seemed to best punctuate his work, from Barbara Stanwyck's gift for making Henry Fonda fall in *The Lady Eve* to the amazing height achieved by William Demarest's pratfalls in *The Miracle of Morgan's Creek.*

Sturges was truly a screwball comedy hybrid, a former Broadway playwright who was also a student of silent film comedy. This combination is best showcased in his last great movie, *The Sin of Harold Diddlebock* (1947), which was reedited and reissued as *Mad Wednesday* in 1950. Part clown comedy (it stars silent comedian Harold Lloyd) and part screwball comedy, it is a fascinating attempt to update what had become of Lloyd's 1920s go-getter persona. Most provocatively, Sturges opens the picture with the final reel of Lloyd's celebrated silent, *The Freshman* (1925), and its visually inventive football game. Now considered a classic, neither *Diddlebock* nor its *Mad Wednesday* edition was a commercial success, due to the interference of sometimes producer Howard Hughes. But Sturges remains a pivotal figure in the history of screwball comedy, as well as a major proponent of the genre's often visual nature.

The fifth antiheroic characteristic in screwball comedy (joining professorial leisure time, childlike nature, male frustration, and physical comedy) is a proclivity for parody and satire. Consistent with the genre's spoofing tone toward romance, screwball comedy affectionately kids both its talent base and the movies themselves. As already noted, both *The Awful Truth* and *Nothing Sacred* burlesque scenes from Capra's *Mr. Deeds Goes to Town* (1936).

The close of Bogdanovich's *What's Up, Doc?* provides a modern-era take on this phenomenon. With batting eyes, Streisand tells

O'Neal, "Love means never having to say you're sorry," which is the signature line from the schmaltzy box-office smash *Love Story* (1970), which also starred O'Neal. The actor's *What's Up, Doc?* comeback, "That's the dumbest thing I ever heard," is the perfect spoof of the earlier picture.

Hawks encouraged this parody nature more than any other screwball director. Entertaining examples highlight most of his outings in the genre. In his *Twentieth Century*, John Barrymore slips onto the train in a disguise that includes a false putty nose. Known as the "Great Profile" in real life, once on the train Barrymore burlesques that famous profile by pulling on his putty schnoz. And he ultimately tops this by then picking his false proboscis.

In Hawks's *His Girl Friday* Grant instructs one of his stooges (the entertaining Abner Biberman) to follow Ralph Bellamy. When Biberman asks for a description Grant says, "He looks like, um, that fellow in the movies, you know, Ralph Bellamy." Later in the same picture Grant has a disagreement with the governor, "Listen, the last man who said that to me was Archie Leach [Grant's real name], just a week before he cut his throat."

At the beginning of Hawks's *Monkey Business,* he spoofs both screwball comedy's predisposition for absentminded professors, as well as Grant's gift for playing them. Having Grant repeatedly come out the front door of his house early, the director (in voiceover narration) admonishes him each time, "Not yet, Cary." By doing the voiceover himself, as well as using the actor's legally adopted name, instead of his *Monkey Business* character name, Hawks further personalized this example of screwball spoofing.

Though the standard example of screwball parody is of the hit-or-miss variety already profiled, the genre is equally capable of a more ambitious take on burlesque. For instance, in *The Awful Truth* McCarey improvised a "Home on the Range" duet between Irene Dunne and Ralph Bellamy. Film theorist Stanley Cavell suggests Bellamy is immediately telegraphed as a loser after the number because he asks Dunne whether she has had lessons.[29]

(Despite having butchered the song, Bellamy is proud of not having had instruction.)

McCarey's derailing of Bellamy, however, is built upon a spoof that asks this question of an actress (Dunne) then equally famous as a singer. She had just starred in the major musical *Show Boat* (1936) the year before *The Awful Truth*! So, this wink, wink example of parody is both more drawn out (including the "Home on the Range" duet) *and* further fleshes out our knowledge of the characters. That is, poor Bellamy is a boob not only for being unaware of Dunne's singing background, but also for being positively vain about his awful "never had a lesson" voice. On the flip side, Dunne's stock with the viewer goes up because she makes no attempt to lord it over no-talent Bellamy, even though his behavior merits payback.

McCarey's use of a more complex screwball comedy spoof is not without later precedent in the genre. In Hawks's *Monkey Business* Cary Grant's wife (Ginger Rogers) accidentally joins him in drinking some of the youth serum randomly concocted by a lab monkey. The young again Rogers suddenly has a need to dance. This is an imaginative parody nod to Rogers's 1930s dance film teaming with the celebrated Fred Astaire.

Parody is an *affectionate* kidding of a well-known commodity, whether it is Dunne's past association with singing or Rogers's earlier dancing partnership with Astaire. Spoofing is without malice. Instead, it is more a comic celebration of a cinematic in-joke—an added bonus for the attentive viewer who knows his or her film history.

Of course, at its most fundamental level (as previously cited), screwball comedy's use of parody involves its continuous razzing of romance. But even here there are special individual jabs and/or throwaway lines that spoof love in other pictures. For example, early in Billy Wilder's *The Major and the Minor* star Ginger Rogers walks by an extra leafing through a movie fan magazine in Grand Central Station. As Rogers passes said character, the extra randomly reads an article title aloud, "'Why I Hate Women' by Charles Boyer." The line works on two parody levels. First, it kids the fact that screwball comedy males are forever frustrated by women. Second, and more pointedly, it takes a period performer (Boyer) associated with romantic comedy (such as *Love Affair*, 1939) and supposedly reveals even he does not like women.

Screwball films, however, frequently trade moments of parody for lengthier patches of biting satire. Indeed, the genre sometimes has a satirical component that stretches the entire length of the individual film. Unlike the affectionate fun of parody, satire is a more darkly comic corrective, lampooning what is meant to be perceived as negative behavior and/or a reproachable institution.

While the parody moment often went unacknowledged, screwball's almost satirical base invariably rated critical comment. For instance, the *London Daily Telegraph* praised *Twentieth Century*'s takeoff on theatre excesses.[30] The *New York World-Telegram* anchored their rave review of *My Man Godfrey* in its satire of the upper classes, a critical slant that could be applied to numerous screwball comedies.[31] The same *World-Telegram* keyed its kudos for *True Confession* in the movie's satire of courtroom law, another popular screwball comedy target.[32] (Former lawyer McCarey included courtroom scenes in both *The Awful Truth* and *My Favorite Wife*.)

An army of film critics focused their *Nothing Sacred* reviews on that picture's send-up of print journalism. For example, *The New York Post* said it "takes effective pot shots at the hypocrisy of sensational journalism."[33] *Variety* celebrated the movie's satirical scriptwriter Ben Hecht—"poking fun in the typical Hechtian manner of half-scorn at the newspaper publisher, his reporter, doctors, the newspaper business, phonies, suckers, and whatnot."[34] And the *New York Times* merely recycled Hechtian journalism barbs, such as describing a city editor as "a cross between a ferris wheel and a werewolf."[35] (With many screwball comedy screenwriters once having been reporters, such as Hecht, journalism is often a popular target for the genre.)

Given all the apparent differences between screwball comedy's use of parody and satire, there is still sometimes confusion. This is especially true of satirical situations that involve individuals instead of institutions. For instance, while Ralph Bellamy's *Awful Truth* performance sometimes inspired parody situations, such as the previously noted "Home on the Range" scene, some period critics found the totality of Bellamy's role a satire of crackerbarrel populist Will Rogers.[36] Besides spouting folksy truism, as populist types like Rogers are want to do, his whole body language bespoke the "aw-shucks" bashfulness of the rural rustic.

The topper, however, to this dig at Rogers was in having Bellamy's character be full of praise for his Oklahoma ranch. Rogers was that state's most famous citizen. And his down home humor was often peppered with references to Oklahoma and/or his ranch. But what made Rogers such a topical source of satirical digs was the near populist deification that had occurred after his 1935 death in a plane crash. Thus, Bellamy's gently satirical take on Rogers suggests homespun wisdom, regardless of its ties to an earlier purer America, often proven inadequate in the complexly antiheroic modern world.

This then daring Rogers dimension to Bellamy's role also helps explain his somewhat surprising Oscar nomination in the supporting actor category. Though he would lose to Joseph Schildkraut (as Captain Dreyfus in *The Life of Emile Zola*, 1937), Bellamy's satirical *Awful Truth* turn would define his Hollywood career for years. His most entertaining later variation of this character would, of course, be in *His Girl Friday*, with Cary Grant again being his nemesis.

These then have been the five key antiheroic characteristics that help define screwball comedy (professorial leisure time, childlike nature, male frustration, physical comedy, and a tendency for parody and satire). None of these components are limited to screwball comedy. But when grouped together they best describe this genre of derailed romantic eccentricity. The thread that links them is a propensity for the unconventional, whether it is time-to-burn childish behavior or the "nothing sacred" behavior associated with parody and satire.

This air of the unconventional is not the iconoclasm of the early Marx Brothers, but it is in the same crazy comedy neighborhood. Unlike, however, the comedy juggernaut that is Groucho, Harpo, and Chico, screwball comedy also highlights those slapstick speed bumps along the way—which is where physical shtick and male frustration come in. While a much battered (or is that *batty*?) affair of the heart is a less-than-respected part of the screwball mix, only *romantic* comedy gets serious about love.

Notes

1. Herb Sterne, *I Married a Witch* review, *Rob Wagner's Script* (December 19, 1942), in *Selected Film Criticism, 1941-50*, ed. Anthony Slide (Metuchen, N.J.: Scarecrow Press, 1983), p. 85; Richard Schickel, *Cary Grant* (New York: Applause Books, 1999), p. 56.
2. Douglas W. Churchill, "Laughter at So Much per Tickle," *New York Times*, February 6, 1938, Section 10, p. 5.
3. Leo McCarey, "Comedy and a Touch of the Cuckoo," *Extension*, November 1944, p. 34.
4. Henri Bergson, "Laughter" (1900), in *Comedy*, ed. Wylie Sypher (Garden City, N.Y.: Doubleday, 1956), pp. 68, 147.
5. Bergson, "Laughter" (1900), pp. 174–75.
6. Bergson, "Laughter" (1900), pp. 69, 178–79; George Meredith, "An Essay on Comedy" (1877), in *Comedy*, ed. Wylie Sypher, p. 44.
7. Miguel de Cervantes, *The History of Don Quixote of the Mancha*, trans. Thomas Shelton (New York: P. F. Collier & Son, 1969), pp. 18–19.
8. Bergson, "Laughter" (1900), p. 155.
9. Molly Haskell, "Man's Favorite Sport? (Revisited)," in *Focus on Howard Hawks*, ed. Joseph McBride (Englewood Cliffs, N.J.: Prentice-Hall, 1972), p. 136.
10. Haskell, "Man's Favorite Sport?, p. 136.
11. Haskell, "Man's Favorite Sport?, p. 136.
12. Stanley Cavell, *Pursuits of Happiness: The Hollywood Comedy of Remarriage* (Cambridge, Mass.: Harvard University Press, 1981), p. 119.
13. James Thurber, "The Car We Had to Push," in *My Life and Hard Times* (New York: Bantam Books, 1947), p. 41.
14. Eric Hatch, *My Man Godfrey* (Boston: Little, Brown, 1935), p. 65.
15. *Turnabout* advertisement, *Photoplay*, July 1940, p. 5.
16. Cavell, *Pursuits of Happiness*, p. 66.

17. Cavell, *Pursuits of Happiness*, p. 66.

18. *My Man Godfrey* review, *New York Times*, September 18, 1936, p. 18.

19. *The Awful Truth* review, *Time*, November 1, 1937, p. 45.

20. Wanda Hale, "'The Awful Truth' Now at Music Hall," *New York Daily News*, November 5, 1937.

21. *The Awful Truth* review, *New York Times*, November 5, 1937, p. 19.

22. Joseph McBride, *Hawks on Hawks* (Berkeley: University of California Press, 1982), p. 69.

23. Cary Grant (with the unaccredited assistance of Joe Hyams), "Archie Leach," *Ladies Home Journal*, January/February 1963 (first of three-part series; see also March and April issues of 1963), p. 136.

24. Pete Martin, "How Grant Took Hollywood," *Saturday Evening Post*, February 19, 1949, p. 59.

25. Martin, "How Grant Took Hollywood," p. 57.

26. Bosley Crowther, "When Satire and Slapstick Meet," *New York Times Magazine*, August 27, 1944, pp. 14–15, 37.

27. Frank Nugent, "Genius with a Slapstick," *Variety*, February 7, 1945, pp. 2, 23.

28. Nugent, "Genius with a Slapstick," p. 23.

29. Cavell, *Pursuits of Happiness*, pp. 246–48.

30. "New Films in London," *Daily Telegraph*, July 9, 1934.

31. William Boehnel, "Music Hall Film Spoofs Upper Classes," *New York World-Telegram*, September 18, 1936, p. 26.

32. William Boehnel, "Law Given Same Digs in 'True Confession,'" *New York World-Telegram*, December 16, 1937.

33. Archer Winsten, "'Nothing Sacred at the Radio City Music Hall," *New York Post*, November 26, 1937, p. 31.

34. *Nothing Sacred* review, *Variety*, December 1, 1937.

35. *Nothing Sacred* review, *New York Times*, November 26, 1937, p. 27.

36. For example, see Marguerite Tazelaar, "'The Awful Truth'—Radio City Music Hall," *New York Herald Tribune*, November 5, 1937, p. 19.

CHAPTER THREE

ROMANTIC COMEDY

> I came here tonight because when you realize you want to spend the rest of your life with somebody, you want the rest of your life to start as soon as possible.
>
> —The seriousness of love from Billy Crystal in *When Harry Met Sally . . .* (1989)

Using screwball comedy as an ongoing contrast, this chapter more fully fleshes out romantic comedy's fundamental configuration. This necessitates examining five pivotal components of the genre: the accenting of sentiment over silly, a propensity for serious and/or melodramatic overtones, more realistic characters (often employed), traditional dating ritual (less controlling woman), and slower story pacing (especially near the end of the picture).

Though romantic comedy has its fair share of funny scenes, it is dead serious about the importance of love. For instance, when gifted writer/director James L. Brooks went on the talk show circuit promoting his inspired romantic comedy *As Good As It Gets* (1997, co-scripted with Mark L. Andrus), he addressed just this subject. Brooks found the first cut of the picture *too* funny. While this might be an enviable position for most filmmakers, he felt the comedy distracted from the budding relationship—from romance. The finished film is still often brilliantly comic, but the love story comes first.

This earnestness about love is what prompted the use of the Billy Crystal quote (scripted by Nora Ephron) that opens this chapter. If such sentiments were to surface in the "nothing sacred" world of screwball comedy, they would immediately be subject to satirical rebuke. For example, in the screwball *What's Up, Doc?* (1972) the traditional love interest (Madeline Kahn) observes, "As the years go by, romance fades, and something else takes its place. Do you know what that is?" "Senility" is the devastatingly funny put-down from her fiancé (Ryan O'Neal, no less).

This having been said, romantic comedy is still dependent upon a passion for love, often best showcased in fervent dialogue. After directing *Sleepless in Seattle* (1993, which she also coscripted), Nora Ephron observed that in the old days "talk was the sex of the romantic movie. People fell in love from what they said to one another. Now sex is more problematic, and maybe we're going back to romantic comedies."[1]

Ephron's claim for talk being the "sex of the [old] romantic movie" might best be equated to a letter excerpt from *The Shop around the Corner* (1940), which she later successfully updated (with coscripter and sister Delia Ephron) and directed as *You've Got Mail* (1998). The *Shop* scene in question has Jimmy Stewart sharing a love letter quote from his anonymous pen pal with a close friend. The sexy suggestiveness of the excerpt is both in the wording and the reading by Stewart—"My heart was trembling as I walked into the post office and there you were lying in box 237. I took you out of your envelope and read you. Read you right there. Oh, my dear friend."

This ardor for love further characterizes the genre by suggesting one's life is not complete without finding that significant other person. This phenomenon of being in love with love is often clearly stated early in the picture. Even in an otherwise journeyman effort like the Drew Barrymore romantic comedy, *Never Been Kissed* (1999), this naive but earnest belief is poignantly presented at the start of the movie. Barrymore describes the bells and whistle moment that will occur when she finally kisses Mr. Right:

> The only thing in focus is you and this person. And you realize that person is the only person that you're supposed to kiss for the rest of your life. And for one moment, you get this amazing gift. And you want to laugh, and you want to cry, because you feel so lucky that you found it and so scared that it'll go away, all at the same time.

In accenting the sentiment inherent in romantic comedy's celebration of love, the genre sometimes mixes a reality base with a certain suspension of disbelief—not unlike the feel-good acceptance one brings to a Frank Capra populist picture. The Capra oeuvre is dependent upon what is sometimes called a "fantasy of goodwill." This is equated not with literal fantasy but rather with a belief in the inherent goodness of people. When consigned to romantic comedy, it means an easy acceptance of idealized love.

Fittingly, romantic comedy also often borrows another basic component from Capra populism—an older, experienced figure of practical wisdom. When transferred to romantic comedy, this character (already synonymous with feel-good sentimentality) becomes a benevolent facilitator and/or supporter of love. Moreover, this character also gives greater credibility to the genre's sometimes gossamer-like musings on the nature of love.

In *Hands across the Table* (1935), Ralph Bellamy's older handicapped flier ultimately orchestrates the romance between Carole Lombard and Fred MacMurray. What makes this pop culture celebration of love all the more tender is that Bellamy had also wanted to marry Lombard but felt she would be happier with MacMurray.

The grandmother (Maria Ouspenskaya) of Leo McCarey's *Love Affair* (1939) is not exactly a matchmaker, but she touchingly serves that same general purpose. Irene Dunne likes playboy Charles Boyer, but it is not until she sees him through the eyes of this loving grandmother that he becomes relationship material. This grandmother also accents the sentimental depiction of love in an additional manner often associated with romantic comedy: she is an ongoing symbol of the

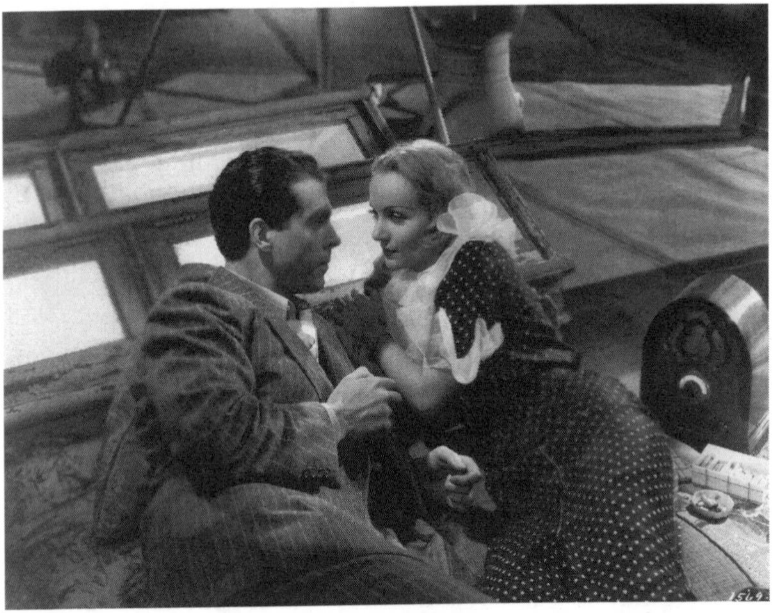

Rooftop romance in Hands Across the Table *(1935, with Carole Lombard and Fred MacMurray).*

eternal purity of love. Long widowed, she remains very much in love with her late husband, something that is warmly communicated to those around her without any degree of mawkishness. Plus, in death, her promise of a special scarf for Dunne is what brings the couple back together—Boyer delivers it and finally discovers why Dunne did not make their Empire State Building rendezvous.

Besides being central to *Love Affair*, as these older poignant figures often are, Ouspenskaya's performance is all the more moving given the actress's convincing naturalness in the part. This was a fact not lost on period reviewers. *New York Post* critic Archer Winsten observed, "This role is so deeply felt, so brilliantly paced and projected, that it will be remembered when parts ten or twenty times as big have long been forgotten."[2] A *Brooklyn Eagle* reviewer added, "Her playing of Boyer's grandmother . . . is a joy to watch—delicate, sincere and eloquently restrained."[3]

The significance of the part is retained in the movie's two remakes—*An Affair to Remember* (1957) and *Love Affair* (1994). Indeed, the role continued to have the power to usurp the featured romantic couple. For instance, the title for syndicated critic Roger Ebert's review of the latter film said it all: "[Katharine] Hepburn Steals Show in 'Love Affair.'"[4] Ebert went on to say of Hepburn, "the magnificent spirit is still there, and the romantic fire, and she's right for this eccentric [youthfully free-spirited] old woman."[5]

Therefore, in each of these three *Love Affair* movies, a charming older person represents not only a testimonial to the movie's romantic male lead but also a corroborative witness for a sentimental celebration of love. The most entertainingly inspired update on the latter perspective occurs in *When Harry Met Sally. . . .* Peppered throughout the movie are a series of interviews with elderly couples briefly but warmly chronicling their love story. In each instance, they are fittingly seated on a love seat looking straight at the camera. The first such instance has an older man observing,

> I was sitting with my friend Arthur Kornblum, in a restaurant—it was a Horn and Hardart Cafeteria—and this beautiful girl walked in [he points to the woman beside him], and I turned to Arthur and I said, "Arthur, you see that girl? I'm going to marry her." And two weeks later we were married. And it's over fifty years later and we're still married.

When Harry Met Sally . . . further underlines the importance of these segments by opening and closing the picture with them. Moreover, by making the finale duo Harry and Sally, it further suggests the permanence of their relationship. That is, the viewer identifies them with all the proceeding golden-aged testimonials to love.

The *When Harry Met Sally . . .* close also makes for a more artistically satisfying movie—the pleasing symmetry of an effective device (witnesses for love) coming full circle to include the focus couple. In addition, it is a legitimate reason to include a postscript, which reinforces the love story by having them still together. Four years after scripting *When Harry Met Sally . . .*, Nora Ephron could still observe,

> I just love that you can ask a married couple how they met and it's their favorite story. You know—the little circumstances that brought them together. Even the most miserable married couples get all warm and cuddly when they tell you that story.[6]

This phenomenon is also at the heart of Ephron's *Sleepless in Seattle*. For her, the movie "examines our tendency to hold on to our little romantic impulses enough to make a grand romantic story out of the accidents that brought us to the one person we're now attached to."[7] This position suggests that our need to believe in love often bests a more realistic take on relationships.

A variation upon Ephron's moving use of an army of elderly witnesses for love in *When Harry Met Sally* . . . occurs in Bonnie Hunt's *Return to Me* (1999). The latter movie has Carroll O'Connor and Robert Loggia running an Irish-Italian eatery and looking out for their granddaughter/niece Minnie Driver. Surrogate parents O'Connor and Loggia are assisted in their matchmaking duties by several restaurant regulars, who come to represent an extended family for Driver and eventual beau David Duchovny. Fittingly, the group not only represents a celebration of love vis-à-vis the young couple, but also, by the picture's close, two members of this senior group have also become a romantic couple.

Return to Me and *When Harry Met Sally* . . . notwithstanding, however, the typical romantic comedy is still more apt to key upon a single older quasi-catalyst, as demonstrated with the various *Love Affair* productions. Other solo examples would include Charles Coburn in *The More the Merrier* (1943), Myrna Loy's uncle (Ray Collins) in *The Bachelor and the Bobby-Soxer* (1947), Maurice Chevalier as the private eye dad of Audrey Hepburn in *Love in the Afternoon* (1957), Vittorio De Sica in *It Started in Naples* (1960), the wheelchair philosopher Al (Dominic Chianese) in the little known but hilarious *If Lucy Fell* (1996), and Helen Hunt's mother (Shirley Knight) in *As Good As It Gets* (1997). (Occasionally the wise older figure even becomes the lover, such as Sally Fields falling for crackerbarrel type James Garner in 1985's *Murphy's Romance*, for which he received an Oscar nomination.)

The wisdom of this veteran love merchant is not, however, always heeded by the younger party. And this only adds to the comic charm of the characterization—the older figure persistently pushing for what turns out to be the right development. I am especially reminded of Shirley Knight popping out of nowhere, yet again, near the close of *As Good As It Gets*, to remind her daughter love is not perfect. But a more whimsical wisdom occurs in *Sleepless in Seattle*, when Meg Ryan's mother gently suggests love should strike like a thunderbolt. But the modern daughter (Ryan) simply dismisses this as old-fashioned . . . only to eventually experience it herself with Tom Hanks.

Maybe the most inventive take on the senior individual as catalyst occurs in Norman Krasna's *Princess O'Rourke* (1943), where an always off-camera President Franklin Roosevelt helps Olivia De Havilland's title character get married in the wartime White House. This whimsical plot device, after the picture's nominal matchmaker (Charles Coburn again) decides against matching De Havilland and Robert Cummings, might seem dated today. But it was a period twist that no doubt contributed to Krasna winning an Oscar for Best Original Screenplay.

Of course, the brass ring for most intelligent older matchmaker has to be Walter Matthau's winsome turn as Albert Einstein in the diverting romantic comedy *I. Q.* (1994). With the assistance of three septuagenarian scientist friends, Matthau's Einstein helps facilitate a romance between his niece (Meg Ryan) and a bookish auto mechanic masquerading as a genius (Tim Robbins). Though some critics might fault the storyline as being "too cute," this period (1950s) piece about a mechanic falling in love at first sight is well worth a screening, especially with Matthau's cagey scientist running the show.

My personal favorite orchestrator of romance for this genre, however, is *Pretty Woman*'s (1990) Hector Elizondo, who is the manager of the exclusive hotel Richard Gere stays at for much of the picture. Ostensibly only looking out for a wealthy resident's paramour (Hollywood hooker Julia Roberts), Elizondo brings an affectionately parental sensitivity to the Pygmalion-style remaking of Roberts. Thus, when he plays a major part in bringing Gere and Roberts together by the film's conclusion, it seems a natural evolution of his character. *Pretty Woman* director Garry Marshall has long considered Elizondo *good luck* for a production, and has cast him in eleven of his pictures. Never has this faith been more obvious than in *Pretty Woman*. Fittingly, Elizondo has added, "Working with him [Marshall], you're not afraid to fail, and that's the important thing. As an actor, you're not afraid to take a chance. He has that kind of confidence in you and in himself."[8]

Before leaving this first pivotal component of romantic comedy (accenting sentimental over silly), one must briefly address the genre's use of music. Now, rare is the movie that does not attempt to occasionally score plot points with music. This is especially true of the comedy genres, from the theme songs of various personality comedians (such as Laurel and Hardy's "Cuckoo Song" and Groucho Marx's "Hooray for Captain Spaulding") to the ironic juxtapositioning of music and visuals in dark comedy, like Malcolm McDowell warbling "Singin' in the Rain" while he beats a person in *A Clockwork Orange* (1971).

Despite the memorableness of these examples, one could argue that no other genre (comedy or otherwise) is so continually tied to music as romantic comedy. Plus, as benefits a section on sentiment, the majority of this music pulls upon the proverbial heart strings, such as Irene Dunne's movingly memorable rendition of "Wishing" in *Love Affair*. This revival of an old song, personally selected by Dunne, became a popular late 1930s hit. In the modern era, one of the most effective romantic comedy packaging of pertinent music occurs in *Sleepless in Seattle*, which had critics scrambling to document its phenomenal soundtrack sales.[9]

The *Sleepless* swoony mix of musical standards includes Louis Armstrong's "A Kiss to Build a Dream On," Nat King Cole's "Stardust," and Jimmy Durante's "As Time Goes By" and "Make Someone Happy." As the normally more cynical *New Yorker* said of this sentimental musical outing, "Ephron is a magpie of useful tunes, all of them guaranteed to put lumps in throats."[10] While this soundtrack produced great numbers, it merely reflected what most successful romantic comedies attempt—to pepper a love story with comparable music.

Probably the only thing unusual about the *Sleepless* soundtrack is the absence of a Dean Martin song. For years now his voice has been synonymous with the genre, from his "That's Amore" over the opening and closing titles of *Moonstruck* (1987) to his "Return to Me," also providing Bonnie Hunt with the title for her enchanting 1999 romantic comedy. Fittingly, the characters in *Return to Me* are even self-referential about Dean Martin, discussing his importance as a romantic singer.

Music in romantic comedy is so significant that central characters often have song-related careers, such as Irene Dunne being both a nightclub singer and voice instructor in *Love Affair*, Dudley Moore as a songwriter in *10* (1979), and Adam Sandler playing the title character in *The Wedding Singer* (1998). The fact that all three are musically gifted (Dunne and Sandler as singers and Moore as a pianist) merely enriches the pictures. But maybe the most innovative use of a song-related career in a romantic comedy occurs in John Cusack's brilliant but neglected *High Fidelity* (2000), which he also coscripted from Nick Hornby's inspired novel of the same name. Cusack's character owns a used record shop, which legitimizes his ongoing use of past recordings as a constant commentary on relationships.

The second key trait of the genre is a tendency for serious and/or melodramatic overtones—as if creating some supreme test by which love must prove itself. These decidedly somber story developments sometimes act as an opening prologue to the romantic comedy film. For instance, Warren Beatty's character dies in an accident at the start of *Heaven Can Wait* (1978). *Benny & Joon* (1993) has a title character (Mary Stuart Masterson) suffering from mental illness. *Sleepless in Seattle* opens with a funeral and is predicated upon the poignant early comments of a recent widower (Tom Hanks) on a radio call-in show. *Return to Me* also begins with both the gut-wrenching loss of a beloved wife and also a touch-and-go heart transplant.

Some romantic comedies introduce ominous plot twists later in the movie. For example, in *Love Affair* and its two high-profile remakes, a crippling near fatal accident halfway through the movie threatens to derail the romance. In each case the wheelchair-bound heroine is reluctant to continue a relationship in which pity might be a factor. (Each of the *Love Affair* installments also includes the moving loss of the grandmother, though the last version makes her the *aunt* of the male lead.) *Return to Me* actually has it both ways—the aforementioned somber opening, and Minnie Driver's later realization that the heart transplant she received was from her lover's (Duchovny) first wife! This seemingly perverse development initially threatens their relationship. But ultimately, when reframed (rethought), it is perceived as the ultimate romantic twist—the heart of Duchovny's first love beats on in the chest of his new love. Indeed, the implication is that the Duchovny-Driver coupling is directly related to a *heart* that would not be denied.

The genre's embracing of somber plot developments need not, however, go beyond the sometimes painful experiences associated with one's search for love. Audrey Hepburn's title character attempts suicide in *Sabrina* (1954) when the hurt for romance becomes more than she can stand. The owner (Frank Morgan) of the business in *The Shop around the Corner* tries to kill himself when he discovers his wife has been unfaithful. And in *Better Off Dead* (1985), as implied in the title, a very young John Cusack nearly hangs himself over the loss of his high school sweetheart.

Even when there is no attempted suicide, the threat of taking one's life is often bantered about. Nicolas Cage's loose cannon character in *Moonstruck* still bitterly claims he will go this route five years after losing his first love. In *If Lucy Fell*, the two central characters (Sarah Jes-

A pivotal romantic comedy Love Affair *(1939, with Irene Dunne and Charles Boyer).*

sica Parker and Eric Schaeffer) have a mutual death pact if they do not find themselves in meaningful relationships by the age of thirty.

In *The Truth about Cats and Dogs* (1996) Janeane Garofalo addresses this quiet desperation over love with darkly comic asides. For instance, when asked "What's wrong?" (why no relationships for three years), she replies, "Nothing that a roof top and an AK47 [rifle] won't take care of." Comedy coping notwithstanding, much of her romantic frustration has *Cyrano de Bergerac* overtones—she is displeased with her appearance. And she goes to comic extremes to have someone else physically double for her when a young man shows interest based on her radio personality (she has a call-in program).

Of course, the genre's ultimate *Cyrano* story is Steve Martin's touchingly funny *Roxanne* (1987), which he also scripted. Sporting a beak that would have impressed even Jimmy Durante, his appearance has forever foiled any chance for love—though he is the most romantically sensitive of men. Naturally, this begins to change when he is asked to become something of a romantic ghostwriter, only to have his passion finally recognized and appreciated.

One does not, however, have to possess such an obvious trait as a monster proboscis to feel physically unattractive. Drew Barrymore's *Never Been Kissed* frequently utilizes flashbacks to her ugly duckling high school years, which are excruciating painful. But the resonance of the flashbacks is tied neither to overly realistic situations nor to performances. Instead, there is a built-in empathy based upon the various anxieties most people have had to soldier through during rite of passage dating, especially in high school.

Cusack's *High Fidelity* provides a quick-witted crash course in romantic pain. It is reminiscent of the late 1970s style of Woody Allen, with both direct address first-person narration and antiheroic fascination over the complexities of modern romance. Cusack's frustrated lover has an "all-time top five" mentality about everything—a natural mind-set for a record shop owner.

Maybe the ultimate take on just how painful love can be occurs in *Moonstruck*, when Cage expresses his feelings for Cher in a long revisionist monologue about romantic misconceptions:

> I love you. Not, not like they [poets] told you love is. . . . Love don't make things nice. It ruins everything. It breaks your heart. It makes things a mess. We—we aren't here to make things perfect. The snowflakes are perfect. The stars are perfect. Not us. . . . We are here to ruin ourselves and to break our hearts and love the wrong people. And—and die. I mean, the storybooks are bullshit.

So why do we persist with such painful romantic games? A decade prior to *Moonstruck*, Woody Allen penned the most comically insightful explanation for taking risks of the heart in his classic *Annie Hall* (1977):

> This guy goes to a psychiatrist and says, "Doc, uh, my brother's crazy. He thinks he's a chicken." And, uh, the doctor says, "Well, why don't you turn him in?" And the guy says, "I would, but I need the eggs." Well, I guess that's pretty much how, how [sic] I feel about relationships. You know, they're totally irrational and crazy and absurd and . . . but, uh, I guess we keep goin' through it because, uh, most of us need the eggs.

Relationships do not always work. Even Alvy (Woody Allen) and Annie Hall (Diane Keaton) do not end up as a couple at the close of the picture. But romantic comedy teaches that despite all this love-related heartache, a relationship is well worth the risk. Anything less is not living. Thus, Dominic Chianese's sidewalk sage in *If Lucy Fell* advises a demoralized young romantic (Eric Schaeffer):

> I once had a girl. I'll never forget the day she told me, "I don't love you anymore." I never wanted to feel the way my gut felt that day, so I never took a chance. I stopped breathing, for Christ's sake . . . that's how much it hurt. So you can sit here with me, and not breathe the rest of your life, or you can give it a try [go after your love].

Before exiting romantic comedy's predisposition for serious or melodramatic overtones, one must note the genre's occasional revengeful moments—because not all victims want to roll over and die. At its most artful, such as with Spencer Tracy and Katharine Hepburn, it can be a thing of twisted comic beauty. A classic example occurs late in *Adam's Rib* (1949), after defense lawyer Hepburn has defeated fellow lawyer and husband Tracy in a court case involving attempted murder suspect Judy Holliday. Married to a womanizing Tom Ewell, Holliday shot her husband when she caught him in a romantic tryst.

Though Ewell's actions are despicable, Holliday's violent reprisal should in no way have been condoned by the court, which Hepburn had comically manipulated by turning the proceedings into a then pioneering study of gender double standards. But Tracy was later entertainingly able to make Hepburn recant when he caught her in a compromising romantic dalliance with wanna-be lover David Wayne.

Tracy pulls a gun on the couple in an apparent copycat rendition of the Judy Holliday shooting. Hepburn and Wayne's fear over what is about to transpire is the catalyst for her to realize and admit she was wrong about justifying violent revenge. With this victory, an apparently satisfied Tracy then changes the couple's fear to horror when he turns the gun on himself. Tracy tops what becomes a priceless dark comic moment by inserting the gun in his mouth, and then biting off the barrel of the pistol—the handgun was made of licorice!

Though simmering with black humor overtones, the strength of this defining scene is that Hepburn and Tracy overcome their differences and remain a romantic comedy couple. But when the comic revenge becomes an end in itself, as with *The War of the Roses* (1989) or *I Love You to Death* (1990), the film is best pigeonholed as a dark comedy. The only possible exception along these lines would be when the payback revenge leads to a *new* romance. For instance, in *Addicted to Love* (1997), Meg Ryan and Matthew Broderick join forces to stalk and disrupt the lives of their ex-lovers (who are now a couple), only to fall in love with each other.

The third central component of romantic comedy is a tendency to have more realistic characters, especially when compared with the screwball genre. Indeed, a commonality one finds while sifting through reviews of significant romantic comedies is a believability factor. For instance, the *New York Times* called 1935's *Hands across the Table* "close to the American scene," while the *Brooklyn Daily Eagle* labeled the film's star Carole Lombard a "believable manicurist."[11]

The *New York Sun* described the characters in *The Shop around the Corner* as "so completely natural that we accept their problems as our own."[12] Though set in Budapest, "It might just as well be in New York, or Middletown [Muncie, Indiana]."[13] The *New York Post* credited Spencer Tracy's sports writer in *Woman of the Year* (1942), the first of several Hepburn-Tracy romantic comedy collaborations, as a character "who has no pretensions but is able to do a good job at being a normal man."[14] The *New York Sun* said of the same film, director "George Stevens has directed with so light and sure a touch that the Sam Craig and Tess Harding characters [Hepburn and Tracy] become very real people."[15]

The high visibility of romantic comedy's realistic component is even a major argument for a revisionist reassessment of *It Happened One Night* (1934) being included in this genre, *instead* of in the

A calmer moment in Adam's Rib *(1949, with Spencer Tracy and Katharine Hepburn).*

screwball comedy camp. Period critics were taken with the naturalness of Capra's characters. For instance, the *New York World-Telegram* reviewer posited,

> He [Capra] is an observant student of human nature, and the players, as a result of his cunning advice, behave like real human beings and not like so many actors pretending to be characters. . . . Every one of them [the actors], from Miss Colbert and Mr. Gable down to the lowest extra, is right and complete.[16]

The fact that Capra has Gable entertainingly teaching Colbert common man talents, such as how to dunk donuts and hitchhike, is no little part of the movie's realistic charm.

This character believability even makes the film's unlikely conclusion—where heiress Colbert runs out on her wedding to be with

Clark Gable and Claudette Colbert on the verge of the hitchhiking scene in It Happened One Night.

Gable—seem quite natural. *Liberty Magazine* addressed just this issue in its 1934 review: "Through them [Gable and Colbert] the story reaches a climax that is at once improbable and entirely plausible."[17] (As a romantic comedy footnote to this conclusion, Gable and Colbert's union is orchestrated by yet another older matchmaker—her father, Walter Connolly.)

Consistent with that, supporting players are equally important in creating a believable romantic comedy story. For example, one 1930s critic described Maria Ouspenskaya's *Love Affair* performance as Boyer's grandmother as "so real it hurts."[18] Even more touchingly natural is the affection between the grandmother (Cathleen Nesbitt) and Cary Grant in the 1957 remake, *An Affair to Remember.* The loving embraces and hand-holding between Grant and Nesbitt, almost like sweethearts, showcases a movingly authentic relationship common in real life (I was reminded of the rapport I had with my own maternal grandmother) but sadly rare in the movies. Leo McCarey, who directed both *Love Affair* and *An Affair to Remember*, was, however, gifted at sensitively portraying older characters in a true-to-reality style. (This McCarey talent is best demonstrated in the shatteringly true-to-life melodrama, *Make Way for Tomorrow*, 1937.)

Supporting players at the other end of the age spectrum (children) represent another way in which romantic comedy often has a believable slant. Once again, McCarey was a pioneer in this area, effectively using children in both *Love Affair* and *An Affair to Remember*. Both pictures showcase a comically precocious little boy on the ocean liner (where the focus couple meet), as well as later informal sessions with children as the heroine teaches music while she is recovering from her debilitating accident.

McCarey enjoyed working with children because he was a student of the spontaneous and forever encouraged improvisation. The director/writer felt no one was more natural than a child, which he probably proved most effectively in his populist classic *Going My Way* (1944). McCarey's portrayal of a sidewalk gang of kids in that film was a contributing factor to it winning the best picture Oscar, while he took home statuettes for direction and original story.

Besides the believability factor, the romantic comedy casting of children through the years serves several other purposes. First, it demonstrates the new couple's potential for being good parents, which in movie shorthand means "nice people." This is especially true of Irene Dunne in *Love Affair*, which reinforced the public's already motherly perception of the actress after her 1936 adoption (with husband Dr. Francis Griffin) of a one-year-old baby girl. More recent examples of the genre's predisposition for using youngsters as a parental barometer occur in *You've Got Mail* and *Jerry Maguire* (1996).

The latter film brings one to a second reason children are cast in the genre—they represent a romantic catalyst. Indeed, Tom Cruise's Maguire falls for Renee Zellweger's little boy before he finds genuine love for her. Along the same lines, Clark Gable is first taken with the little boy in the underrated *It Started in Naples* before embracing romance with the child's surrogate mother, Sophia Loren. *Naples* writer/director Melville Shavelson was reworking material from his earlier *Houseboat* (1958), where children are also pivotal to a romantic comedy involving Loren and another aging male lead (Cary Grant). But in *Houseboat* Loren falls for widowed Grant's children first.

Sometimes the child even orchestrates the romance, such as in *The Courtship of Eddie's Father* (1963) and *Sleepless in Seattle*. An ironic twist on the child as catalyst occurs in the Tracy-Hepburn film *Woman of the Year*. Her career as a famous political commentator overpowers their young marriage, with sportswriter Tracy coping as best he can. But her neglect of their newly adopted son is the last straw. It triggers the first of what would become a standard component in their romantic comedies—Tracy bringing Hepburn down to earth.

A third explanation for casting children in the genre brings one full circle back to the reality factor. With divorce so much a part of today's society, the modern romantic comedy merely documents the frequency with which one or both partners in a new relationship have youngsters from a previous marriage. Such is the case in the charmingly underrated *One Fine Day* (1996), where Michelle Pfeiffer and George Clooney are two self-absorbed New Yorkers who meet during one of those hectic days when juggling parenthood and a career seems impossible.

A final reason for the genre's use of children is to underline, in yet another way, the ultimately serious foundation of romantic comedy. Whereas screwball comedy parodies the process, such as the custody fight over a dog in *The Awful Truth* (1937), romantic comedy's sometimes inclusion of children reminds us that there are broader (reality-based) ramifications for our love. Tom Hanks's son (Ross Malinger) in *Sleepless in Seattle* is an ongoing study in how new relationships impact youngsters. Of course, this is a natural extension of Hanks's lovingly open tendency to share with his son, such as his take on dating: "This is what single people do. They try other people on and see how they fit, but everybody's an adjustment. Nobody's perfect."

The romantic comedy equation that posits that children underline the genre's ultimately serious foundation receives a provocative twist in Nancy Meyers's *What Women Want* (2000). Mel Gibson plays a womanizing male chauvinist who, through a freak accident, acquires the ability to hear women's thoughts. This gift has many repercussions, both romantic and professional. But the most poignant effect involves reconnecting with a teenaged daughter (Ashley Johnson) he had formerly neglected after his divorce. Johnson's testy fifteen-year-old is also a throwback to McCarey's original reason for casting young people: her teen-with-an-attitude is very real.

Consistent with romantic comedy's character believability, whether discussing the focus couple or children, is the genre's portrayal of the pivotal best friend category, another case in point. In screwball comedy this figure is often pleasantly potted, such as Hugh Grant's zany flatmate (Rhys Ifans) in *Notting Hill* (1999), who has an inability to write down phone messages or distinguish mayonnaise from yogurt gone bad. As Grant affectionately says of Spike (named after Peter Sellers's eccentric *Goon Show* sidekick Spike Milligan), "There's no excuse for him." In contrast, the romantic comedy sidekick is often amusing but from planet earth. For example, in *Sleepless in Seattle*, Hanks's carpenter best friend (Rob Reiner) gives him amusing but honest advice on the current dating scene:

> Things are a little different now. First, you have to be friends. You have to like each other. Then, you neck. This could go on for years. Then you have tests, and then you get to do it with a condom. The good news is you split the check.

On other occasions the realistic romantic comedy sidekick is there to say something logical and believable . . . simply to better set up a surprising comic comeback by one of the film's lead characters. For instance, Billy Crystal's best friend (Bruno Kirby) in *When Henry Met Sally* . . . tells him: "Marriages don't break up on account of infidelity—it's just a symptom that something else is wrong." Crystal replies, "Really? Well, that symptom is fucking my wife." (As a realistic footnote to this film, every effort was made to anchor the story in authenticity, including an attempt to present each of the aforementioned elderly witness scenes as "Documentary Footage.")[19]

A realistic characteristic of most romantic comedy characters (whether major or minor figures) is that they are usually gainfully employed. This contrasts markedly from the high-living, nebulous employment background of screwball comedy players, such as the ever-present idle rich or the genre's generous sprinkling of absent-minded professors. Thus, in *Hands across the Table,* Carole Lombard is a manicurist, while in *The Shop around the Corner* Jimmy Stewart is a gift shop clerk. In *Pretty Woman*, Richard Gere is a business tycoon, and in *You've Got Mail,* Tom Hanks operates a large chain of bookstores. This believability factor, with relationship to romantic comedy employment, allows the genre to occasionally flirt with fairy-tale developments, confident that a working-class foundation will still make the movie realistically palatable to the typical viewer. In 1993, shortly after starring in *Sleepless in Seattle*, Tom Hanks (who so often today reminds both critics and public alike of Jimmy Stewart) made a generalization about his often employed movie persona that is more than applicable to most romantic comedy players:

> If there has been any bona fide kind of sit-down, analyzed plan to this . . . career of mine, it has probably been that whatever I'm in, it's not too farfetched for everybody to believe.[20]

A fourth key component of romantic comedy (after accenting sentiment over silly, a propensity for the melodramatic, and realistic characters) is a more traditional dating ritual. Whereas the zany screwball heroine dominates the courtship game of that genre, romantic comedy follows a more conventional, male-directed path. This is not to suggest that the man immediately pushes for some sort of relationship, unlike the aggressive Katharine Hepburn in the screwball classic *Bringing Up Baby*. In romantic comedy, both parties tend to be hesitant in their maneuvering toward couplehood. Still, it is usually the man who ultimately goes the extra mile to guarantee the love match, because the romance was waiting for one of four things to happen.

The first and most frequent reason the genre has a male catalyst is the fact that the leading man often needs to mature. For instance, in *10*, Dudley Moore is in a wonderful relationship with Julie Andrews. But he is having a midlife crisis and is obsessed with young women, particularly the physically perfect Bo Derek. Consistent with this, Moore is also fascinated by a neighbor's seemingly ongoing sexual orgy on which he periodically spies with a telescope throughout the movie. However, by the film's close, after getting a chance to both join the orgy and bed Bo Derek, he finds it all incredibly shallow and wisely returns to Andrews.

In Rob Reiner's *The Sure Thing* (1985), a sexually inexperienced college student (John Cusack) has the opportunity to bed another physically perfect young woman. But first he must travel crosscountry with a classmate (Daphne Zuniga) who is meeting her fiancé. In a road romance update of *It Happened One Night*, they fall in love.

But it does not initially register with him until he attempts to proceed with his "sure thing." Like Dudley Moore ultimately rejecting Bo Derek, Cusack does not complete his sexual odyssey because of his love for Daphne Zuniga, which allows their romance to bloom.

Cusack later imaginatively returns to the same material in *High Fidelity*, when as a thirty-something record store owner he is no more romantically mature than his *Sure Thing* college student. But as Cusack comically reexamines his personal "top five" failed relationships—inspired by the exit of his latest love (Iben Hjejle)—he finally finds both maturity and an overdue ability to commit to a romantic partner. Not surprisingly, Cusack and Hjejle end up back together. This male need to grow up surfaces in countless other romantic comedies, from the world of Woody Allen (see especially *Manhattan*, 1979) to the watershed, Allenesque *When Harry Met Sally* . . . .

The genre's second reason for a male catalyst is that the leading man sometimes has other issues to work through. For example, in *Return to Me*, widower David Duchovny must process the discovery that his lover literally possesses the heart of his late wife. In *Pretty Woman* Richard Gere has to decide not only whether to commit to a permanent relationship but a permanent relationship with a hooker. Tom Cruise's title character in *Jerry Maguire* must decide whether he is with Renee Zellweger out of love or merely from an incredible devotion based on both her cute child and the loyalty she displayed when no one else supported him.

The most basic topic in need of male brainstorming, however, is when he has not processed being over a past failed love . . . and now is ready for the right love. In *Addicted to Love*, Matthew Broderick is so busy tormenting his old girlfriend's new beau (as well as hoping to get her back), that he is initially oblivious to falling in love with his co-conspirator in romantic revenge (Meg Ryan). In *If Lucy Fell*, Eric Schaeffer's super crush on the woman across the courtyard (supermodel Elle Macpherson) blinds him to the real love he ultimately feels for his longtime apartment mate and friend (Sarah Jessica Parker).

A third explanation for the male being the ultimate romantic comedy instigator is to correct behavior by the heroine that threatens the relationship. This is best demonstrated by *Love Affair* and its two remakes. In all three versions the heroine does *not* share the reason why she missed the Empire State Building rendezvous with the male lead. She is so afraid he will feel only pity for her (after the crippling accident) that she does not make allowances for his (or more precisely—their) love.

In *Woman of the Year* and *Adam's Rib*, the best of the Hepburn-Tracy romantic comedy teamings, Tracy has to rectify Hepburn's behavior, which in each case threatens their marriage. In both stories her career drive and the actress's patentedly regal manner had gotten in the way of being a spouse. Or, as her sportswriter husband (Tracy) observed in *Woman of the Year*:

> You know, it's too bad I'm not covering this dinner of yours tonight, because I've got an angle that would really be sensational: The outstanding woman of the year isn't a woman at all.

This defrosting of the ice goddess formula, which became a Tracy-Hepburn norm, had gotten its start in the memorable *Philadelphia Story* (1940), where Cary Grant is responsible for bringing Hepburn down to earth. Fittingly, the surname of Hepburn's *Philadelphia Story* character is Lord, which a supporting player nicely ties to the picture's title with the observation: "The unapproachable Miss Lord—the Philadelphia Story." Moreover, in an odd bit of foreshadowing, given the later significance of her *Taming of the Shrew* type teamings with Spencer Tracy, her full *Philadelphia Story* name is *Tracy* Lord.

A fourth reason for romantic comedy to ultimately have a male prompter is for him to correct negative behavior of his own that threatens the making of a relationship. In *The Shop around the Corner*, Jimmy Stewart has been short in his conversations with fellow clerk Margaret Sullavan, and there is a decided chill in the air whenever they interact. But as if to give him time to make up for his shortcomings, a plot twist enables Stewart to discover that Sullavan is his writing companion, while she remains in the dark. This allows him to methodically mend his ways and gradually win her heart, which also occasionally involves Stewart entertainingly kidding her about this idealized pen pal. (Is he chubby, or balding? And so on.) Thus, by the time Sullavan discovers his true identity she has fallen for her longtime coworker.

When the picture was loosely remade as *You've Got Mail*, Tom Hanks's transgressions against Meg Ryan (with whom he has a warm but anonymous Internet online relationship) move beyond the petty shop differences of the original. Hanks's corporate bookstore chain first threatens and then drives from business Ryan's longtime family owned children's bookstore. (As a cinematic footnote to the earlier film, Ryan's store is called The Shop around the Corner.) Hanks's need to repackage himself represents a major challenge be-

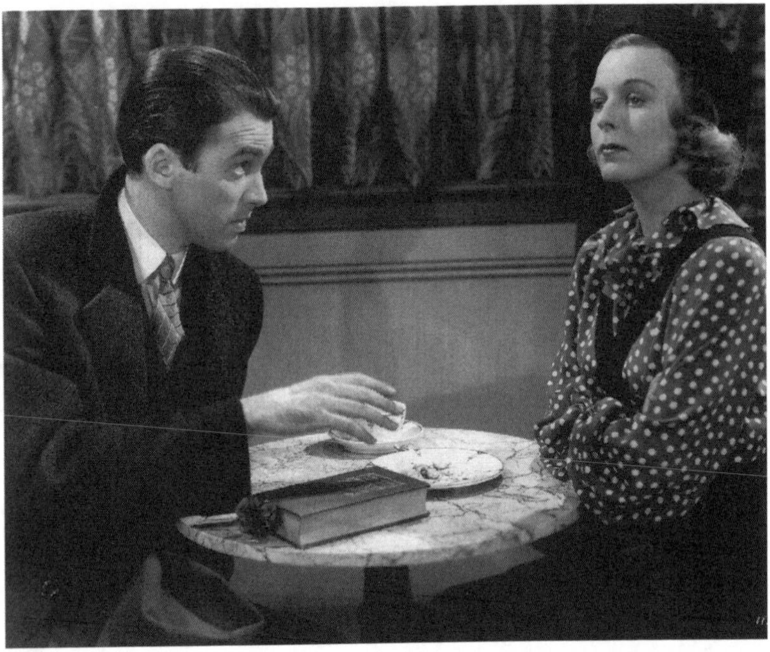

A stressful moment from The Shop around the Corner *(1940, with Margaret Sullavan and pen pal Jimmy Stewart).*

cause when they first officially meet (shades of the original movie) they do *not* get along. Hanks is assisted, however (as was Jimmy Stewart in the first version), by discovering early that Ryan is his formerly unknown Internet pen pal . . . while she remains outside the loop. Thus, Hanks has no choice but to be the catalyst for romance.

What Women Want provides another entertaining slant on a romantic comedy male having to correct past mistakes that could prevent the creation of a perfect match. Mel Gibson's ability to hear women's thoughts has enabled him to take an advertising position away from his inhouse agency rival (Helen Hunt). But the romantic catch is that somewhere along the line he fell in love with her. Like Dustin Hoffman's title character in *Tootsie* (1982), Gibson's thinking like a woman has made him a better man.

Once again, as with *The Shop around the Corner* and *You've Got Mail*, the male must make things right because the heroine does not realize what has transpired. Thus, Gibson confesses his wrongdoing (gives Hunt the soughtafter position), and convinces her of his love. But consistent with the genre's often realistic slant, he does not share that his cheating was an outgrowth of being able to hear women's thoughts. Hunt would have thought he was nuts! So the fantasy element is completely minimized.

A final central component for romantic comedy (joining sentiment over silly, melodramatic tendencies, realistic characters, and a traditional dating ritual) is a propensity for slower story pacing, especially near the end of the film. In contrast, the narrative movement of screwball comedy invariably escalates near the close. For instance, in *Notting Hill* Hugh Grant must endure a comic white knuckle, high-speed drive through London traffic in order to make Julia Roberts's press conference and confess his love.

Romantic comedy courts a slower story pacing for several reasons. First, it is an effective narrative ploy, particularly near the movie close, to keep the romantic outcome in question. Will Richard Gere decide to marry the Hollywood hooker in *Pretty Woman*? Can Tom Hanks overcome countless negatives to win Meg Ryan's love in *You've Got*

Mail? Will the male lead in each of the three screen versions of *Love Affair* ever discover the real reason why the heroine did not meet him at the top of the Empire State Building? Along related lines, will Tom Hanks and Meg Ryan both make it to the top of said building in *Sleepless in Seattle*, enabling their natural chemistry to run its course?

The romantic comedy naysayers might deny this point—suggesting there is no narrative tension involved. The audience's wanna-be couple, according to this line of thinking, will naturally get together. But it is never a given. There are countless quasi-romantic comedies that suddenly dovetail into downbeat conclusions. Examples include the drowning of Kevin Costner at the close of *Message in a Bottle* (1999) and the shooting death of Robert Redford at the end of *Up Close & Personal* (1996).

The second reason the genre assumes a slower pace is to underline yet again the more serious nature of love in romantic comedy, as opposed to the frivolous manner of courting in screwball comedy. One might say, if we're to believe in the reality of love, it cannot come easily. Consequently, the genre almost flirts with melodrama in the number of potential roadblocks that surface. For example, David Duchovny has to cope with the loss of his wife twice in *Return to Me* (both after it happens and later when the recipient of her heart is revealed) before he can embrace love again.

A third take on romantic comedy's less harried storyline is an outgrowth of more realistic, three-dimensional characters. Regardless of how entertaining screwball comedy can be, the genre is generally populated with one-note figures, such as Katharine Hepburn's scatterbrained heiress in *Bringing Up Baby* and the absentminded professor (Cary Grant) with whom she falls in love. Compare the charming cartoon simplicity of Hepburn and Grant in *Baby* to their teaming in *The Philadelphia Story*, where they are entertainingly complex and ever so articulate about this multiplicity. For instance, at one point Grant tells Hepburn, "There are more of you than people realize. A special class of the American female: the married maidens." The observation is made all the more insightfully memorable by Hepburn later paraphrasing it to Jimmy Stewart. Impressively, Stewart (who would win an Oscar for his performance) manages to be even more eloquent, such as in this description of Hepburn in the same film:

> There's a magnificence in you, Tracy . . . a magnificence that comes out of your eyes and your voice and the way you stand there and the way you walk. You're lit from within, Tracy. You've got fires banked down in you, hearth fires.

Compare that to Hepburn's direct but ever so meager description of Grant in *Bringing Up Baby*—"You're so good-looking without your glasses."

Moreover, one might further associate romantic comedy's more three-dimensional characters with the added time it takes to get to know and appreciate a potential companion. Thus, in *When Harry Met Sally* . . . Billy Crystal observes with warm detail:

> I love that you get cold when it's 71 degrees out. I love that it takes you an hour and a half to order a sandwich. I love that you get a little crinkle above your nose when you're looking at me like I'm nuts. I love that after I spend a day with you I can still smell your perfume on my clothes. And I love that you are the last person I want to talk to before I go to sleep at night.

A fourth reason romantic comedy embraces a reduction in pacing is the need to juggle so many life choices. For all the emotionalism associated with matters of the heart, this is still a genre that takes a great deal of time for soul-searching *thought*. In *What Women Want*, Mel Gibson must not only decide what his true feelings are toward Helen Hunt, he needs to contemplate giving up his new, much soughtafter agency position.

In the various configurations of *Love Affair*, the male lead, despite long believing he has been rejected by the heroine, finds it necessary to rethink his life. This involves everything from giving up his shallow playboy ways to finally attempting to realize his gift as a painter. Naturally, this makeover is a direct outgrowth of his love for the heroine . . . even though she seems lost to him.

In *High Fidelity* John Cusack agonizes so hard over what he thinks is the right relationship that one is reminded of the John Lennon song title, "Watching the Wheels Go Round." In fact, the genre's cerebral component is best articulated in the novel of the same name from which *High Fidelity* is closely drawn:

> Just because it's a relationship, and it's based on sappy [emotional] stuff, it doesn't mean you can't make intellectual decisions about it. Sometimes you just have to, otherwise you'll never get anywhere. That's where I've been going wrong. I've been letting the weather and my stomach muscles and a great chord change in a Pretenders [record] single make up my mind for me, and I want to do it [rationally] for myself.[21]

This contemplating component is in marked contrast to the helter-skelter emotional decisions of screwball comedy, where the breakneck narrative leaves no time for thinking.

A final explanation for romantic comedy's slower pacing is a conclusion more realistically grounded than the standard screwball comedy close. The latter genre's finale is often so outrageous (however entertaining) that the film quickly rushes through it (as in *Bringing Up Baby*), before the viewer has time to ponder the improbability factor. Indeed, Preston Sturges goes as far as to satirize this phenomenon in *The Palm Beach Story* (1942), which starts where a traditional screwball story ends—with a marriage, or the promise thereof. Sturges then proceeds to showcase a comically struggling relationship. He seems to suggest, "I never believed these screwball comedy conclusions, either."

In contrast, by the conclusion of the more drawn-out romantic comedy ending, it seems reasonable that the relationship will endure: Tracy and Hepburn work out their marital differences in *Adam's Rib*, and Tom Hanks and Meg Ryan move toward a Tracy and Hepburn–like relationship in both *Sleepless in Seattle* and *You've*

Got Mail. When one also factors in the aforementioned historical witnesses for love that were so warmly and effectively profiled in *When Harry Met Sally . . .*, even time and tradition seem fated to guarantee the permanence of these unions.

These, then, have been the five pivotal components of romantic comedy: sentiment over screwball silliness, a propensity for serious and/or melodramatic overtones, more realistic (often employed) characters, a traditional dating ritual (fewer controlling women), and slower story pacing, especially at the end of the movie.

Despite the "Gee whiz, ain't love dreamy?" stereotype sometimes associated with romantic comedy, this genre (as demonstrated by this chapter) has much more to do with reality than its sister format, screwball comedy. Bottom line, screwball comedy is a distraction from the real world while romantic comedy promises something special in the most familiar of settings . . . the proverbial, "this could happen to me."

Notes

1. Kitty Bean Yancey, "'Seattle' Director Seduces with Old-Fashioned Romance," *USA Today*, July 8, 1993, p. 12-D.
2. Archer Winsten, "'Love Affair' Opens at Radio City Music Hall," *New York Post*, August 17, 1939.
3. Herbert Cohn, *Love Affair* review, *Brooklyn Eagle*, March 17, 1939, p. 11.
4. Roger Ebert (syndicated *Chicago Sun Times* reviewer), "Hepburn Steals Show in 'Love Affair,'" *Cedar Rapids Gazette*, October 21, 1994, p. 6w.
5. Ebert, "Hepburn Steals Show in 'Love Affair,'" p. 6w.
6. Robert W. Butler, "And She Lived Happily Ever After," *Kansas City Star*, June 28, 1993, p. D-5.
7. Butler, "And She Lived Happily Ever After," p. D-5.
8. Samantha Critchell, "'Bride' Gives Elizondo 11th Marshall Film," *Indianapolis Star*, July 30, 1999, p. F-7.
9. For instance, see Susan Wioszczyna, "'Sleepless' Awakens Demand for Old Tunes," *USA Today*, July 20, 1993, p. 1-D.

10. Anthony Lane, "Brief Encounter," *The New Yorker*, July 19, 1993, p. 80.

11. Andre Sennwald, *Hands across the Table* review, *New York Times*, November 2, 1935, p. 13; John Reddington, "Comedy in a Romantic Vein . . .," *Brooklyn Daily Eagle*, November 2, 1935.

12. Eileen Creelman, "A Lubitsch Comedy . . .," *New York Sun*, January 26, 1940, p. 24.

13. Creelman, "A Lubitsch Comedy . . .," p. 24.

14. Archer Winsten, "'Woman of the Year' Opens at Radio City Music Hall," *New York Post*, February 6, 1942, p. 17.

15. Eileen Creelman, "Spencer Tracy in 'Woman of the Year' . . .," *New York Sun*, February 6, 1942, p. 19.

16. William Boehnel, "'It Happened One Night' Proves Worthy of Fine Acting," *New York World-Telegram*, February 22, 1934.

17. *It Happened One Night* review, *Liberty Magazine*, March 7, 1934.

18. Winsten, "'Love Affair' Opens at Radio City Music Hall."

19. Nora Ephron, *When Harry Met Sally . . .* (New York: Alfred A Knopf, 1997), pp. 3, 36, 54, 60.

20. Lisa Schwarzbaum, "The Nice Man Cometh" (cover article), *Entertainment Weekly*, July 9, 1993, p. 19.

21. Nick Hornby, *High Fidelity* (New York: Riverhead Books, 1995), p. 318.

CHAPTER FOUR

CARY GRANT AND KATHARINE HEPBURN

Ah, that's the old redhead, no bitterness, no recrimination, Just a good swift left to the jaw.

—Grant, reacting to one of Hepburn's insults in *The Philadelphia Story* (1940)

Cary Grant (1904–1986) and Katharine Hepburn (born 1909) starred together in three bona fide classics—the screwball comedies *Bringing Up Baby* and *Holiday* (both 1938), and the romantic comedy *The Philadelphia Story*. (Their first pairing had been in the offbeat comedy drama *Sylvia Scarlett*, 1935.) One could make a case for *Baby* and *Philadelphia* being the definitive example of each genre. Of course, Grant put his stamp on screwball comedy like no other performer. In the genre's heyday he seemed to appear in every other watershed film. Besides the aforementioned works, there were also *The Awful Truth* and *Topper* (both 1937), and *His Girl Friday* and *My Favorite Wife* (both 1940).

In the postwar era (after 1945), when screwball comedy was less frequently produced, he starred in two excellent revisionist examples of the genre—*I was a Male War Bride* (1949) and *Monkey Business* (1952). But changing entertainment tastes now made romantic comedy a more marketable genre. Thus, the late 1940s would find him surfacing in both a traditional romantic comedy, *The Bachelor and the Bobby-Soxer* (1947), and a romantic fantasy *The Bishop's Wife* (1947). And late in his career he would appear in a memorable string of romantic comedies, including *An Affair to Remember* (1957), *Indiscreet* and *Houseboat* (both 1958), and *That Touch of Mink* (1962).

Hepburn was an excellent screwball companion to Grant in *Baby* and *Holiday*, with her part in the former film being "the final evolution" of the genre's zany heroine.[1] But her importance to the text more fully takes off with *The Philadelphia Story*. In a production originally hand tailored for her as a stage play, she found her defining screen persona—the ice goddess in need of a comeuppance, or, as Grant observed in that film: "No, you're slipping, Red [Hepburn]. I used to be afraid of that look—the withering glance of the goddess."

This cutting-Hepburn-down-to-size phenomenon, first ushered in by Grant in *The Philadelphia Story*, became the defining component in a now celebrated series of romantic comedies with real-life love Spencer Tracy. The most pertinent of these teamings are *Woman of the Year* (1942), *Adam's Rib* (1948), *Pat and Mike* (1952), and *The Desk Set* (1957). But variations of the Hepburn comeuppance scenario also occur in the offbeat romantic comedy masterpiece *The African Queen* (1951, with Humphrey Bogart) and the underrated *Iron Petticoat* (1956, with Bob Hope).

In terms of both screwball and romantic comedy over time, therefore, no two actors are more central than Grant and Hepburn. They are to these genres what Humphrey Bogart and Lauren Bacall are to film noir, or Fred Astaire and Ginger Rogers are to the musical. This film-actor-as-icon status is a unique achievement and invites a closer examination of Grant and Hepburn, for to know them better is to more fully understand screwball and romantic comedy.

Thawing the ice goddess (Katharine Hepburn) of The Philadelphia Story *(1940), with Cary Grant (left) and Jimmy Stewart.*

Becoming Cary Grant

One of the actor's most tellingly insightful observations on his film success linked Grant's freelance career to quality directors apprecia-tive of his improvisational skills:

> I gravitated to men such as Hitchcock, George Stevens, George Cukor, Howard Hawks, Stanley Donen, and Leo McCarey. They understood me. They permitted me the release of improvisation during the rehearsing of each scene. They let me discover how far out I could go with confidence . . . and I am deeply indebted to each of them.[2]

McCarey's last place position, however, is ironic for two reasons. First, when McCarey gave Grant a major big-screen improvisational chance in *The Awful Truth* (1937), the actor initially balked at the chance. The catch for Grant was that McCarey was *too* improvisational. The director would come in each day during the production with story ideas scribbled on scraps of paper, in lieu of a script!

This approach so shook up Grant that he attempted to buy out his contract, but Columbia Studio chief Harry Cohn would have none of it. Grant's *Awful Truth* costar Irene Dunne told the actor "if he would just stay with it, he would give a wonderful performance, which he did. It upset him that McCarey didn't have a script. I was able to calm him down."[3]

Another concerned *Awful Truth* cast member, Ralph Bellamy, approached McCarey about the absence of a script even before the production started:

> When I went to Leo's house, he met me with his perpetual gleeful grin and dancing eyes. . . . He said nothing much about the story or the part. He just joked and said not to worry—we'd have lots of fun, but there wasn't any script. . . . There never was a script. Each morning Leo would appear with a small piece of brown wrapping paper . . . and throw us lines and business. . . . We were quickly won over to him and had the fun he'd promised. And we made the film in six weeks, a record for that kind of picture.[4]

Bellamy went on to say that "after four or five days, we realized he [McCarey] was a comedy genius." Not surprisingly, except maybe to Grant, *The Awful Truth* was a huge critical and commercial success. McCarey would win an Oscar for his direction, with the film also receiving Academy Award nominations for Best Picture, Actress (Dunne), and Best Supporting Actor (Bellamy). Period conjecture suggests Grant missed a nomination because of a reputation for difficulty, such as attempting to bail out of McCarey's production. Irene Dunne remembered,

> Cary used to be very apprehensive about nearly everything in those days. So apprehensive in fact he would almost get physically sick. If the script, the director, an actor or a particular scene displeased him, he would be greatly upset.[5]

Be that as it may, McCarey's unorthodox style provoked an Oscar caliber performance from Grant. For example, in one scene the director told Dunne to open the door of her apartment and:

> discover Grant standing there and say with surprise, "Well, if it isn't my ex." He did not tell Grant what to reply, but the actor ad-libbed one of the film's best-remembered lines, 'The judge says this is my day to see the dog."[6]

The point is not, however, that McCarey taught Grant improvisation. The director merely helped the actor tap into a natural talent. Indeed, even as a child performer with Pender's Knockabout Comedians, he had impressed the veteran Bob Pender with his "gift for comedic improvisation."[7] But Grant had not been using this skill in film before *The Awful Truth*.

Along related lines, McCarey's "do it visually" philosophy also coaxed out the inspired slapstick portion of Grant's *Awful Truth* performance. For instance, in one scene, at Dunne's music recital, Grant tips over his chair, followed by a Laurel and Hardy–like moment when he has comic difficulty disengaging himself from the chair. Once again, physical and visual shtick had been second nature to the actor since childhood, but it was McCarey who made it part of the Grant *film* persona.

Leo McCarey (right), a student of all kinds of comedy, is pictured on the set of his Ruggles of Red Gap *(1935) with actor Charles Laughton (left) and crackerbarrel humorist Irvin S. Cobb (center).*

The irony of McCarey's placement in Grant's personal pantheon of directors is only partly addressed with the subject of improvisation and slapstick—despite their significance for the actor in *The Awful Truth*. McCarey's ranking in this Grant grouping is also paradoxical for a much more provocative reason—the actor seems to have drawn part of his screen persona from the real-life personality of the director.

That is, McCarey's improvisational approach was also aided by his ability to enthuse performers with his mesmerizing on-the-set storytelling. But this magical spinner of tales went beyond being merely someone fun with whom to work. McCarey seems to have been pleasantly overpowering with his storytelling mix of both verbal and mime skills. In a telephone interview with Irene Dunne over forty years after the making of *The Awful Truth*, she still literally bubbled over with both affection for this "dear sweet man" (McCarey), as well as his unintended knack for getting performers to mimic his mannerisms.[8] (In fact, one of the stills used in the Peter Bogdanovich interview anthology *Who the Devil Made It* actually documents Grant attempting to parrot his director on the set of *The Awful Truth*.)[9]

The best description of imitating McCarey mannerisms, however, occurs in Joe Adamson's entertainingly insightful *Groucho, Harpo, Chico, and Sometimes Zeppo*. McCarey, the comedy mastermind behind the Marx Brothers's greatest film, *Duck Soup* (1933), had in the late 1920s already gifted cinema with the teaming and molding of Laurel and Hardy. And Adamson's most telling point keys upon McCarey and Stan Laurel:

> McCarey had a habit of dominating every film he directed, in ways that were spontaneous, graceful, and various. . . . Sometimes his constant pantomimes in the course of his conversation were infectious enough to show up on film being performed by the actors. (Many of Stan Laurel's familiar mannerisms, in fact, were originally familiar mannerisms of McCarey's. The director had a "Let's go have a beer" gesture and an "Anybody want to play tennis?" gesture that friends and associates haven't shaken even yet.)[10]

Hollywood dates the birth of Grant's film persona to *The Awful Truth*. No less an artist than writer/director Garson Kanin later said, "How much of that [Grant] personality was directed into him by

Leo McCarey, I'm not prepared to say . . . [but] he polished that [*Awful Truth*] personality, and he played it over and over and over again—each time more skillfully."[11] For years after *The Awful Truth*, it was not unusual for critics to link Grant's superior comic performances with McCarey. For instance, *New York Times* critic Bosley Crowther made just that connection in his 1947 review of *The Bachelor and the Bobby-Soxer*—"reminiscent of some of those gay, galvanic larks that . . . McCarey used to make 10 or more years ago."[12]

Grant's screen penchant for everything from flirtatiously self-deprecating humor to the amusingly expressive use of his hands and eyes were all signature trademarks of McCarey long before they became synonymous with the actor. Moreover, the formerly moody-on-the-set Grant soon metamorphosed into a more gregarious, McCarey-like joker during film productions—someone who entertainingly dominated every moment. (Period humorist H. Allen Smith remembers one visit with McCarey when the storytelling was so diverting that the identity of another guest was hardly noted. Later, Smith realized he had missed talking to Ingrid Bergman![13] Soon there would be Grant stories like this.)

A provocative historical footnote to McCarey's apparent influence on Grant is that period critics even saw the two men as looking alike. Here is one such description of the director from 1939—"the handsome McCarey, with his twinkling Irish eyes and his resemblance to Cary Grant."[14] While this proves nothing concrete, in relation to McCarey's molding of Grant, one could certainly argue that similar appearances might have made the actor more predisposed to mimic the mannerisms of the director.

Fittingly, given this McCarey-Grant connection, one of the most insightful takes on the actor comes from the director. When asked to compare his two greatest romantic comedies, McCarey observed,

> The difference between *Love Affair* and *An Affair to Remember* is very simply the difference between [the two male leads:] Charles Boyer and Cary Grant. Grant could never really mask his sense of

humor—which is extraordinary—and that's why the second version is funnier.[15]

Director and author Peter Bogdanovich's description of Grant is a more succinct take on the McCarey description, but with an all-important reference to the actor's good looks: "What makes him so desirable as a player and so inimitable was the striking mixture of a comedian's talents with the looks of a matinee idol."[16] Bogdanovich knew of what he spoke. He made this observation just a few years after loosely remaking *Bringing Up Baby* as *What's Up, Doc?* (1972), with the latter film's male lead (Ryan O'Neal) under specific orders to play his part like Cary Grant.

Cary Grant as Screwball Comedy Player

Though McCarey's screwball comedy *The Awful Truth* firmly established the Grant screen persona as we now know it, the actor essentially offered up two variations of himself for this genre—depending upon the director. When working with any megaphone man other than Hawks, Grant tended to follow McCarey's saving grace of plausibility. While screwball comedy's farcelike nature often flirts with absurdity, the McCarey Grant begins, at least, with one foot in reality. Thus, in *The Awful Truth* his character is merely trying to keep wife Irene Dunne from knowing where he really vacationed . . . with the implication being that he has had an affair.

In director George Cukor's *Holiday* Grant simply wants a break from the world of big business, while the McCarey-produced *My Favorite Wife* (which Garson Kanin directed) has Grant comically coping with the return of formerly missing wife Irene Dunne. In all these screwball films, Grant's good looks and comic tendencies are way above average, but the special appeal, according to director Cukor, came from Grant acting "as though he were just an ordinary young man."[17] This everyman perspective also meshes nicely with McCarey's plausibility factor for the genre.

George Cukor (left) on the set of Holiday *(1938), with (from right to left) Cary Grant, Doris Nolan, Henry Kolker, Lew Ayres, and Katharine Hepburn.*

In contrast, when Grant appeared in a Hawks screwball comedy, the actor's persona begins by being both more dignified and distracted—the world of the absentminded professor. Not surprisingly, this leads to a more extreme ritualistic humiliation for Grant, or what critic/historian Richard Schickel has so entertainingly described as a "dignified fellow reduced to ninnyhood by desperate circumstances."[18]

The absentminded professor character is what drove Hawks's screwball comedies, even without Grant, be it Gary Cooper's take on comic academia in *Ball of Fire* (1942), or Rock Hudson's professor-like author in *Man's Favorite Sport* (1964). Hawks even did a musical remake of the former film called *A Song Is Born* (1948), with Danny Kaye leading a band of dowdy intellectuals who need to learn about jazz for an encyclopedia entry.

Hawks's best professorial screwball outings, however, star Cary Grant—*Bringing Up Baby* and *Monkey Business.* In fact, even the Hawks-Grant collaboration *I Was a Male War Bride* succeeds in part through its absentminded professorlike scenario—the military has reduced the actor's character to the same leaf-in-the-wind status he muddled through in his academic settings. Regardless, each of Grant's *Awful Truth* nuances, which soon became stylized for humor—such as the quizzical cocked head, the eye-popping expressions, the forward lunge of surprise, inspired double-takes, and an athleticlike agility—are showcased most *broadly* in Hawks. The one Hawks addition to Grant's comedy persona, the actor's horselike whinnying when things get a little too crazy, was born in *Bringing Up Baby.*

Hawks was sort of a comic D. W. Griffith—he invented little but insightfully maximized what was appropriate for an actor like Cary Grant. Regardless, the director encouraged exaggeration and speed in all of his screwball films to increase the sense of comic absurdity. In the screwball dark comedy *Arsenic and Old Lace* (1944) director Frank Capra pushed these Hawksian excesses even further—producing a Grant performance too over-the-top for some viewers but beloved by many others.

Only in Hawks's *His Girl Friday* does Grant dodge the *distracted* professor role, and with it the extremes of ritualistic humiliation normally associated with this genre. It is also an unusual screwball outing in that the heroine does not rule. In fact, *Friday* costar Rosalind Russell usually never knows what hit her, with Grant dominating in a way normally associated with the genre's leading ladies.

Among these screwball heroines, Grant was probably at his best opposite Irene Dunne—a fact no doubt assisted by the presence of McCarey. Grant's other romantic teamings in the genre, with Russell, Hepburn, and *Topper*'s Constance Bennett, are also winning arrangements. But his couplings with Dunne are bolstered by their special rapport—a give-and-take that smacked of being affectionate equals, despite the genre's propensity to have the heroine dominate.

Dunne's lady mother hen persona, moreover, both on screen and off (critic Pauline Kael once called her "the ancestor of Julie Andrews"), provided the perfect parental contrast for Grant's often childlike shtick—McCarey borrowings that remind us of Laurel and Hardy. For instance, in *My Favorite Wife* Grant has just had a pep talk with Dunne on how to tell his second wife their marriage is off. As he rehearses his lines little boy style near the hotel stairs between his two rooms (for wives one and two), Grant is very demonstrative with his hands, including a "we can still be friends" sort of outward handshake thrust of his right arm. At this exact moment a suspicious hotel clerk appears, and Grant milks the scene to comic perfection. Amusingly leaving his extended hand outward like an inanimate prop, he looks first at the clerk, then returns his gaze to said hand, followed by yet another stare at the clerk. Stan Laurel could not have executed it more comically, though it was actually a little routine McCarey sometimes used among friends.

In Kael's imaginative *New Yorker* profile of Grant, "The Man From Dream City," which remains the key essay examination of the actor, she beguilingly describes screwball comedy as a genre that "turned love and marriage into vaudeville acts and changed the movie heroine from sweet clinging vines into vaudeville partner."[19] This screwball comedy as vaudeville metaphor is best realized in the teaming of Grant and Dunne. Indeed, the all-important *Awful Truth* even finds Dunne literally recreating a nightclub/vaudeville routine that had occurred earlier in the picture.

True to McCarey's improvisational style, the director also incorporated a Dunne adlib into the scene. That is, during a preliminary run-through, which involved both a song and an oomph hip movement by the actress, Dunne blurted out, "I never could do that [physical shtick]." McCarey so liked the comic confession that he had Dunne repeat a variation of the line in the final take.

The in-film audience for her performance includes several people at a social gathering, but Dunne's focus is entirely on Grant for two reasons. First, she is obsessed with winning her soon-to-be ex-husband

Cary Grant and screwball comedy's most underrated actress (Irene Dunne) in The Awful Truth *(1937).*

back. Second, her recreated vaudeville turn is dependent upon the fact that only she and Grant had already seen it performed by another . . . and found it wanting. Thus, Dunne's ongoing comic asides during the number reflect their winsome rapport, with regard to a past shared experience, as well as documenting how far she will go (public humiliation) to get him back. Moreover, with Dunne's routine being so Grant-directed, it makes the performance reminiscent of Kael's vaudeville *team* reference with regard to screwball couples.

In addition, the Grant-Dunne screwball package beats other teamings in the genre for another reason also associated with McCarey. Celebrated French director Jean Renoir affectionately observed of his friend, "No one knows people like McCarey." The implied meaning here is that no director created such likeable screen characters as McCarey, no small accomplishment in a genre where eccentric behavior can often prove abrasive to many viewers.

Grant's greatest gift to the genre, regardless of leading lady or director, was his physical comedy skills. Critic Kael observed, "The assurance he [Grant] gained in slapstick turned him into the smoothie he had aspired to be. He brought elegance to low comedy, and low comedy gave him the corky common-man touch that made him a great star."[20] One cannot emphasize enough the double-edged insightfulness of this statement—a slapstick marriage that both elevated low comedy and gave Grant a touch of the everyman. We so wanted to believe that we could be like Grant!

The physical comedy "elegance" Kael speaks of is what separates Grant from the slapstick shenanigans of a Henry Fonda in the acclaimed screwball comedy *The Lady Eve* (1941). While both actors are at home in the genre replicating Laurel and Hardy–like low comedy, Grant also radiates a sex appeal that Fonda and other physical comedy-oriented male screwball alumni cannot muster. Fittingly, Kael once referred to Grant as a "slapstick Prince Charming." Plus, while a pratfall from Fonda, or the screwball low comedy male lead of your choice, often makes the viewer feel affectionately superior to this figure, the Grant physical miscue merely adds to what another critic called his "perplexed intelligence."[21]

One should hasten to add that while slapstick Grant moments occur in other genres, including his Hitchcock thrillers, screwball comedy is both where it was born and best utilized as part of his screen persona. This is the genre of Grant's youth, and his knockabout exuberance perfectly matched an equally youthful comedy type bent on distracting the nation from the Great Depression. When a markedly older Grant returned to screwball comedy in 1952's *Monkey Business*, his still youthful energy level now needed an explanation—which was provided by way of a script about discovering an elixir of youth.

That Grant intuitively recognized his natural ties to screwball comedy is borne out by the fact that, as a pioneering Hollywood freelancer, he was responsible for selecting all his aforementioned classics in the genre (notwithstanding his initial reservations about McCarey and *The Awful Truth*). Grant further bolstered this period association with screwball comedy by recreating for *The Lux Radio Theatre* during the late 1930s and early 1940s some of his celebrated roles in the genre; he even starred in radio productions of popular screwball comedies in which he had not originally appeared, such as *Theodora Goes Wild* and *Here Comes Mr. Jordan*. Appropriately, Grant's watershed *Awful Truth* proved to be the genre's most popular vehicle transferred to radio, where it was done three times, with Grant starring twice.[22]

Cary Grant and Romantic Comedy

The romantic comedy Grant is an older, more subdued version of his screwball comedy leads. For instance, the physical comedy shtick is still often present but it is not as pervasive or as central to the part. For instance, in *Indiscreet* there is Grant's inspired comic dance sequence; while *Charade* (1963) includes both the fruit-passing scene and his shower in a drip-dry suit. Though all delightful, one feels as if the bits are there strictly because some sort of low comedy is expected of Grant, even in roles near the end of his career. Indeed, that is part of their charm, that he can still do these scenes of agility—and as a leading man—at a point in time when most of his contemporaries have been relegated to less physically demanding character parts.

As with *Topper*'s inclusion in Grant's screwball comedy filmography, the actor's list of romantic comedies includes a fantasy film, too—the aforementioned *Bishop's Wife*. But the latter film is by far more metaphorically significant when examining the Grant persona, especially as it pertains to his post–World War II romantic comedy image.

In *The Bishop's Wife* he plays the angel Dudley, who has come in answer to the prayers of an Episcopalian bishop (David Niven), troubled over raising funds for a new cathedral. The frazzled Niven has begun to both lose faith and have concerns that his marriage (to Loretta Young) is failing. Naturally, Grant successfully addresses these issues, and additionally gives a new purpose to the life of an old professor (Monty Woolley).

So how does this impact romantic comedy, à la Grant? His angel brings happiness to everyone through a courtshiplike relationship with Young. (Niven's bishop is the only one who knows Dudley's true identity.) Grant's character is such a dashingly charismatic figure one almost expects something blasphemous to occur—with no competition from the milquetoast Niven. But then the film's 1940s feel-good populist values kick in without a hint of controversy. The aforementioned concerns the romantic comedy image of Grant as so handsome and charming that he is downright *heavenly*. Though unstated, this was what Pauline Kael implied when she entitled her pivotal Grant essay "The Man from Dream City."

It could be argued that a semblance of Grant's other world romantic uniqueness first clicked into place when Mae West invited him up to see her in *She Done Him Wrong* (1933). But it really took both the 1937 McCarey molding of Grant and the 1940s' usurpation of screwball films by romantic comedy for the full actor-as-dreamboat metamorphosis to take place. Thus, the heavenly Dudley seems a fitting starting point for this phenomenon. Or, maybe one should just document this development from 1947, the release date for both *The Bishop's Wife* and *The Bachelor and the Bobby-Soxer*, because the latter picture also has a touch of Grant fantasy, too.

This other 1947 film finds Grant in a compromising situation with bobby-soxer Shirley Temple. That is, after he visits her school as a guest lecturer, a smitten Temple crashes Grant's apartment when he is out. But as luck would have it, the authorities show up just after Grant's return. To avoid the threat of jail, he agrees to pretend to be Temple's boyfriend long enough for the infatuation to pass. This unorthodox arrangement is the product of a judge who also doubles as Temple's older sister (Myrna Loy).

Romantic comedy thrives on differences, as demonstrated by this scene from The Bachelor and the Bobby-Soxer *(1947, with Cary Grant and Myrna Loy playing bookends to Shirley Temple).*

While this film ends with the pleasant predictability of Grant and Loy as the romantic couple, both Temple and Loy share the same *vision* of their leading man—a knight in shining armor. Twice during Grant's visit to Temple's school he appears, in her eyes, as this most basic of romantic fantasy figures. Later in the picture, after it seems that Grant has won an athletic event, it is Loy's turn to also see him as a knight in the brightest possible armor.

This is an entertainingly memorable way to showcase Grant as a love object for three reasons. First, nothing gets his desirability across more effectively than seeing him through the infatuated eyes of Loy and Temple. Second, that two such diverse women (with a real-world difference in age of twenty-three years) should have the identical Grant fantasy is comedy based in the ludicrous. *Yet*, it still serves a romantic purpose because both women celebrate the same man. Third, by portraying the idealized Grant in a costume that can also be seen as cartoonish, one can admire the actor with bemused detachment, without getting caught up in the cloying soft-focus sentimentality of Barbra Streisand revering Robert Redford in *The Way We Were* (1973). But then that is a basic difference between the straight love story, à la *The Way We Were*, and the world of romantic comedy.

The romanticized Grant received further polishing in Hitchcock's *To Catch a Thief* (1955) and *North by Northwest* (1959), as well as the Hitchcock-like *Charade* (1963, directed by Stanley Donen). Though not pure romantic comedies—Kael once called them "romantic suspense comedies"—there is enough sexual innuendo to qualify these films for at least cross-referencing purposes. Moreover, following Hitchcock's penchant for exotic locations, such as the French Rivera of *To Catch a Thief*, the case for Grant as the ultimate male sex symbol is made all the easier. Just as McCarey once said the Grant intangible was his gift for comedy, Hitchcock might have noted the actor's knack for sophisticated sexuality. But then he would only have been stating the obvious.

Grant had become a benchmark for the romantic comedy male long before he retired from the screen, and this legacy continues today. For example, when the Tom Hanks of *Sleepless in Seattle* (1993) reenters the dating game after the death of his wife, he asks his best friend (Rob Reiner) for relationship advice. Near the close of this poignantly funny scene Reiner gives his most sage suggestion: "Think Cary Grant." When Woody Allen wants to comically undercut the less than romantic nature of his antiheroic persona in *Broadway Danny Rose* (1984), he makes the most ludicrous of comparisons, "I'm never going to be Cary Grant. I don't care what anybody says."

Grant's ability to become the model for both the romantic comedy male as well as the screwball leading man (à la Tony Curtis's take on the professorial Grant in *Some Like It Hot*, 1959) even qualifies as a phenomenon in the comedy theory of philosopher Henri Bergson. He suggested, "What is most comic of all is to become a category oneself into which others will fall, as into a ready-made frame; it is to crystalize into a stock character."[23] Grant has very much become a "category" in both these genres . . . though no one has yet to measure up to his standard.

Ironically, the actor did not always feel like he measured up, either. It was not until late in his career that the actor who started life as the antiheroic Archie Leach felt comfortable as a creation, the sexy Cary Grant, worthy of Thurber's Walter Mitty. But Grant was a quick study in what worked on screen. And just as he focused on screwball comedy after the breakthrough with McCarey's *The Awful Truth*, late in his career he started the aforementioned incredible romantic comedy run that began with 1957's *An Affair to Remember*.

Now, while the standard romantic comedy male is more assertive than his screwball comedy counterpart (a pattern also true of Grant's career), the actor's late movies did allow for a greater leading lady directness than the romantic comedy norm. Part of this was by design, given that Grant felt self-conscious about being so much older than the women with whom he was being teamed. (For instance, Grant was a quarter century older than Audrey Hepburn, his costar in *Charade*.) Thus, his scripts were often tweaked to eliminate what he feared would be perceived as a "dirty old man" phenomenon. That is, these much younger leading ladies left no question as to how they felt about him. For example, in *Charade* Hepburn asks him, "Do you know what's wrong with you?" When he does not have an answer, she matter-of-factly states, "Nothing."

In *North by Northwest* Grant wonders why Eva Marie Saint (twenty years his junior) is so nice to him. Her response is a sexually provocative come-on, "It's going to be a long night . . . and I don't particularly like the book I started." Of course, one might counter by asserting her character is a double agent under orders to make contact with Grant. But since she immediately falls in love with him, this becomes a moot point.

I hasten to add that even while these romantic comedy heroines late in Grant's career are more assertive then the genre norm, the actor gave as good as he got. For instance, when Grant surprises Eva Marie Saint in her hotel room, after the famous crop-dusting plane sequence in *North by Northwest*, she insists that his suit be cleaned. Acquiescing to this point, he adds, "Now, what can a man do with his clothes off for twenty minutes?"

Consistent with that quote, film comedy historian James Harvey defined Grant as "a kind of [witty] intelligence on the loose—threatening to all, even to himself. A kind of uncontrolled alertness."[24] One might only qualify this pocket definition with the corollary that Grant was more a threat to himself in the earlier screwball comedies where, despite the alertness, women ruled. By the time of his mature romantic comedies he had that witty "intelligence on the loose" down to an exact, sexually-in-control science. Indeed, it was precisely this control factor that initially made both Deborah Kerr (in *An Affair to Remember*) and Doris Day (in *That Touch of Mink*) proceed slowly in their relationships with Grant. But in the end they, too, succumbed like all the rest.

Again, this is a far cry from the early screwball comedies where Howard Hawks even resorted to a code term when directing Grant in scenes verbally dominated by women, "we finally got so that I'd say, 'Cary, this is a good chance to do Number Seven.' Number Seven was trying to talk to a woman who was doing a lot of talking." Or, to be more succinct, Hawks added, "I think it's fun to have a [screwball] woman dominant and let the man be funniest."[25]

A final component in Grant's romantic comedy arsenal is a bemused ability to play along with the heroine's lead, however misguided. This became a running gag in *Charade*, where he seems to constantly pooh-pooh Hepburn's ongoing honesty about the stolen gold, only at the film's conclusion to turn out to be the American official in charge of recovering it. Grant's knack for playing along with his leading lady (what Hawks once described as being a "great receiver"),[26] evolved through the years. In the late romantic comedies Grant operates this "great receiver" trait from a position of control, as demonstrated by the example from *Charade* or by Grant's game of pretending to be married in *Indiscreet*, merely to avoid an official union with screen lover Ingrid Bergman.

In contrast, Grant's "great receiver" quality during the early screwball comedies usually found the heroine in charge. For instance, in Maria DiBattista's tribute to comedy leading ladies of Hollywood's golden age (1930s and 1940s), *Fast-Talking Dames*, she praises Grant for "gallantly" refusing "to expose his wife's masquerade as a boozy vulgarian [sister] in [the all-important] *Awful Truth*."[27] But the term "gallantly" is a misnomer. The title of DiBattista's book says it much more effectively—these screwball comedy heroines are not to be denied. Grant's "great receiver" quality here might better be likened to the awe associated with witnessing a comic force of nature. Only later, especially with Grant's mature romantic comedies, does he manage to control the playing field *before* the heroine even opens her mouth. Then his "great receiver" mug entertainingly telegraphs bemused control, instead of that shocked silly puss synonymous with the screwball comedy male.

One can, however, utilize Hawks's "great receiver" description of Grant along broader stylistic lines for a romantic comedy leading man. Even though nominally in charge during outings in the genre, Grant excelled at making these love matches seem the most democratic of interactions. And while this has become more the norm today, thanks in part to Grant, it was not always the case.

One might best demonstrate this by contrasting Grant's romantic comedy approach with that of contemporary Clark Gable, the only actor to challenge Grant's leading man longevity record (from the 1930s to the 1960s) in this genre. The comparison is further enhanced by the fact that the mature Gable and Grant sometimes starred opposite the same actresses. For example, Doris Day teamed with Gable in *Teacher's Pet* (1958) and Grant in the aforementioned *That Touch of Mink*.

Costarring with Grant, Day is initially very much the professional virgin who inspired actor/author Oscar Levant's celebrated observation, "I knew her before she was a virgin." Her knees-together legacy had coalesced in the late 1950s in a series of romantic comedies that most famously teamed her with Rock Hudson. Naturally, Grant still manages to eventually finesse Day into a relationship and even marriage. But it is a suavely methodical Grant romantic game plan, which allows for Day's need to go slowly.

In contrast, Gable's *Teacher's Pet* plan of attack is just that—a romantic attack. He takes Doris Day in his arms and kisses her, hard . . . and it works. Day sputters and is taken aback, but she is definitely smitten. Granted, he later overplays his hand by attempting the same maneuver less successfully. And, storywise, Gable even backs down from his initial philosophy that experience beats college. Still, by film's close he has returned to his take-charge manner, and Day is his.

While Gable's late career pales in comparison to Grant's last films, in this one instance (*Teacher's Pet* versus *A Touch of Mink*) the Gable picture is clearly superior. That having been said, however, Grant's finesse approach is now the romantic comedy norm for the genre's leading man. No one else has yet matched the amazingly nuanced Grant, who could be vulnerable, sophisticated, witty, and even slapstickingly silly—all in the space of a single scene.

Sadly, it was revealed in later years that the actor's metamorphosis from Archie Leach to Cary Grant had not been as successful in private life. In such candid references as Warren Hoge's 1977 *New York Times* interview with the actor, "Cary Grant: No Lady's Man," or Geoffrey Wansell's 1983 biography, *Haunted Idol: The Story of the Real Cary Grant*, it was documented that the actor was much closer to his woman-dominated screwball antiheroic male than to his suavely capable romantic comedy leading man.[28] Ironically, it seemed that, like most American males, not even Cary Grant could live up to being Cary Grant, that figure largely born of McCarey's *The Awful Truth*. The revelation carried added weight at the time, since the actor had finished his career with the aforementioned string of romantic comedy films.

Interestingly enough, though, one real-life antiheroic Grant trait, which the actor had always been front and center about, continued to serve him well—his whimsical philosophy about Hollywood. It involves Grant's often repeated anecdote drawn from Chaplin's *Pay Day* (1922), a rare example of the silent comedian as a henpecked husband—a provocative choice for Grant to have made in light of the present subject matter. This anecdote, a silent comedy metaphor, makes an analogy between Hollywood success and riding a streetcar.[29] The streetcar has only so much room, and every time someone climbs aboard, someone else falls out the back or is pushed. Even if you manage to stay on the streetcar, it never takes you anywhere; you just go in circles. Grant's view of his position on this "ride" is extremely tenuous—he does not have a seat and he must stand in the aisle and hold onto one of the leather ceiling straps. This is a worldview with which any Walter Mitty–like antiheroic screen male would be most familiar.

Katharine Hepburn Basics

If one were to drop Katharine Hepburn into the Cary Grant streetcar analogy, she would no doubt be the conductor and/or the driver. But make no mistake, she would be in charge. While the real-life Archie Leach tried to be the screen Cary Grant, the film Hepburn was at her best when she played a variation of her dominating private self. For example, her signature movie role, with relationship to her now legendary film persona, was closely based upon the real Hepburn. Of course, this is the aforementioned Tracy Lord of *The Philadelphia Story*. The production's central character (Lord) is a self-absorbed, uppity East Coast young woman of privilege—"Oh, we're going to talk about me, are we? Goody!" The character fit Hepburn like a glove, including a real philosophy of life she often described as "ME, ME, ME," with a single *Me* even being chosen later as the title of her autobiography.[30]

After first starring on Broadway in this 1939–1940 production, which was a huge critical and commercial success, Hepburn bought the movie rights. This allowed her to return to Hollywood in a power position (after Harry Brandt, president of the Independent

Theatre Owners of America, had earlier labeled the actress and several other film stars "box-office poison"). The resulting screen adaptation of *Story* proved to be an even bigger triumph for Hepburn. But it was a calculated victory that took into account the damaging fallout from the "poison" claim, which the national press had unfortunately played up. Thus, *Story* took a tarnished image and used it to return Hepburn to box-office success. The woman whose forcefulness (on screen and off) had previously "won" her the damning press nickname of "Katharine of Arrogance" was given an affectionate comeuppance from *Story*'s Cary Grant. And through bringing her down a peg, an enduring screen persona was born. Before, however, addressing the post-*Story* romantic comedy Hepburn roles, some misperceptions about the actress's previous "box-office poison" status merits attention.

Katharine Hepburn and Screwball Comedy

Ironically, the last two pictures Hepburn made before heading to Broadway in order to revive her career are now considered screwball classics—1938's *Bringing Up Baby* and *Holiday*. Despite their now celebrated status, both films were initial commercial disappointments. And while the comedic parts these movies offered were a major departure from the "soap operas and costume dramas that helped get her named 'box office poison,'" the less than sterling commercial performance of these screwball comedies seemed to underscore the Hepburn poison-at-the-box-office analogy.[31]

The irony, however, does not stop there. Hepburn's period reviews for *Baby* and *Holiday* are generally glowing! For instance, the *Brooklyn Daily Eagle*'s rave critique of the former picture (entitled "Katharine Hepburn Clowns Pleasantly in 'Bringing Up Baby'") observed, "Katharine ('Mary of Scotland') Hepburn chucked her regal robes and royal demeanor for 'Bringing Up Baby.' . . . It is only Katie Hepburn ['who runs away with the picture'] as the wild and zany Connecticut heiress."[32] And the *New York Daily News* added, "it is really Katharine Hepburn and Cary Grant who put over the absurdities of the comedy and are gaily and wackily responsible for most of the laughs."[33] The normally insightful *Variety* even predicted "definite box-office" for *Baby*.[34]

Hepburn's critical comedy kudos continued on *Holiday*. Moreover, since this film opened less than a month after the "box-office poison" attack, period reviews often even defended the actress. For example, *Time* magazine stated,

> By her performance . . . [in *Holiday*], Katharine Hepburn seems highly likely to refute the argument of . . . [the] Independent Theatre Owners Association, who claimed her box-office appeal was practically nil.[35]

Newsweek even led with the same defense in the title of its *Holiday* review—"Miss Hepburn's Answer: Brilliant Playing in 'Holiday' Turns Tables on Critics."[36]

Jack Cohn, vice president of Columbia, which produced *Holiday*, was so taken with Hepburn's performance that he attempted to use the Independent Theatre Owners' attack on the actress to the studio's own ends. The *Holiday* advertising campaign for a time asked the question, "Is it true what they say about Hepburn?"[37] The obvious implication was that this picture would change all that. Sadly, that was not to be the case. Despite the movie's superlative reviews, which often keyed upon Hepburn, it produced (at best) a modest box-office profit.

A closer, three-part look at *Holiday*, however, provides further insight on Hepburn and the "box-office poison" phenomenon. First, *Holiday* was based upon a popular late 1920s play of the same name by Philip Barry—the identical author who, according to one Hepburn biographer, "painstakingly studied her every movement . . . and incorporated them into the [*Philadelphia Story*] character he was writing for her."[38] That being said, Hepburn's *Holiday* character (another young, headstrong, East Coast woman of privilege) also seems written with the actress in mind, though this was obviously not the case. Thus, it should be noted that of all that era's prominent playwrights, Barry seemed the most predisposed toward capturing Hepburn's character on paper, since he had a proven proclivity toward her type.

Screwball comedy's toy factor in Holiday, *with Cary Grant and Katharine Hepburn.*

Second, while Hepburn's bad box-office press did not help *Holiday*'s commercial possibilities, probably a greater liability for the picture was a plotline that had Cary Grant walking away from being a millionaire simply because he wanted an extended "holiday." For a Depression audience, many of whom had already experienced an economically forced "holiday," such 1920s idealism probably seemed ludicrous.

Third, Hepburn literature often states that the actress was largely responsible for putting together the 1938 *Holiday* package, getting Columbia head Harry Cohn to both hire George Cukor to direct and sign Cary Grant to costar with Hepburn.[39] More recent revisionist research would, however, suggest that Cukor was answerable for putting Hepburn in the film.[40] Indeed, late 1937 *Holiday* press material, by way of powerful period movie columnist Louella Parsons, had Cary Grant costarring with Irene Dunne instead of Hepburn.[41]

The same Parsons piece also had Leo McCarey being considered for director, which would have been a natural connection—given that McCarey had recently directed Grant and Dunne in the Columbia mega-hit *The Awful Truth*. A McCarey-Dunne-Grant *Holiday* would no doubt have done better at the box office, too. The public was clamoring for a Dunne-Grant reteaming, and when it did occur (1940's *My Favorite Wife*), they had another major hit on their hands. But maybe more to the point, the year before Hepburn was being called "box-office poison" (1937), *Boxoffice* magazine ranked Dunne a lofty number two in the publication's "most popular film star" poll.[42] Consequently, a previously unexplored explanation for *Holiday*'s disappointing commercial returns might be attached to a public upset that one of its favorite performers was unceremoniously dumped from a coveted port, only to be replaced by an actress in disfavor. And along related lines, "Irene was later quoted as saying she cried her eyes out after losing the part."[43]

Before moving on to the changes in the Hepburn persona that would qualify *The Philadelphia Story* as the beginning of her romantic comedy career, the actress's screwball role in *Bringing Up Baby* also merits further examination along "box-office poison"–related lines. For example, as noted earlier, the actress's zany *Baby* character is now seen not only as being composed of Hepburn traits (domineering, woman of privilege) but also an amalgamation of screwball heroine basics. These fundamentals would include everything from Carole Lombard's patented crazy behavior to Irene Dunne's signature throaty laugh, which went on just long enough to imply, "You have no control over what I'm about to do."

Though Hepburn's recycling of these traits and more in *Baby* seem charming today, not everyone in 1938 saw her performance (or the film in general) as a seemless hybrid. For instance, the *New York Times* review encouraged viewers to play a game called "the cliché expert goes to the movies."[44] The *New York Herald Tribune* complained that "the comic byplay is labored where it should have been inspired."[45] Couple these comments with the fact that by 1938 screwball comedy in general was suffering from a shortage of new ideas and one has another explanation (beyond Hepburn's "box-office poison" excuse) for *Baby*'s disappointing commercial numbers. That is, if period viewers perceived this picture to simply be the recycling of a genre rapidly becoming passé, it would be natural for the box office to be soft.

The one distinctive Hepburn trait in her *Bringing Up Baby* performance, beyond that signature forcefulness, is a gift for the physical in everything she does. Like Cary Grant, Hepburn's athleticism is central not only here but in many of her other films, such as joining Grant for pratfalls in *Holiday*. Thus, in *Baby* she "skips, ambles, strolls, lopes, ducks, crouches, squats, and in general reproduces the entire repertoire of human postures and gaits," not to mention showing off her golf game.[46] Again, as for Grant, this trait for the physical comedy is also present in her romantic comedy persona. But whereas Grant tones it down for the romantic genre, Hepburn is more likely to escalate its significance, such as in *Pat and Mike*, which showcases her skills in several sports.

Netting her man, Katharine Hepburn's gift for physical comedy is showcased in this scene from Bringing Up Baby *(1938, with Cary Grant).*

Katharine Hepburn and Romantic Comedy

Philip Barry's successful reinventing of Hepburn in *The Philadelphia Story* was not merely a kind gesture by a playwright friend. Barry was also in need of both a hit production and a creative makeover, because, as previously suggested, he was predisposed to a type of forceful heroine that had by then (the late 1930s) fallen from favor. Ironically, for this reason, the disappointing box-office performance of *Holiday* was probably fortuitous for both Barry and Grant—it underlined the need for a major change.

The Philadelphia Story opens with heiress Tracy Lord about to marry a pompous social climber. Her transformation from ice goddess to real human being starts when she falls in love with self-made writer/humanist Mike Conners (played in the film version by Jimmy

Stewart) who puts her in touch with the world beyond her nose. But it is not until she reconnects romantically with first husband C. K. Dexter Haven (played by Cary Grant in the movie) that Lord achieves a real "coming out" as a human being. When she becomes sensitive to human frailty in others, such as the philandering of her father, she begins to recognize her own condescending tendencies. Haven is the worldly wise playboy who ultimately makes this happen but with enough compassion that, like his name (Haven), Hepburn's character can change with minimal humiliation.

Paradoxically, the inspiration for this sophisticated makeover of Hepburn might have come from something as basic as the popular culture of the day. For instance, in late 1937 *Motion Picture* magazine did a Hepburn profile entitled "She Who Gets Slapped," with the following provocative opening:

> You know those wooden dolls you slap down and then, after a barely appreciable moment they bob up again, even more gaily and spiritedly than before? . . . They were made to be slapped down. Katharine Hepburn reminds me of them.[47]

Now, the slapping doll analogy was meant as a metaphor for Hepburn's real-world resiliency. But it anticipates the formula utilized in *The Philadelphia Story*—slap Hepburn down and have her rethink who she is.

This Hepburn makeover was so successful that the "slap down" humiliation factor is actually bolstered in her next romantic comedy outing—1942's *Woman of the Year*. And, like Cary Grant's orchestration of his career, Hepburn was again the guiding force behind getting *Woman of the Year* filmed, just as she had shepherded the screen adaptation of *The Philadelphia Story*. In this, her first teaming with Spencer Tracy (who would become her real-life companion for the next twenty-five years, until his 1967 death), Hepburn's character, Tess Harding, is even less initially likeable than *Philadelphia*'s brittle Tracy Lord. For instance, *New York Sun Times* critic Eileen Creelman praised the picture but described Harding as "one hard to bear, a woman who admits she likes to know things before other people do and then to tell them."[48] The critic from the communist newspaper the *New York Daily Worker* took a similar slant but contrasted the character with Tracy's populist sportswriter (Sam Craig)—"He likes just to be with people but she wants to be telling them what's what all the time."[49]

Not surprisingly, Harding's bossiness was modeled upon Hepburn's own patented outspokeness, a given trait since the actress was old enough to talk. The following real-life example, though occurring just after the making of *Woman of the Year*, was quintessential Hepburn. During the shooting of 1942's *Keeper of the Flame,* she kept telling her director friend George Cukor how he should have done numerous scenes. Finally, in a climactic sequence two performers are told the house is on fire:

> "I don't think that they should have to be told about the fire," Hepburn interjected. "They would smell the smoke."
>
> This time Cukor finally responded. "It must be wonderful," he shouted, "to know all about acting and all about fires, too!"[50]

Harding is such a cosmopolitan journalist, specializing in international politics, that she seems positively un-American. But this is not an unexpected story development, given that the film was made at the beginning of America's involvement in World War II, with most period pictures involving narrative openings for patriotic cues. Consequently, Hepburn's evolution here might be subtitled the *Americanization of Harding*, á la the later James Garner/Julie Andrews romantic drama *The Americanization of Emily* (1964).

As implied earlier, this Hepburn/Yankee Doodle factor is best addressed with regard to the national game of baseball, via Tracy's story occupation as a sportswriter. This is also another example of romantic comedy's one-foot-in-reality tradition, since the production of *Woman of the Year* paralleled a then national debate as to whether major league baseball should shut down for the duration of the war. With predictable yet entertaining appropriateness, the two central characters first lock horns over this issue, and the movie is raised to a higher level than mere flag waving. *New York Herald Tribune* critic Howard Barnes observed, "When the sports writer challenges his woman of the year by reminding her that baseball may be the real index of democratic freedom, the film takes on significant meaning as well as comic implications."[51]

To Harding's credit, she quickly embraces the pop culture Americanism of baseball as Craig tutors her at the sport's ultimate shrine (Yankee Stadium) while he covers a game. There is even an element of the populism so inherent to baseball when, during the course of the contest, Hepburn's Harding not only loosens up to Tracy's sportswriter but also a nearby blue collar fan.

Despite these humanizing steps, Harding's progress is negated by what the *New York Time*'s called "the blow-off," "when the great lady . . . permits a little Greek boy she has adopted to languish, unmothered and unloved, in their apartment."[52] This returns the film to a basic romantic comedy theme—defining a character's capacity for love through how he/she interacts with children. Even the self-centered Tracy Lord always had time for comically affectionate interaction with her much younger *Philadelphia Story* screen sister (Virginia Weidler)—the child actress who first wins our approval by way of an entertaining rendition of Groucho's "Lydia, the Tattooed Lady" (from the Marxes's *At the Circus*, 1939).

Fittingly, *Woman of the Year*'s showcasing of another romantic comedy component, utilizing an older couple as a model for what love should be, eventually rescues Harding from her less than passing marks on the child front. The two most important people in Harding's life are her widowed statesman dad (Minor Watson) and a pioneering feminist friend of the family (Fay Bainter). The latter character had served both as a surrogate mother figure for Harding, as well as her prototype for the modern woman—the single and dominatingly independent career track type. But when these two successful loners decide to marry, a lightbulb goes on in Harding's head, and the fundamental axiom for the genre is indirectly acknowledged—everyone needs someone.

What makes *Woman of the Year* such a rich genre work is its ability, therefore, to incorporate so many romantic comedy rudiments in its story. What seems to start off as merely, according to one period critic, "shades of the 'Philadelphia Story,'" with its defrosting of Hepburn's persona, does this and much more.[53] For example, besides the aforementioned plot advancements via Harding's interaction with pivotal young and old characters, not to mention the straight shooting Spencer Tracy, the movie also includes a crucial wedding ceremony.

Unlike screwball comedy, which is famous for marriages that do *not* happen, romantic comedy is equally tied to making the ceremony significant. Interestingly enough, *Woman of the Year* features two weddings. Ironically, it is not Harding's that is central to the story but that of her father. Only then, after Tracy's Craig has left her, does the ceremony's message sink in.

Interestingly enough, it anticipates by four years the celebrated single-take wedding scene from William Wyler's *The Best Years of Our Lives* (1946), "creating action and reaction within the same shot," where one couple's ceremony applies equally to another couple in attendance, all in the same film frame.[54] The opening of the comparable *Woman of the Year* scene accomplishes a variation of the same one-take theme. That is, in a film shot originating from the altar, the center foreground of the film frame has the wedding couple. In the left background of the same shot is an elderly couple (more historic witnesses for love). In the center background of the frame is the small chapel's entrance, through which Hepburn/Harding now slowly enters. The marriage ceremony has already started, and as she lingers by the doorway Harding's aloneness underlines the poignancy of her finally understanding this rite of passage moment. Director George Stevens soon cuts to the traditional subjective close-up of a crying Hepburn to punctuate this lightbulb moment. Consequently, this same-frame long take does not approach the sustained length of the focus ceremony in Wyler's film. Still, Stevens anticipates the later groundbreaking scene and gives the viewer yet another reason to highlight *Woman of the Year* as not only a watershed Hepburn romantic comedy but also as movie equally central to the genre itself.

The successive Tracy-Hepburn romantic comedy is *Without Love* (1945). Though a minor work, which will be addressed later in this chapter, the film is historically important for establishing a variation of the genre's Hepburn as ice goddess persona. In this scenario, the actress needs appreciation, rather than a comeuppance. *Without Love* has Tracy and Hepburn entering a platonic relationship, with love to follow. Elements of this formula surface in such later Hepburn films as *The African Queen* (with Bogart), *Pat and Mike*, and *Desk Set* (both with Tracy). What makes this lesser but entertaining Hepburn take on romantic comedy doubly interesting is that it was again orchestrated by Philip Barry, from his original 1942 play, *Without Love*. Moreover, it was also written for Hepburn, who opened on Broadway in the play on November 10, 1942.

The early 1940s had very much of a Barry connection for Hepburn, including the 1940 screen adaptation of *The Philadelphia Story*, a 1940–1941 stage season tour in the national company of *The Philadelphia Story*, three radio productions of this very popular production (1942, 1944, and 1947), a Broadway stage production of *Without Love* (1942–1943), and the 1945 stage adaptation of *Without Love*!

The next Tracy-Hepburn application of Barry's more popular "slap down" approach to the actress must wait, however, for the film classic *Adam's Rib* (1949). While they had been teamed several times after *Woman of the Year*, their joint enterprises (with the exception of *Without Love*) had been outside romantic comedy, such as Frank Capra's last important populist film, *State of the Union* (1948). Still, the couple's rapport in the latter picture rekindled interest in their returning to a *Woman of the Year*–like production, an influence noted in many reviews of *Adam's Rib*. To illustrate, the *New York Times* stated,

Spencer Tracy and Katharine Hepburn can only avoid romance so long in Without Love *(1945).*

People still think of it [*Woman of the Year*] fondly—including MGM, which obviously thought of it so fondly that it decided to try again. And that it has done, with equal humor and what should surely be comparable success, in *Adam's Rib*.[55]

This new movie was written by real-life husband and wife Ruth Gordon and Garson Kanin, close friends of Tracy and Hepburn, who had patterned their screenplay couple after the two actors. As addressed in the previous chapter, *Adam's Rib* pits Tracy and Hepburn as opposing lawyers in an attempted murder case that soon becomes a comic treatise on woman's equality. Since the duo are married in the movie, there are no neutral corners in this battle of the sexes, which means there are few comedy lulls. Thus, *Variety* advised, "Subtitles or hearing aids are needed to break through the wall of audience laughter that will greet most of the byplay."[56] This would very much include Hepburn's outrageous dark comedy comeuppance by Tracy and his licorice gun.

Adam's Rib proves to be the best of the Tracy-Hepburn films for more reasons, however, than the aforementioned "byplay." There are all those little relationship nuances that ring so true in the picture, from matching pet nicknames ("Pinkie" and "Pinky") to their elaborate midnight snack rituals. This attention to the small details of a marriage also demonstrates how minor variations in habit can signal relationship problems. For example, another *Adam's Rib* ritual has Tracy periodically giving Hepburn a rubdown. During one comically stressful scene he finishes the rubdown with a more enthusiastic than normal slap to her backside. She is outraged:

> Hepburn: "You meant that, didn't you? You really meant that. . . . Yes, you did, I know your type. I know a slap from a slug. . . . I'm not so sure I care to expose myself to typical instinctive masculine brutality. . . . And it felt not only as though you meant it, but as though you felt you had a right to. I can tell."
>
> Tracy: "What've you got back there, radar equipment?"

This could be a capsulization of their comic clashes—preachy overstatement versus a humorously defusing directness.

Along related lines, one review praised how the picture entertainingly showcased a "happy couple who are well settled in their

[law] careers and presumably wholly acquainted with each other's eccentricities."[57] But given what we now know about Tracy and Hepburn (the public was unaware of their private relationship during his lifetime), these comments about a "happy couple" and their special "eccentricities" rings equally true about the performers themselves, especially with parts patterned after the duo in the first place. One is reminded of realist film theorist André Bazin's observation on "transposed autobiography," where an actor brings such naturalness to a role, or a series of roles, that the performance goes leagues beyond merely assuming a character.[58]

Another reason to celebrate *Adam's Rib* is that it marked a clear departure from *Woman of the Year*. Whereas the latter film reinforced the romantic comedy tradition of using an older couple (two, actually) as a role model for love, *Adam's Rib* broke new ground by better defining the special Tracy and Hepburn relationship through a contrast with a comically bad marriage. The movie introduced film audiences to Broadway standouts Judy Holliday and Tom Ewell—who play a truly battlin' couple, with her shooting him during an adulterous affair. It is the ensuing trial that places Adam and Amanda Bonner (Tracy and Hepburn) in opposite camps—with Amanda defending Holliday's Doris Attinger against Adam's prosecuting district attorney.

The case for tying these two diverse couples together is best made late in the movie when Adam catches Amanda and a neighbor in the aforementioned compromising romantic situation and Tracy's character briefly feigns a violent response, à la the gun toting Doris. Consequently, Hepburn/Amanda not only gets her comeuppance but the linking of the couples more effectively proves the Tracy/Adam point—no one is above the law, whether it is the poignantly goofy, victimized Doris, in a movie-stealing performance by Holliday, or an innocent Hepburn getting a heavy romantic rush from songwriter Kip Lurie (David Wayne).

For the Tracy and Hepburn romantic comedies, it does not get any better than *Adam's Rib*, a movie that boasted Hepburn's strongest supporting cast since *The Philadelphia Story*. Indeed, revisionist criticism for the movie now keys upon Holliday, whose role had been beefed up at the insistence of Hepburn, in order to better the chances that this movie novice would get the Billie Dawn lead in the screen adaptation of *Born Yesterday* (1950). Hepburn was outraged that Holliday had not been the automatic choice, given that the younger actress had already won Broadway acclaim in the stage production of *Born Yesterday*. But thanks to Hepburn and the career-making launching pad that was *Adam's Rib*, Holliday not only got to play Billie Dawn in the movies, she also won the Best Actress Oscar for 1950.

Besides the entertaining Holliday, Tom Ewell's ne'er-do-well husband reveals some of the antiheroic flair that would serve him so well in the later screen adaptation of *The Seven Year Itch* (1955). Ewell's mistress in *Adam's Rib* is comedy standout Jean Hagen, whose high-pitched whine registers here as a sneak preview for her tour de silly role in the later movie classic *Singin' in the Rain* (1952). And David Wayne's Kip Lurie also scores points as the character you love to hate. Despite his entertaining abrasiveness, there is an amusing honesty about him that is rare in romantic comedy, from admitting to Hepburn's Amanda that part of her attractiveness lies simply in living so close to him to his darkly comic axiom about lawyers (and the film's funniest observation): "Lawyers should never marry other lawyers. This is called inbreeding, from which come idiot children and more lawyers."

With Tracy's masterful checkmating of Hepburn in *Adam's Rib*, it was like the long distance runner finally hitting the proverbial "wall" (limit); romantic comedy would never again so totally usurp her autonomy. But there would still be provocative variations upon this theme. The greatest such example would be her teaming with Humphrey Bogart in *The African Queen* (1951). As the prim spinster sister of a missionary in German East Africa, she meets her romantic Waterloo in the unlikely guise of a riverboat souse played by Bogart, in an Oscar-winning performance.

It is the beginning of World War I and Hepburn's Rosie concocts the most unlikely of plans—blowing up an enemy ship down river. Normally, this action adventure backdrop, not to mention period setting, would have eliminated the picture from this study's standard contemporary romantic comedy worldview. But *The African Queen* merits inclusion here for several reasons. First, the movie not only showcases elements of the melted ice goddess persona but also the alternative Barry/Hepburn take on romantic comedy (see *Without Love*), where she is simply in need of some heartfelt appreciation. Second, while both *The African Queen* and *Without Love* have war backdrops (from the sinking of a World War I German ship to the invention of a better World War II oxygen mask), they are completely secondary to the slow blossoming love story each film documents. Third, even period critics did not take the war-related story elements seriously. In fact, when reviewing *The African Queen*, where the armed conflict might have merited more attention (versus *Without Love*), the *New York Time*'s otherwise affectionately positive critique referred to any such "attempt at serious portrayal . . . [as] not only incongruous but absurd."[59]

A fourth reason to include *The African Queen* in this romantic comedy study is that the duo of Charlie and Rosie (Bogart and Hepburn) seemingly have even less in common than any of the standard odd couple arrangements in the Tracy and Hepburn teamings. As *Variety* observed, *The African Queen* couple is "completely mismatched in every way except their adventurous hearts."[60] But just as in the opposites attract world of Tracy and Hepburn, Charlie and Rosie manage to defy the odds and surface with love intact.

Fifth, more than one publication referred to the twosome as a "romantic middle-aged couple."[61] Sadly, even today this remains a relatively rare story premise, with popular culture art appearing to be more youth obsessed with each passing year. Consequently, *The African Queen*'s middle-aged love story, a moniker equally at home describing the post–*Woman of the Year* Tracy and Hepburn films, seems more refreshingly new with each screening. And just as

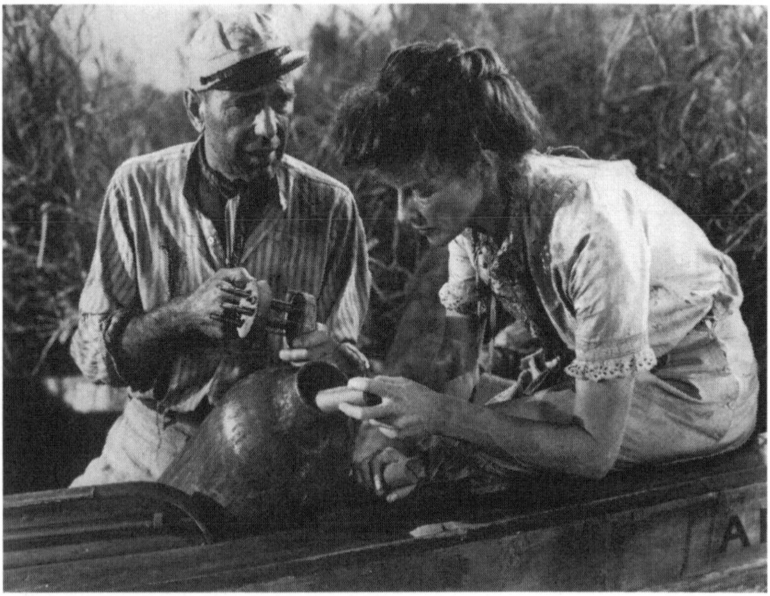

The most unlikely of romantic comedy couples—Katharine Hepburn and Humphrey Bogart in The African Queen *(1951).*

Charlie and Rosie's odd couple topped the ongoing mismatches in the Tracy and Hepburn romantic comedies, *The African Queen* duo would win any middle-aged romance sweepstakes, too. The explanation for this is painfully simple. While scripts for Tracy and Hepburn always include and/or imply the possibility of other romantic partners for them, the Charlie and Rosie love story is something unique for both characters. Moreover, it is a last chance for these two lonely misfits, the aloof, teetotaling, missionary spinster and the hard-drinking riverboat captain, whom *African Queen* director John Huston later described as a "wretched, sleazy, absurd, brave little man."[62]

A final explanation for tucking the movie into this romantic comedy fold brings the student back to an aforementioned basic of the genre—one foot in reality. Granted, period critics found some components of this story lacking in believability, but there is also genuine love in Charlie and Rosie's relationship. Bogart said, "We all believed in the honesty and charm of the story. And I wanted to get out of the trench coat I wear in the [tough guy] movies. . . . We loved those two silly people on that boat."[63] The actor's trench coat comment is especially well chosen given the insightful observations of Bogart biographer and friend, Richard Gehman:

> The Bogart cult do not like it [*The African Queen*] . . . they feel that this film comes closer to being a real experience than those in which he, James Cagney and Edward G. Robinson always were shooting each other. So it does. . . . [*The African Queen*] has moments of warmth and tenderness and humor between Katharine Hepburn and Bogart which seldom have been approached on the screen.[64]

The Philip Barry alternative romantic comedy take for Hepburn of appreciation (versus melting the ice goddess) surfaces again in her next picture after *The African Queen*—*Pat and Mike*, yet another outing with Spencer Tracy. Plus, this picture had the added pedigree of assembling the behind-the-screen talent of *Adam's Rib*—director George Cukor and the screenwriting couple of Ruth Gordon and Garson Kanin. While entertaining, *Pat and Mike* is not in a league with *Adam's Rib*, though few romantic comedies are.

Pat and Mike primarily works today as a showcase for Hepburn's very real athletic skills as she holds her own with celebrated golf pros like Babe Didrikson Zaharias (arguably the greatest woman athlete of all-time) and Betty Hicks, as well as such champion tennis players as Don Budge, Alice Marble, and Gussie Moran. When not competing, Hepburn is a college athletic instructor engaged to a stuffy professor (William Ching), who does not take her very seriously. Thus, when Spencer Tracy's sports promoter approaches her about playing professionally, she joins ranks with him to prove to herself and her fiancé that she is good. As in *Woman of the Year* and *The African Queen*, her romantic lead (Tracy) is not in her social class, or as the *New York Times* so colorfully phrased it—"Mr. Tracy . . . makes happy pretense of being a sporting type—a type several pegs below the lady but none the less a sport."[65]

He also acts the tough training coach, so there is a semblance of the ever popular Hepburn comeuppance. Still, the slow growing romance is more about finding a middle ground than some sort of ritualistic Hepburn humiliation, à la *Woman of the Year* or *Adam's Rib*. Consequently, her eventual love for Tracy's Damon Runyon–like figure breaks Hepburn's character of choking whenever the insensitive fiancé attends an athletic event, while her physical gifts literally save Tracy's sport from a beating at the hands of some equally Runyonesque hoods.

Hepburn's last two romantic comedy outings are a mixed bag. In 1956 she starred opposite Bob Hope in *The Iron Petticoat*, a loose updating of *Ninotchka* (1939, an early prototype for the melting of an ice goddess). Hepburn is a Russian flyer who defects to the West, with any remaining remnants of communism collapsing by way of Bob Hope's entertaining American Air Force officer—who has been assigned to her case. Though a critical and commercial disappointment at the time, it was not without its period champions—*Variety* said, "Hepburn makes an impressive showing as the Soviet pilot."[66] And today's viewer witnesses a film not without some charm. Revisionist movie critic Leonard Maltin credits this to the two "Stars' surprising rapport."[67] Maybe 1950s American's had had enough of defrosting the Hepburn persona. Certainly her earlier romantic comedy outings during the decade (*The African Queen* and *Pat and Mike*) depended much more on the gentler appreciation factor first mapped out for the actress in *Without Love*.

Added evidence for this position comes with Hepburn's last romantic comedy, the box-office and critical hit *The Desk Set*, which is very much in the tradition of *Without Love*. *Desk Set* has Hepburn's character directing a reference department for a major television network. Tracy plays a business efficiency expert and inventor of a new advanced computer. (Again, this represents shades of his inventor in *Without Love*.)

As he constantly quizzes Hepburn and her staff and endlessly measures the physical dimensions of their department, the water cooler conjecture is that everyone will be replaced by Tracy's computer. Meanwhile, he shows a mild interest in Hepburn, who is still hopeful of having a relationship with a network executive—Gig Young in yet another of his likable, second banana roles.

From this thin premise is devised an entertaining, though admittedly lightweight, comedy outing. Tracy essentially wins her by default, because by the time Young is ready to make his commitment move, Hepburn has already been won over by the efficiency experts comfortable attentiveness. But two other factors reinforce this argument for the ascendancy of the *Without Love* position in *Desk Set*. First, the latter film ends with Tracy (*not* Hepburn) flirting with a comeuppance—his computer goes haywire. And second, period critics not only praised the picture, they scoffed at the notion of even a computer topping Hepburn. For instance, the *New York Times*'s review is peppered with such comments—"Hepburn is obviously a woman who is superior to a thinking machine," or "The prospect of automation is plainly no menace to Kate."[68]

For today's audience *Desk Set* merits an additional romantic comedy postscript. The film was adapted from the William Marchant play by Phoebe and Henry Ephron, the screenwriting parents of writer/director Nora Ephron, best known for penning *When Harry Met Sally . . .* (1989) and coscripting with sister Delia *You've Got Mail* (1998, which Nora also directed). Nora and Delia's love of old movies (*You've Got Mail* is a loose remake of *The Shop around the Corner*, 1940) is born of their parents' earlier involvement in writing for both the stage and screen.

After *Desk Set* Tracy and Hepburn teamed one more time—for the problem film *Guess Who's Coming to Dinner* (1967, which addressed interracial marriage). While this movie obviously falls outside the parameter of a romantic comedy study, there is a Tracy line near the close of the picture that works as a moving summation/tribute to the long-term Tracy-Hepburn relationship, both on screen and off. Tracy's *Guess Who's Coming to Dinner* character supports an interracial marriage by telling his screen daughter's lover (Sidney Poitier),

"You have to get married, because if you love her [Katharine Houghton] the way I love *her*" and he looks directly at a now crying Hepburn. The film's director (Stanley Kramer) said, "That unintended personal identification made it a scene of fantastic power."[69] *The New Yorker* critic added that this moment, and Tracy's final comments at the climax, when "he turns to her [Hepburn] and tells her what an old man remembers having loved; it is, for us who are permitted to overhear him, an experience that transcends the theatrical."[70]

By this point in time (1967), it seems inconceivable that Hepburn had once been branded "box-office poison." Indeed, even by the time of 1945's *Without Love*, period critics had scoffed at the very idea. For instance, *Variety*, with tongue firmly in check, had observed, "And of course, Hepburn-Tracy on the marquee ain't exactly b.o. poison."[71] The couple's status was further elevated by the 1950s when reviewers begin to routinely refer to them as "Mr. and Mrs. America." They had become, in effect, romantic comedy royalty. They were further deified after Tracy's 1967 death, particularly with the publication of Garson Kanin's *Tracy and Hepburn: An Intimate Memoir* (1971), in which the general public first learned of the couple's private relationship.[72]

For the avid fan of romantic comedy this revelation constituted an added genre bonus, bringing one full circle back to Bazin's aforementioned "transposed autobiography," though Tracy and Hepburn aficionados had long assumed they were more then just a screen couple. Moreover, unlike the Cary Grant disclosures on the difficulty of moving from Archie Leach to a facsimile of his movie persona, the reality factor associated with the Tracy-Hepburn films simply reinforced the fact that the actress's parts were often patterned upon herself.

Ultimately, if one enjoys the romantic comedy world of Hepburn (be it comeuppance directed, or the woman in need of appreciation), the joy comes from viewing life lessons in love that are movingly consistent. If age we must, it would be comforting to grow old in a relationship not unlike that of screen duo Tracy and Hepburn. Of course, *The Picture of Dorian Gray* phenomenon that is Cary Grant (not aging) has its followers, too. But since that *Dorian Gray* scenario is not likely to occur for most of us, Hepburn wins the romantic comedy cigar for being the most reality-based. Thus, a balance is achieved, since Grant had a greater influence on screwball comedy.

Notes

1. Gary Carey, *Katharine Hepburn: A Hollywood Yankee* (New York: Dell, 1983), p. 98.
2. Nancy Nelson, *Evenings with Cary Grant* (New York: William Morrow, 1991), p. 217.
3. Nelson, *Evenings with Cary Grant*, p. 98.
4. Ralph Bellamy, *When the Smoke Hit the Fan* (Garden City, N.Y.: Doubleday, 1979), pp. 129–30.
5. Geoffrey Wansell, *Haunted Idol: The Story of the Real Cary Grant* (New York: William Morrow, 1984), pp. 121–22.
6. Wansell, *Haunted Idol*, p. 122.
7. Albert Govoni, *Cary Grant: An Unauthorized Biography* (Chicago: Henry Regnery, 1971), p. 47.
8. Wes Gehring, "Phone Interview With Irene Dunne," July 1979.
9. Peter Bogdanovich, *Who the Devil Made It* (New York: Ballantine Books, 1997), p. 380.
10. Joe Adamson, *Groucho, Harpo, Chico, and Sometimes Zeppo* (New York: Doubleday, 1979), pp. 129–130.
11. Nelson, *Evenings With Cary Grant,* p. 98.
12. Bosley Crowther, *The Bachelor and the Bobby-Soxer* review, *New York Times*, July 25, 1947, p. 12.
13. H. Allen Smith, "A Session with McCarey," *Variety*, January 7, 1970, p. 23.
14. Incomplete McCarey interview, No publication cited, March 23, 1939, in the McCarey file, Billy Rose Special Collection, New York Public Library at Lincoln Center.
15. Wansell, *Haunted Idol*, p. 231.
16. Peter Bogdanovich, American film Institute Seminar, Beverly Hills, July 1975. (Variations of this quote have surfaced in several sources since this AFI event.)

17. Richard Schickel, *Cary Grant: A Celebration* (New York: Applause Books, 1999), p. 62.

18. Schickel, *Cary Grant*, p. 100.

19. Pauline Kael, "The Man From Dream City," *The New Yorker*, July 14, 1975, p. 54.

20. Kael, "The Man From Dream City," p. 45.

21. David Thomson, "Charms and the Man," *Film Comment* (cover story), February 1984, p. 65.

22. Donald Deschner, *The Films of Cary Grant* (Secaucus, N.J.: Citadel Press, 1973), p. 274.

23. Henri Bergson, "Laughter" (1900), in *Comedy*, ed. Wylie Sypher (Garden City, N.Y.: Doubleday, 1956), pp. 157–58.

24. James Harvey, *Romantic Comedy in Hollywood: From Lubitsch to Sturges* (New York: Da Capo Press, 1998), p. 304.

25. Joseph McBride (ed.), *Hawks on Hawks* (Berkeley: University of California Press, 1982), p. 70.

26. McBride, *Hawks on Hawks,* p. 70.

27. Maria DiBattista, *Fast-Talking Dames* (New Haven: Yale University Press, 2001), p. 19.

28. Warren Hoge, "Cary Grant: No Lady's Man," *Des Moines Register* (*New York Times* copyright), July 6, 1977, pp. 1A, 8A; Geoffrey Wansell, *Haunted Idol.*

29. The best rendering of this Grant story is in the Pete Martin article, "How Grant Took Hollywood," *Saturday Evening Post*, February 19, 1949, p. 66.

30. Katharine Hepburn, *Me: Stories of My Life* (New York: Alfred A. Knopf, 1991), p. 154.

31. Jerry Vermilye, *Cary Grant* (New York: Pyramid, 1973), p. 63.

32. Herbert Cohn, "Katharine Hepburn Clowns Pleasantly in 'Bringing Up Baby,'" *Brooklyn Daily Eagle*, March 4, 1938, p. 17.

33. Kate Cameron, "Babies, Just Babies, On Music Hall Screen," *New York Daily News*, March 4, 1938, p. 46.

34. *Bringing Up Baby* review, *Variety*, February 16, 1938.

35. *Holiday* review, *Time*, June 13, 1938, p. 24.

36. "Miss Hepburn's Answer: Brilliant Playing in 'Holiday' Turns Tables on Critics," *Newsweek*, June 13, 1938, p. 21.

37. "Miss Hepburn's Answer," p. 21.

38. Carey, *Katharine Hepburn*, p. 106.

39. For instance, see the Gary Carey biography of Hepburn, pp. 100–01.

40. For example, see Marge Schultz's *Irene Dunne: A Bio-Bibliography* (Wesport, Conn.: Greenwood Press, 1991), p. 13.

41. Louella Parsons, "Cary Grant Gets Lead in 'Holiday': Irene Dunne is Slated for Top Spot, too," *Philadelphia Inquirer*, December 24, 1937, p. 9.

42. Schultz, *Irene Dunne*, p. 180.

43. Schultz, *Irene Dunne*, p. 13.

44. *Bringing Up Baby* review, *New York Times*, March 4, 1938, p. 17.

45. Howard Barnes, "'Bringing Up Baby'—Music Hall," *New York Herald Tribune*, March 4, 1938, p. 14.

46. DiBattista, *Fast-Talking Dames*, p. 196.

47. Gladys Hall, "She Who Gets Slapped," *Motion Picture*, December 1937, p. 26.

48. Eileen Creelman, "Spencer Tracy in 'Woman of the Year' . . .," *New York Sun*, February 6, 1942, p. 19.

49. Milton Meltzer, "Hepburn, Tracy Star in Woman of the Year," *New York Daily Worker*, February 7, 1942, p. 7.

50. Christopher Anderson, *An Affair to Remember: The Remarkable Love Story of Katharine Hepburn and Spencer Tracy* (New York: William Morrow, 1997), p. 161.

51. Howard Barnes, "'Woman of the Year'—Music Hall," *New York Herald Tribune*, February 6, 1942, p. 13.

52. Bosley Crowther, *Woman of the Year* review, *New York Times*, February 6, 1942, p. 23.

53. *Woman of the Year* review, *Variety*, January 14, 1942.

54. Bernard F. Dick, *Anatomy of Film* (New York: St. Martin's Press, 1998), p. 239.

55. *Adam's Rib* review, *New York Times*, December 26, 1949, p. 33.

56. *Adam's Rib* review, *Variety*, November 2, 1949.

57. *Adam's Rib* review, *New York Times*, December 26, 1949.

58. André Bazin, "The Grandeur of Limelight," in *What Is Cinema?*, vol. 2, selected and trans. Hugh Gray (Berkeley: University of California Press, 1967), p. 136.

59. *The African Queen* review, *New York Times*, February 21, 1952, p. 24.

60. *The African Queen* review, *Variety*, December 26, 1951.

61. For example, see *Variety*'s December 26, 1951, review of *The African Queen*.

62. John Huston, *An Open Book* (New York: Ballantine Books, 1981), p. 229.

63. Stephen Humphrey Bogart (with Gary Provost), *Bogart: In Search of My Father* (New York: Plume, 1996), p. 259.

64. Richard Gehman, *Bogart* (Greenwich, Conn.: Fawcett, 1965), p. 140.

65. *Pat and Mike* review, *New York Times*, June 19, 1952, p. 32.

66. *The Iron Petticoat* review, *Variety*, July 11, 1956.

67. Leonard Maltin (ed.), "The Iron Petticoat Entry," in *Leonard Maltin's Movie and Video Guide: 1999 Edition* (New York: Signet Book, 1998), p. 672.

68. *Desk Set* review, *New York Times*, May 16, 1957, p. 28.

69. Bill Davidson, *Spencer Tracy: Tragic Idol* (New York: E. P. Dutton, 1987), p. 210.

70. Donald Deschner, *The Films of Spencer Tracy* (Secaucus, N.J.: Citadel Press, 1972), p. 251.

71. *Without Love* review, *Variety*, May 21, 1945.

72. Garson Kanin, *Tracy and Hepburn: An Intimate Memoir* (New York: Viking Press, 1971).

CHAPTER FIVE

SECREWBALL AND ROMANTIC COMEDY IN THE MODERN ERA: SINCE 1960

> Wanda, do you have any idea what it's like being English? Being so correct all the time, being so stifled by this dread of doing the wrong thing? . . . You see, Wanda, we're all terrified of embarrassment. That's why we're so . . . dead.
>
> —Archie Leach (John Cleese) to
> Wanda (Jamie Lee Curtis) in
> *A Fish Called Wanda* (1988)

Both screwball and romantic comedy genres continue to be alive and well in the modern era. Many traditional examples of each type, throwbacks to the golden age of the 1930s and 1940s, continue to be produced. But all genres, by the very nature of artistic and social change, are works in progress. Consequently, while entertainment formulas are a valuable part of genre study, these equations should remain open-ended for the inevitability of change. The following pages address both conventional and new variations of each genre.

The Traditional Screwball Mold

Any number of movies can be included in this category. One group would include remakes of earlier classics, such as *What's Up, Doc?* (1972), a loose update of *Bringing Up Baby* (1938). There are also self-conscious homages to the past, such as *Seems Like Old Times* (1980). Other vehicles simply bring to mind prior watershed works.

For instance, the pioneering antiheroic fantasy makeover that was *Topper* (1937) has much in common with the "spirited" *All of Me* (1984), where Steve Martin rediscovers life by becoming densely populated with the soul of Lily Tomlin. Carole Lombard's pathological liar in *True Confession* (1937) seems reborn in Goldie Hawn's master fibber from *Housesitter* (1992, with the actresses even physically resembling each other). Plus, as an addendum to the similarity factor, after such screwball comedies as *Four Weddings and a Funeral* (1994) and *Notting Hill* (1999), antiheroic leading man Hugh Grant was hailed as "the new Cary Grant."

One could argue that the most pivotal of recent screwball films have had a British slant, including *A Fish Called Wanda*, *Four Weddings and a Funeral*, *Notting Hill*, and *Bridget Jones's Diary* (2001), the latter three of which Richard Curtis had a hand in scripting. Though a critic might be tempted to interpret this English connection as a major genre makeover, these movies merely reinforce the most basic of screwball values. That is, the genre's central male is often portrayed as initially in need of life. And as suggested with John Cleese's chapter opening quote, each of these movies play upon the popular stereotype that British males are even more romantically dead than their American antiheroic counterparts. While Cleese is the most tightly wound of the three male principals addressed here, the other two (befuddled Hugh Grant of *Four Weddings*, and the ever-so-rigid Colin Firth of *Bridget*) are both in need of screwball revitalization.

That being said, one should note there are story components in each movie that arguably distracted from their screwball status. *Wanda* had the cartoon-like dark comedy subplot involving Michael Palin and the falling safe that flattens a pooch. *Four Weddings* had the poignant drama of a popular character dying. And *Bridget* was marketed as the latest incarnation of the everywoman picture, with title character Renée Zellweger playing even more of an antihero than the aforementioned Colin Firth.

There seems to be a greater propensity for such story distractions to occur in modern screwball comedy, such as each of the secondary plots attached to the different matching bags in *What's Up, Doc?* Still, quirky developments, seemingly contrary to the genre, were not unheard of during screwball's golden age. Examples would range from Lombard standing trial for murder in *True Confession* to celebrated writer/director Preston Sturges's patriotic smoke screen in *The Miracle of Morgan's Creek* (1944).

In chapter 2 screwball comedy is defined by examining five pivotal components of the comic antihero: abundant leisure time, childlike nature, basic male frustration (especially in relationships), a general propensity for physical comedy, and a tendency toward parody and satire. The vast majority of examples used to flesh out this model were taken from the original heyday of the genre (especially the late 1930s and early 1940s). This section briefly documents how these same components are equally important to any number of modern screwball comedies.

The genre's use of extensive leisure time is still a given, from Dudley Moore's nonstop partying as the spoiled millionaire in *Arthur* (1981, with John Gielgud as the acid-tongued valet) to the upper-class world of *Four Weddings and a Funeral.* And even if the central character is lacking the wealth associated with free time, his or her position seemingly green lights the most casual of lifestyles. Examples include Ryan O'Neal's absentminded professor in *What's Up, Doc?*, Hugh Grant's underwhelmed bookstore owner in *Notting Hill*, Renée Zellweger's book publication representative in *Bridget Jones's Diary*, and Richard Gere's freelance writer in *The Runaway Bride* (1999). (This genre has never taken the world of the printed page too seriously.)

Along related lines, the genre often embraces professions that middle America does equate with work, à la the seemingly leisure life of the absentminded professor. A more recent variation of this screwball tendency is to look at what appears to be the decadent downtime of film stars, such as the movie press junket world of *America's Sweethearts* (2001, from a script cowritten by Billy Crystal).

Second, the childlike nature of the genre has, if anything, become more pronounced in the modern era. Dudley Moore's screwball adventures often encouraged this mind-set, from the toys and parental Gielgud of *Arthur* to his childishly comic orchestra conductor who suspects his wife of an affair in the 1984 remake of Sturges's 1948 *Unfaithfully Yours*. At the heart of Moore's little boy persona is a diminutive size (5'2") and teddy bear good looks, which are reflected in such 1980s press nicknames as "Cuddly Dudley" and the "Miniature Cary Grant." His childlike persona was further cemented by playing characters beset by a youngster's indecision, as if he were an undersized comic Hamlet, without a sense of what to do. These times of boyish bafflement would include not being able to pick his favorite bride in *Micki & Maude* (1984, à la Cary Grant's situation in *My Favorite Wife*, 1940), and weighing his *Arthur* inheritance against poverty with his blue-collar girlfriend (Liza Minnelli).

Since the mid-1990s Hugh Grant has become the designated poster *boy* for the screwball comedy male. Though a more conventional leading man in both size and appearance than Moore, Grant's screen persona has its own very definite childlike components. They range from that unruly shock of hair that he is forever brushing out of his eyes to Grant's signature stammer in moments of shock and/or embarrassment, such as dealing with his goofy *Notting Hill* roommate.

Hugh Grant even has a man-child element missing from the Dudley Moore screen persona—a total sense of naiveness. No one radiates not having a clue better than Grant the younger. When his *Four Weddings and a Funeral* romantic interest (Andie MacDowell) chronicles her legion of past lovers, poor Grant's jaw is totally on the floor. He could not have been more surprised if she had smacked him with a sock full of nickels. Not since Barbara Stanwyck lowered a similar litany of lovers on a wonderfully naive Henry Fonda in Sturges's *The Lady Eve* (1941) has a screwball comedy male been so completely dumbfounded.

Barbara Stanwyck gets comic revenge by convincing poor Henry Fonda she has had an army of lovers in The Lady Eve *(1941).*

Hugh Grant would then often top such deer-in-the-headlight expressions by adding an amusingly inane comment (actually more of a self-deprecating aside), such as his response to an early *Notting Hill* rejection by Julia Roberts, "That would be a no, then." In contrast to Grant's gift for playing the naively childlike, Dudley Moore's boyish persona has a tendency to cover his caught-by-surprise demeanor with a certain Puckish bravado, no matter how misguided things have become.

Another take on Hugh Grant's ability to play at being childlike is an outgrowth of a talent first credited to Cary Grant—being a great "receiver," which meant they were both good at playing verbal punching bags, responding with visual pluck to the nonstop chatter of the screwball heroine. Seen another way, each male is reduced to a status not unlike a little boy receiving directions from a controlling mother. In fact, the pioneering dark comedy/sometimes screwball *Harold and Maude* (1972) literally posits a domineering mother (Vivian Pickles) against a darkly rebellious son (Bud Cort) who discovers life and love via a seventy-nine-year-old swinging eccentric (Ruth Gordon). An inspired *Harold and Maude* moment of receiving occurs during yet another rambling tirade by Pickles—Cort gives a brief direct address look at the camera and silently nods to the viewer, as if to say with childish glee, "She might win the verbal battle but I'll control the war of adolescence."

While both Hugh Grant and Dudley Moore are English—yet another parallel with Cary Grant—only Hugh Grant actively uses that fact as part of his little boy screwball persona, especially as it pertains to language. For instance, there is a child's fixation on taboo terms, such as the use of the word "bugger" in *Four Weddings and a Funeral*. And there is Grant's hopelessly English inability to ditch his proper diction for the colorful speech patterns of the Italian American mobster in *Mickey Blue Eyes* (1999), despite having his girlfriend's gangster father, James "Fuhgeddaboutit!" Caan, for a teacher.

One should also note in passing that Dudley Moore and Hugh Grant, like Cary Grant before them, have been equally adept at playing both screwball and romantic comedy leading men. Basic story developments often dictate the genre in which to pigeonhole their individual films. Thus, space herein devoted to their adventures in screwball comedy should not preclude their occasional ties to romantic comedy, which will be discussed later in the chapter.

A third fundamental component of screwball comedy's antihero is frustration, most often in relationships. Again, this Thurberesque battle of the sexes has only escalated in modern depictions of screwball comedy. The only major change here is that in an age of gender enlightenment, screwball comedy provides more equal time for both sexes in the area of comic gender relationship angst. Consequently, years ago screwball audiences would have been more conditioned for a male perspective along the lines of Thurber's "The Secret Life of Walter Mitty" or his story collection, *The Middle-Aged Man on the*

Flying Trapeze. Today's audience has more of an opportunity for an antiheroic woman's perspective in *Bridget Jones's Diary*.

Still, this is not a radical change, and *Bridget Jones's Diary* continues to follow the traditional screwball pattern. That is, Renée Zellweger's free spirit title character manages to both loosen up the genre's classically rigid male (Colin Firth), as well as free him from another basic of the genre—the dominatingly deadening fiancée. The film even has a comic fashion link with the genre's pioneering *It Happened One Night* (1934). The earlier picture has a disrobing scene that reveals star Clark Gable is not wearing an undershirt. Period sales of this garment dropped almost immediately. Coincidentally, *Bridget Jones's Diary* has a steamy love scene that discloses Zellweger is wearing oversized tummy-control "granny" undies. Sex partner Hugh Grant is initially shocked by this but then decides they are sexy. Suddenly, "granny" undies were in. The *USA Today* article on the phenomenon said it all in the title: "Bridget's Bloomin' Undies Bring Oversized Sales Surge."[1] (And speaking of Grant, the film also provides him with an entertaining opportunity to play against type. Instead of essaying his standard staid British antihero, the Firth part, he shines as a comic cad—Bridget's manipulative playboy publisher boss.)

The Runaway Bride, however, provides a more ambitious balance of both male and female relationship antiheroes. A throwback to screwball's golden age, when the genre was frequently about marriages that *didn't* happen, as well as the newspaper racket (Gere plays a former *USA Today* columnist), the picture has both Gere and Julia Roberts doing battle over his reporting of her knack for leaving grooms at the altar. Naturally, they fall in love, but that does not stop her from leaving him at the altar once, too. So the movie becomes a comic dual-focus narrative on the relationship blues.

This is also the path taken in Roberts's more recent screwball farce, *America's Sweethearts*, which chronicles both her antiheroic woes as the plain assistant to her movie star sister (Catharine Zeta-Jones), and the ever more entertainingly problematic life of her sister's estranged actor husband (John Cusack). Again, there is the inevitable predictable romance between Roberts and Cusack, but not before the film is peppered with a legion of eccentrics seemingly fresh from Hollywood's golden age, from Alan Arkin's zany shrink to Christopher Walken's certifiable nut case film director.

America's Sweethearts also boasts a darkly comic relationship breakdown that rivals a battle of the sexes in *Bluebeard's Eighth Wife* (1938), which results in Gary Cooper's character being institutionalized. In *America's Sweethearts* the unraveling marriage of the country's favorite movie couple (Cusack and Zeta-Jones) has sent Cusack to a sanitarium. But whereas Cooper and his love interest (Claudette Colbert) eventually reunite, Cusack's character moves on to a healthier partner (Julia Roberts).

A fourth antiheroic basic associated with screwball comedy is a propensity for physical and/or visual comedy. No one has yet approached the pantomime skills of Cary Grant, but the genre still showcases a great deal of slapstick. Dudley Moore demonstrated the greatest gift along these lines (regardless of the part), though he was especially memorable as a comic drunk in *Arthur*.

Leo McCarey disciple Blake Edwards was very much in the "do it visual" tradition of the older director, so it really did not matter who the actor was. If Edwards was making a screwball comedy, the visual shtick was there, from Bruce Willis's debut film, *Blind Date* (1987), to John Ritter and those amazingly bright condoms in *Skin Deep* (1989). Of course, in both cases, Willis and Ritter had already demonstrated physical comedy skills on American television—Willis on the 1980s series *Moonlighting* and Ritter on *Three's Company* (1977–1984). Fittingly, the visually orientated Edwards is the grandson of silent film director J. Gordon Edwards. Combine that with a writing apprenticeship for Leo McCarey, and Edwards had an excellent mind-set for slapstick screwball comedy, which is probably best showcased in *Victor/Victoria* (1982) and *Micki & Maude* (1984).

Garry Marshall is another modern-era director with a penchant for visual humor, especially when he megaphones screwball comedy. Though neither of his *Runaway Bride* stars (Julia Roberts and

Richard Gere) has a special gift for physical shtick, they are constantly showcased in entertainingly visual scenes. The most high-profile examples for Roberts, of course, are the various weddings from which she flees—all nicely incorporated into the picture via comic home movies. As with screwball classics from Hollywood's golden age, *Runaway Bride*'s striking visual imagery sometimes also inspired great verbal lines. For instance, when Roberts runs from her first marriage with Gere, she is amusingly last seen escaping in a FedEx truck. When a wedding guest asks where Roberts is going, Marshall cast regular Hector Elizondo responds, "Wherever it is, she'll be there by 10:30 tomorrow."

Even in such modest *Runaway Bride* scenes as Gere's first information gathering visit to Joan Cusack's beauty parlor (the comically titled "Curl Up and Dye") or his stop at the automotive garage of Roberts's first jilted groom, Marshall stages the action with an inventively visual touch. For example, in the latter case he surprises the viewer by Gere's up-in-the-air placement inside a car on a hydraulic hoist. More comedy follows with Roberts's arrival and attempt to physically retrieve a controversial photo now in Gere's possession—something his high perch makes all but impossible. But maybe that is just delayed tit-for-tat revenge—for the comedy payoff moment of the aforementioned beauty parlor scene, when Gere discovers his hair has not been washed but rather brightly dyed.

In those rare *Runaway Bride* segments not given to a particularly striking visual orientation, Marshall still often manages to punctuate them with physical comedy. Thus, near the close of Gere's visit to a high school football practice (Roberts's latest fiancé is a coach), she also shows up and eventually finds herself on the back of a mobile blocking sled. When Marshall wants her comically out of the scene, she is literally "blocked" out by the practicing players pushing the sled. And as she makes this impromptu exit, she also gifts us with her patented squeal of surprise.

Screwball comedy's greatest slapstick turn in a single modern-era film belongs to Steve Martin in *All of Me*. The highlight reel would have to include footage of the sidewalk scene where he first attempts to walk after the spirit of Lily Tomlin enters his body. This man, comically possessed, elevates *All of Me* to modern screwball classic status. Interestingly enough, even when Tomlin finally exits his body, the movie closes on another visual gem—an out-of-control Martin and Tomlin dance sequence that slapstick prone director Carl Reiner keeps in the picture despite (or, possibly because of) the spontaneous fall they take.

The beauty of *All of Me*, beyond Martin's amazing physical performance, is how closely the picture assimilates the slapstick into a classic screwball formula. This includes a dominating fiancée whose presence is synonymous with the rigidity of death (she even gifts Martin with an ancient African tombstone for his birthday) to his need to leave a life-sapping job as a lawyer to pursue the youthful dream of being a jazz musician.

Martin took his special affinity for screwball slapstick in new directions with *L.A. Story* (1991), another fantasy take on the genre in which he both wrote and starred, as well as acted as the coexecutive producer. Instead of the *All of Me* physical comedy difficulties connected with relearning motor skills when sharing body space with another spirit, *L.A. Story* is about a zany California weatherman who simply enjoys choreographed slapstick in unusual places. For instance, he and a friend visit various art galleries and when the coast is clear she videotapes him comically roller skating through these high art settings. The joy Martin's character associates with this physical release could be likened to Cary Grant's periodic need to do cartwheels and handstands in *Holiday* (1938).

Martin's ability to revitalize the slapstick form even applies to California's most basic activity—travel by car. Each day he takes a back way shortcut that involves driving his car across lawns, down concrete steps, and through every possible Los Angeles pathway not normally associated with automobiles. He ups the comedy factor by both the nonchalant manner in which he drives this cockeyed route, as well as the equally casual response of people along the way—they appear used to this drive-by eccentric.

Fittingly for someone bringing such a refreshing slant to slapstick, *L.A. Story* also has a provocative opening up of the traditional screwball story. Again there is the standard killjoy fiancée. But in this case his character's life is recharged by *two* other heroines—Sarah Jessica Parker's sexy, kooky, clothing clerk and Victoria Tennant's quirky British journalist. Though Martin ends up with Tennant (his then real-life wife and costar from *All of Me*), Parker steals the show through a physically wacky performance. Like Lombard in *My Man Godfrey* (1936), or Hepburn in *Bringing Up Baby*, Parker is literally comedy in motion. Whether she is measuring Martin for slacks, or reacting to an invitation for a weekend getaway, she is all bobbing and weaving—a female reincarnation of the young pre-Vietnam Muhammad Ali. Her joy in movement, often a screwball comedy hallmark, is a perfect match for Martin's roller skating-through-art tendencies.

A final antiheroic trait connected to the genre is a proclivity for parody and satire. While both components are prevalent in modern screwball comedy, satire seems to be in the ascendancy. And a popular satirical target as of late is the film industry, from the occasional asides in *L.A. Story* and *Notting Hill* to a center stage send-up in *America's Sweethearts*. While the latter picture keys upon the chaos of a movie press junket, it makes satirical space for such additional Hollywood targets as the intense arty director (Christopher Walken), the movie entourage (especially Hank Azaria's macho Spanish lover—"I am extreme-a-lee well-*chung*."), the amoral studio chief (Stanley Tucci), the spin control head of studio publicity (Billy Crystal), and the spoiled, old-school glamour queen (Catherine Zeta-Jones).

Junkets by their very nature are ripe for satire, beginning with the redundancy of questions to which the stars are subjected. As Julia Roberts observed on a real press junket for *America's Sweethearts*, "If I did a movie and I have to do seventy-five takes of the same scene over and over again, that's what a junket is."[2] This movie comically compounds such junket truisms with added satirical twists, from the wonderfully warped Walken refusing to let *anyone* see the picture before the press screening to the married but estranged stars of the film within the film pretending to be friendly for the sake of business. And, as with most satires (regardless of the main target), this movie includes a generous helping of additional send-ups, from Alan Arkin's hilarious take on New Age off-the-wall therapy to the feeding frenzy that passes for the modern press.

Of course, to work as a screwball comedy one cannot forget the antihero of the picture. As cowriter Billy Crystal observed, "At the core of it there's a . . . story of a lost guy, Eddie [John Cusack], who has realized that his marriage was really the longest location romance."[3] As with most screwball comedies, Eddie rediscovers life by finding someone (Julia Roberts) who likes him simply for who he is. But even when Cusack's Eddie is down, Crystal has given him a wit worthy of an earlier screwball age. For instance, when Eddie is asked why he does not have an entourage, he explains, "I'm a paranoid schizophrenic. I am my own entourage." This is worthy of Thurber's greatest antiheroic work—*My Life and Hard Times* (1933).

In *L.A. Story* Steve Martin's antihero is adrift in a world that satirizes everything associated with that city, from restaurants so expensive and trendy that potential diners must pass a credit check to darkly comic pokes at freeway shootings and silicone makeovers (deceased L.A. women are said to decay very little). Hollywood and L.A. notwithstanding, most modern screwball comedies satirize golden age subjects, such as the *Runaway Bride* send-up of both small town, Capraesque America and the world of newspaper journalism. *What's Up, Doc?* comically undercuts academic life, from flaky grant proposals and professional students, as well as the court system.

The latter target, lawyers and the law, has been a popular screwball satire subject since former lawyer McCarey made the courtroom an integral part of *The Awful Truth* (1937) and *My Favorite Wife* (1940). In both these pictures comic judges attempt to make sense of screwball relationships. In the modern era, however, the genre's use of the law might better be equated with the comic rigidity normally associated with screwball comedy's portrayal of academia. Thus,

Steve Martin's lawyer in *All of Me* and John Cleese's *A Fish Called Wanda* barrister are nearly sexless robots robbed of vitality by both the law and dominating women.

Interestingly enough, however, the best post-1960s use of a courtroom in a screwball comedy, from *What's Up, Doc?*, is a throwback to the 1930s. Character actor Liam Dunn gives an inspired performance as the most antiheroic of judges, trying to piece together the mad hatter comedy chase/riot of *What's Up, Doc?*. Whether fielding one surprising revelation after another from the mob of participants or downing a vast array of nerve medicine pills, Dunn's neurotic judge is a comic microcosm of all the anxieties that afflict us in the ongoing battle that is day-to-day life. The fact that this powerful man of the law can neither make sense of the mob in his courtroom, nor the world outside it, is just a typical satirical outing in screwball land.

When the "nothing sacred" story of this genre is not being peppered with satire, there are often elements of parody—an affectionate kidding of a given genre and/or auteur. As with golden age screwball comedies, spoofing in modern-era examples of the genre begins with a takeoff on romantic comedy. This sentiment is nicely captured in *The New Yorker*'s description of Colin Firth's character in *Bridget Jones's Diary*: "You catch in his eye not just affection but, more subversively, a semi-suppressed amusement at the whole exhausting charade of modern romance."[4]

In *America's Sweethearts* Julia Roberts's character represents a segue into a spoof of the hoariest romantic story on record—*Cinderella*. She plays the mousey, unappreciated sister with a former weight problem (assisted in flashbacks by a fat suit). *L.A. Story* parodies a Shakespearean love sonnet, with Steve Martin's revisionist character revealing that the Bard was actually from Los Angeles. However, when modern screwball comedies are not spoofing the obvious (romance), they often parody other genres; *Honeymoon in Vegas* (1992), *Mickey Blue Eyes*, and *Analyze This* (1999) all do takeoffs on gangster films, too. By casting celebrated actors associated with mobster movies in each film—James Caan in both *Honeymoon in Vegas* and *Mickey Blue Eyes*, and Robert DeNiro in *Analyze This* (both alumni of *The Godfather* saga)—the movies play their parody card much more effectively. One is, of course, reminded of Billy Wilder's classic mix of screwball comedy and gangster parody in the celebrated *Some Like It Hot* (1959). Wilder also cast a famous mobster-associated actor in a prominent part (George Raft). During screwball's golden age no less a director than John Ford intertwined the genre with the world of gangsters in *The Whole Town's Talking* (1935), with notable mobster actor Edward G. Robinson playing both a gangster and a meek look-alike clerk.

Of the aforementioned more recent trilogy of screwball films carrying on the genre tradition of spoofing mobster movies, the best is inventive writer/director Andrew Bergman's *Honeymoon in Vegas*. As *Newsweek* raved at the time, "to those who are keyed into his lunatic sense of humor, the arrival of any new Bergman movie is a major comic event."[5] But what makes this a notch above the always quality Bergman film is his ability here to create a romance that allows the viewer to both empathize with the antihero (Nicolas Cage) and his gangster rival (Caan) as well as create an inspired contemporary screwball world. For instance, one period review presented this summarization: "Add a running motif of Elvis impersonators, a hilarious turn by Peter Boyle as a Hawaiian chieftain obsessed with Broadway musicals, and a cameo from [controversial] UNLV basketball coach Jerry Tarkanian and you have a sunny comedy of anxiety."[6] Ultimately, as regional critic Joan Bunke observed, Cage's screwball everyman, "a poor, helpless schmo . . . [eventually, as is the case with most antiheroes] knocks himself out to do the right thing when he finally knows what he wants."[7]

Still, for this writer, the highlight of the movie came early with a cameo by Anne Bancroft. In a viciously comic bit as Cage's mother, she demands on her deathbed that he never marry—because no woman could love him as his mother did. While screwball males often have a fear of romantic commitment, rare is the movie that actually gives the audience an explanation, let alone such a wonderfully loopy one.

Modern-Era Variations in Screwball Comedy

As with most film types, screwball comedy often operates in a compound genre world. For example, this chapter's previous section briefly addressed screwball comedy's tendency to contain elements of satire and/or parody. But occasionally, especially in the post-1960 period, the genre has taken on a schizophrenic nature. Thus, films like *Irreconcilable Differences* (1984), *My Best Friend's Wedding* (1997), and *Forces of Nature* (1999) all start out as screwball comedies but then dovetail into other genres.

Irreconcilable Differences's screwball beginnings chronicle the life and fun times of an entertaining young couple (Ryan O'Neal and Shelley Long) who find success as Hollywood filmmakers. But as their marriage starts to unravel, the movie slides into melodrama and is topped off with their daughter (Drew Barrymore) suing them for divorce! This ultimately bittersweet comedy is loosely based upon the marriage breakup of onetime screwball director Peter Bogdanovich (of *What's Up, Doc?* fame) and screenwriter/art director Polly Platt.

Both *My Best Friend's Wedding* and *Forces of Nature* start off as traditional screwball comedies, too. In the 1930s the leading ladies for these pictures (Julia Roberts and Sandra Bullock) would have broken up each film's focus wedding and saved the males (Dermot Mulroney and Ben Affleck, respectively) from a life of comic rigidity. Instead, each leading man opts for the less flashy and less eccentric fiancée. In a genre that normally paints the fiancée as a life-sucking drone, these pictures showcase her as much more positive and flexible—especially Cameron Diaz's ever-so-loving wanna-be bride in *My Best Friend's Wedding*. Ultimately, each movie breaks with screwball comedy and essentially embraces the world of romantic comedy.

The latter development is most surprising in *Forces of Nature*, since the vast majority of the screen time is devoted to a road picture mentality that seems to be building toward an Affleck-Bullock relationship. It begins with the about-to-be-wed Affleck stranded in New York with fellow plane passenger Bullock. Their flight to Savannah, Georgia, has crashed on attempted takeoff, and while no one was seriously injured, the unharmed but very antiheroic Affleck has decided against anymore flying . . . ever.

With both Affleck and Bullock having Savanah business (his wedding, the sale of her bagel shop), they end up traveling south together. In a movie that borrows a chaos-ridden page from the road wreck comedy *Planes, Trains & Automobiles* (1987), everything about the haphazard Affleck-Bullock travel itinerary goes bad. Or, as he observes at one point, when he mistakenly thinks they are going their separate ways, "Other than the plane crash and the drug bust, it's been fun."

Though a hurricane is also thrown into this zany narrative as well, the real *Forces of Nature* title character is Bullock, whose comically bad karma seems to sideswipe everything from modes of transportation to the weather. After several misadventures with her on this screwball odyssey, Affleck mumbles to no one in particular, "I just happen to be travelin' along beside a natural disaster." Yet, both he and the audience are drawn toward this screwball heroine, with her physical nonstop energy and her creative manipulation (lying) for every problem. It is Carole Lombard's *True Confession* character by way of Goldie Hawn in *Housesitter*.

With such "forces of nature" one naturally assumes Affleck will succumb to Bullock's screwball charm. Besides all that genre tradition, including Affleck's tightly wound antihero, Bullock is the top billed, terribly attractive star of *Forces of Nature*. Ultimately, however, the movie becomes not only a romantic comedy but a moving manifesto for antiheroes to remain antiheroes—not leaving the rut in which they are comfortable. Both these subjects (security and love) are wrapped together as marriage in a closing quote by Affleck. Spoken in voiceover and attributed to a sixteenth-century bishop, he says,

> Marriage has less beauty but more safety than the single life. It's full of sorrows and full of joys and it lies under more burdens. But it is supported by all the strengths of love, and those burdens are delightful.

Then, as if thinking his character has become too deep-dish in his philosophizing, he adds, in sort of a Woody Allen romantic comedy aside, "In the end all you can do is commit to the people you love and hope for a little luck and some good weather."

So what does this revisionist take on screwball comedy mean? The late *New Yorker* film critic Pauline Kael once explained a comparable unusual genre twist as simply a misfire by the filmmakers, unsure of which direction to take.[8] While this always remains a possibility, *Forces of Nature* registers more as a provocative pushing the envelope picture, as in maybe the antihero knows what is best for him—without being overwhelmed by the screwball heroine. Moreover, by defusing the normally problematic screwball fiancée with a very likeable beautiful character (played here by the charming Maura Tierney), the transition to a status-quo romantic comedy is made more palatable.

Since the 1990s there also seems to be a tendency for audiences to gravitate more readily toward the less manic comedy leading ladies, whether one is studying golden age screwball comedies or more recent variations. As a longtime film professor, this has been reflected for some time in the tastes of my students, who consistently prefer the more controlled Irene Dunne of *The Awful Truth* (1937) to the nonsensical Katharine Hepburn of *Bringing Up Baby*.

There is also, of course, the ongoing safe-sex pitch that has encouraged monogamy and a more traditional romantic comedy approach to relationships (versus the spontaneous, anything goes screwball genre) ever since AIDS has become a global concern. In addition, one could argue that embracing a less demanding and complex fiancée (versus the strong career woman Julia Roberts plays in *My Best Friend's Wedding*) would suggest modern screwball is soft on feminism. All these factors notwithstanding, *Forces of Nature* offers an additional comic argument for the antihero to play it safe—the screwball heroine could be hazardous to his health. While the danger factor is not new to the genre (think of Katharine Hepburn exposing Cary Grant's professor to leopard liabilities in *Bringing Up Baby*), *Forces of Nature* breaks new ground by having Affleck's antihero periodically articulate comic commonsense rebuttals to Bullock's typical screwball heroine mind-set about the "need to get some thrills in your life."

Though there are several such Affleck comebacks, probably the most entertaining one involves Bullock's attempt to get him on a twisting, turning, truly "dizzy" amusement park ride called the "Spinning Sombrero." Affleck, suddenly like an apprentice crackerbarrel philosopher, observes there are two kinds of people—"The kind that look at the 'Spinning Sombrero' ride and think there is some maybe amusement to be had there. And the kind that look at it and think, 'Where will I throw up after?'" (This is refreshingly comic stuff, since most earlier screwball antiheroic males have been reduced to a stun gun mentality by the zany heroine.) Not surprisingly, Affleck stays off the "Spinning Sombrero." But more important (with regard to change in the genre) is the metaphorical meaning—Affleck opts to *not* drop his fiancée (Tierney) for free spirit Bullock.

Likening the eccentric screwball heroine to a fun and/or scary thrill ride is an excellent analogy that is applicable to most films in the genre, including, of course, the nontraditional examples. Certainly the Julia Roberts of *My Best Friend's Wedding* is a rollercoaster ride not unlike Bullock in *Forces of Nature*. And that movie's antiheroic leading man (Dermot Mulroney) also opts for the security blanket–oriented fiancée (Cameron Diaz). Thus, as modern-era screwball comedies qualify as compound genres, there is now a chance that the put-upon male will opt for the safer, noncontroversial romantic route.

A second new age twist for the genre is a proclivity for one member of the screwball couple to be famous. Other than a random princess or two during the Depression, genre players in the pre–modern era were not showcased as famous people. Since the 1960s the genre has taken a more high-profile path, from the movie personalities of *Irreconcilable Differences*, *In & Out* (1997), *Notting Hill*, and *America's Sweethearts* to television personalities (Dudley Moore in *Micki & Maude*, Steve Martin in *L.A. Story*, and Tom Selleck in *In & Out*), as well as Richard Gere's prominent newspaper columnist in *Runaway Bride*. There are numerous explanations for this change.

First, fame provides the genre with a two-part catalyst for eccentricity. Screwball comedy is always about finding new ways to document zany behavior in a romantic context, whether the absurd behavior of the ideal rich or the later use of fantasy (as in the *Topper* series) for the same results. Being associated with the film industry has long been equated, for much of the general public, with oddball behavior. So on one level, if screwball comedy embraces a movie milieu, it is easy for an audience to accept the kooky characters, such as *America's Sweethearts*'s permanently off-the-wall director (Christopher Walken) or John Cusack's temporarily deranged lovesick actor.

There is also a flip side to using fame (especially related to Hollywood) to showcase zany behavior in new-wave screwball comedies. Normal, everyday people frequently turn goofy when confronted with notables, such as Julia Roberts's movie star in *Notting Hill*. This film becomes the most entertaining of case studies along these lines, especially when Hugh Grant's "aw-shucks" bookstore owner takes her to a small dinner party for his sister's birthday. People become unglued, especially his screen sister.

Besides the diverting antics provoked in common folks by the celebrity types, screwball notables also make the easy rapport among modern characters in the genre more palatable. For instance, Richard Gere's superstar journalist in *Runaway Bride* gets easy access to everyone and everything in Julia Roberts's Capresque hometown precisely because of who he is. In an earlier, more trusting age, this was hardly necessary. To illustrate, Clark Gable's *It Happened One Night* (1934) reporter did not need celebrity status to charm his way through several screwball people encounters.

As a corollary to the fame factor, it seems most fitting that the age of modern screwball comedies should make space for a variation of Andy Warhol's "15 minutes of fame" prophecy. While this observation is merely made as a historical reference, there are also cases of screwball comedy characters riding this camped outside Hugh Grant's modest flat hopeful for a chance to spot Julia Roberts's movie star. When his nutty roommate discovers this army of press, he immediately goes out to mug for the cameras. (Both *Runaway Bride* and *In & Out* also have scenes of feeding frenzy paparazzi.) And Richard Gere's *Runaway Bride* journalist implies to townspeople as he gathers information on Roberts's title character that, with a little assistance, their names will appear in the forthcoming article.

A third new modern-era screwball comedy development asks the question, "How does someone act with a romantic partner when they are used to getting what they want from everyone?" This is, of course, a direct outgrowth of the previous point about one member of the screwball couple being famous. At its most basic, this question encourages the viewer to look at specific screwball films and characters more realistically in two ways.

First, the celebrity figure attempts to argue he/she is like everyone else when it comes to romance. Thus, Julia Roberts's *Notting Hill* movie star tells Hugh Grant's anithero, "I'm just a girl standing in front of a boy asking him to love her." It is an effective comeback to Grant's reluctance to get involved with a film actress. Plus, it is similar to how Roberts perceives her real-life relationships. That is, when she later discussed her amicable private life split from longtime companion Benjamin Bratt for the first time, she told *Late Night* host David Letterman, "We're both two kids trying to find our way in the world."[9] It was a perspective that would not have been out of place in *Notting Hill*. But regardless of one's take on this perspective, Roberts's inability to simply walk in and out of Grant's life is what gives *Notting Hill* a comically touching appeal. Her sense of bafflement, which elicits the aforementioned quote, is a refreshing twist on the movie star stereotype.

Second, film theorist and critic David Denby has suggested that a star performer is sometimes most believable playing some sort of celebrity.[10] Whether one buys this view or not, it is an effective argument for a number of modern screwball players, including Richard Gere's nationally known journalist in *Runaway Bride*. Gere received the best reviews of his career for this part. High-profile critic Leonard Maltin credited Gere with being "more engaging than he's ever been onscreen," while the always critical *New Yorker* observed that Gere's "work is freer and looser than ever before. He may not be a great actor, but he's become, at last, an extremely likeable man."[11]

One explanation for Gere's "freer and looser" nature is the Denby slant on a star playing a star. Regardless, part of the easy charm Gere brings to a celebrity not always getting his way is what allows his character to evolve from a smug womanizer at the beginning of *Runaway Bride* to the sympathetic jilted groom near the picture's close.

Being the victim of a "runaway bride," or having your former spouse (Rita Wilson) fire you are both classic screwball comedy examples of ritualistic humiliation that Gere must survive. While a legion of earlier antiheroes in the genre have been tested along similar lines, what makes Gere's position new age is the greater degree of humiliation (as a famous person) involved. Consequently, the viewer is further drawn to Gere's character by his ability to roll with this greater comic adversity and still remain such a likeable romantic character.

One does not, however, have to limit Gere's *Runaway Bride* charm factor to his ability to entertainingly weather what was once unheard of in his world—being rebuffed by women. There is also a winning rapport to his interactions with everyday people, whether it is the bantering T-shirt salesman near his New York office or the bakery lady (Laurie Metcalf) in Julia Roberts's hometown.

A fourth new, modern-era development for screwball comedy involves the subject of homosexuality. During the classic age of the genre it was often kiddingly addressed but never taken seriously, such as the *Bringing Up Baby* scene in which Cary Grant, dressed in a frilly woman's bathrobe, jumps in the air and yells, "I just went gay all of a sudden." But while film characters might think Grant or comparable figures in other films were gay, the movie audience always knew this was *not* the case.

Post-1960s screwball comedies, however, are sometimes peopled with real gay characters. Writer/director Blake Edwards's 1982 *Victor/Victoria* represents a pivotal transition work on the subject. On one hand, it plays the traditional screwball game of having characters think the antiheroic male lead (James Garner) is gay after he falls for the masquerading-as-a-man Julie Andrews. The sexual revisionism comes from Andrews having a gay mentor (Robert Preston), while Garner's bodyguard (Alex Karras) comes out of the closet with comic poignancy when he thinks his boss is homosexual.

More recently, Rupert Everett's gay pal of Julia Roberts steals the show in *My Best Friend's Wedding*. Since the genre traditionally spoofs the love story, having a gay Everett pretend to be Roberts's fiancé (when she is trying to sabotage her old boyfriend's wedding) adds an inspired irony to the parody. Moreover, with the film's unconventional close (the screwball Roberts *not* getting the guy), Everett's amusing supportive presence still manages to make the ending both upbeat and screwy—the best looking and most charismatic couple at the wedding party are not a traditional couple at all.

The wittiest take on the phenomenon in the post–*Victor/Victoria* age is director Frank Oz's *In & Out*. A young actor (Matt Dillon) wins an Oscar and thanks his Capraesque small-town high school teacher (Kevin Kline)—who, he adds, is gay. Comically, this is news to Kline. In fact, he is just days away from marrying his longtime sweetheart (Joan Cusack). If this had been an old-fashioned screwball comedy, the rest of the story would be an amusing negating of Dillon's nationally broadcast statement. But the new age perspective on the genre has Kline discovering, after much comic soul-searching, that he actually is gay. (However, not to dampen the close, Cusack and Dillon seem headed for a romantic future.)

One might even make a case for *The Birdcage* (1996) as a gay-orientated modern screwball comedy, though Nathan Lane's entertainingly over-the-top characterization (to Robin William's unusually restrained lover) pushes the movie more toward the personality comedian (clown) genre. However, the fact that the genre question is even being asked here is symptomatic of modern screwball comedy's tendency to flirt with gay themes.

Adding the gay card to screwball comedy becomes even more unorthodox in *The Object of My Affection* (1998), when a heterosexual woman (Jennifer Aniston) invites a gay male friend (Paul Rudd) to share her Brooklyn apartment after his professor companion dumps him. They are platonic soulmates excited about raising a baby—Aniston is pregnant by a boyfriend for whom she has lost interest. *Newsweek* comically retitled the picture "Falling for Mr. Wrong," because while he has no problem with her seeing other men, she is jealous of his affairs.[12]

The straight woman/gay man dichotomy is a fresh but challenging new direction for screwball comedy. Wendy Wasserstein's screen adaptation of Stephen McCauley's *The Object of My Affection* novel is both funny and sensitive. But the subject matter is easy to fumble. Witness the initially promising *The Next Best Thing* (2000), about the yoga instructor (Madonna) having a child with her gay best friend (Rupert Everett). This film bumbles along in entertaining screwball fashion until she falls for another man (Benjamin Bratt), then it turns to mawkish melodrama. Instead of trying to take the genre into a new era, as *Affection* does with the entertainingly out-of-control Aniston, *The Next Best Thing* becomes anything but "the next best thing." New age screwball comedy has a larger potential amusement arsenal but an equally greater chance of misfiring.

The Traditional Romantic Comedy Mold

The post-1960 formula for romantic comedy largely continued to key upon the same five golden age components that differentiated the genre from screwball comedy: emphasizing sentiment over silly, a tendency for serious and/or melodramatic overtones, more realistic characters (frequently employed), traditional dating pattern (more male influence), and slower story pacing.

This ongoing romantic comedy equation is best documented in the work of today's greatest auteur in the genre—writer and/or director Nora Ephron. She grew up in the genre via the screenwriting of her parents (Henry and Phoebe Ephron) and frequently has gone on record championing the superiority of golden age romantic comedies. Consequently, her *Sleepless in Seattle* (1993) uses an earlier classic of the genre (*An Affair to Remember*, 1957) as its centerpiece, while *You've Got Mail* (1998) is actually a remake of the celebrated *Shop around the Corner* (1940). Critics, moreover, celebrate this sense of romantic traditionalism in her work—such as Roger Ebert's comment on *Sleepless in Seattle* accenting sentiment:

> Ephron develops this story with all the heartfelt sincerity of a 1950s tearjerker. There is no irony, no distance, no angle on the material. It is about two people who are destined for one another, and that's that. And that was fine with me.[13]

But one need not go further than a perusal of review titles for her golden age roots to be acknowledged, from "'Sleepless': Ephron Makes 'em Like They Used To" to "'Seattle' Director Seduces with Old-Fashioned Romance."[14]

Naturally, the aforementioned romantic comedy basics are all front and center in her work, from Ebert zeroing in on her preference for sentiment to a balancing act with realistic characters and slower story pacing. In fact, the latter two elements often go hand-in-hand. For instance, *You've Got Mail* poses a very real question about Internet relationships. On one hand, it allows an individual to open up further and faster than in a normal face-to-face situation, a fact comically endorsed by Ephron:

> It's very much about safety and being free to say whatever you want to, without ever thinking that you're going to be faced with

> the fact that the person wears really ugly shoes or whatever your nightmare may be.[15]

But this speed factor, ironically, can still lead to slower plot development. A key here is the Internet infidelity factor. In the case of *You've Got Mail*, both lead characters are in relationships when they start their Internet romance. Granted, both of their live-in companions are portrayed as shallow and self-centered. Moreover, each relationship has the earmarkings of being over even before the Ryan-Hanks Internet connection begins to heat up. Still, the stars later agreed that an Internet romance, à la *You've Got Mail*, constituted a form of infidelity. Hanks observed, "If you're giving up intimate secrets to this other person, then, yes, it is cheating," while Ryan added, "a case could be made that it is cheating. If you're being more intimate with these people than you are with your significant other, it probably is cheating. Nasty cheating at that."[16]

Even if this were not a morality point to be pondered, Internet anonymity brings one back to the element of slower pacing. That is, Hanks and Ryan eventually have to brave what Ephron jokingly referred to as the "ugly shoes" phenomenon—the fear that this electronic pen pal has something glaringly wrong with him/her. Neither party wishes to rush into this potentially traumatic situation. But when it is time to reveal the *You've Got Mail* identities, the movie continues to follow the traditional *Shop around the Corner* blueprint—Hanks both finds out first and orchestrates the upbeat romantic comedy fadeout.

Instead of further tracking the genre's ongoing continuity in the modern era by way of high-profile romantic comedy auteurs (à la Ephron), one can also draw reinforcement from the most unlikely of sources. A case in point would be Adam Sandler's *The Wedding Singer* (1998). Normally one simply includes his lowbrow film outings under the personality comedian umbrella—a comic phenomenon to his many fans, an embarrassment to most critics. But in this one breakthrough picture Sandler manages to fashion the most entertainingly traditional of romantic comedies. And by utilizing Sandler's interest in music (especially comic numbers), the movie fully embraces this genre's frequent focus on song.

Sandler plays an underemployed wedding singer comically broken up over losing his fiancée. But things begin to improve when he befriends a novice waitress (Drew Barrymore). Not only does *The Wedding Singer* include all the aforementioned basic romantic comedy components, but the added nuances are there, too. The significance of older witnesses of love is common in classic Hollywood romances, such as Charles Boyer's grandmother in *Love Affair* (1939). Their mutual love is what alerts Irene Dunne to the fact Boyer is not simply a playboy.

In *The Wedding Singer* Sandler has a surrogate grandmother (Ellen Albertini Dow) to whom he gives singing lessons. The comic bond they have (including payment in homemade meatballs) is one of the reasons Barrymore is drawn to him. Moreover, Dow's delightful little old lady, Rosie, is yet another elder symbol for love: the reason for the lessons is to be able to serenade her husband on their fiftieth wedding anniversary. Her gift of song is "'Til There Was You," which she delivers with poignant style later in the picture.

Music, of course, is another corollary to the theme of sentiment over silly. And between Rosie and Sandler's title character, few romantic comedies (past or present) have better linked song to story. The payoff number for Sandler is when he does some serenading of his own—winning Barrymore over with an actual Sandler composition—"Grow Old With You."

Music can also be used as a bridge for examining the second basic romantic comedy component showcased in *The Wedding Singer*—a proclivity for serious or melodramatic overtones. A common example of this for the genre is the broken relationship. When this happens to Sandler, the movie gives us several entertaining renditions of the rock 'n roll classic "Love Stinks." Seemingly the perfect musical match for his comic anger, it only gets funnier when he includes "Love Stinks" in his repertoire of numbers at a wedding. (In a related footnote, legendary rocker Billy Idol, appearing as himself, assists Sandler in his romantic misadventures.)

A more traditional melodramatic example from *The Wedding Singer* is the fact that Barrymore is initially engaged to a world-class jerk (Matthew Glave). Sandler, who has fallen in love with her by now, agonizes over whether he should tell Barrymore any of this. Moreover, Barrymore is both in love with Sandler and having second thoughts about her fiancé. But each time Barrymore and Sandler try to act upon their emotions, they misread the situation—thinking the other person is perfectly content.

The romantic comedy resolution to this melodramatic scenario is both laughter and the application of another basic component of the genre—male assertion in a traditional dating pattern. Sandler flies to Las Vegas to stop Barrymore's wedding, not initially realizing she and Glave are on the same flight. Between Sandler's song, "Grow Old With You," and some timely blocking of Glave by Billy Idol, Barrymore and Sandler become a couple. Their scene-closing kiss then cuts to their wedding kiss.

The other pivotal romantic comedy elements found in *The Wedding Singer*—more realistic working characters and slower pacing—have already been implied. Barrymore is a beginning waitress and Sandler a lowly wedding singer. And if their "career" choices are not enough to slow story pacing, there are all those melodramatic tangles to be straightened out by romance and comedy. But Sandler, the most unlikely catalyst for a film in this genre, has succeeded admirably.

Yet another way to document the ongoing popularity of the traditional romantic comedy, beyond the huge commercial success of both a pivotal auteur (Ephron) and an unlikely one (Sandler), is to examine a rare romantic comedy excursion into fantasy—the box office smash *What Women Want* (2000). Normally, fantasy is more likely to surface in the less reality-based screwball comedy, from Cary Grant's "spirited" performance in *Topper* (1937) to Steve Martin sharing his body with another spirit (Lily Tomlin) in *All of Me* (1984).

When a fluke accident gives Mel Gibson the ability to hear women's thoughts, the fantasy element is forever downplayed. Indeed, there is every attempt to ground the cause in reality—Gibson falling into a water-filled bathtub with an electric hair dryer. Consistent with this, when he loses his mind-reading skills late in the picture, the plausibility card is played again—only now it is a downed power line. While this is hardly Italian neo-realism, it contrasts sharply with screwball comedy's tendency to revel in exotic fantasy—such as an invisible Cary Grant changing a flat tire in *Topper*—which became a mere exercise in special effects.

In addition, when fantasy occurs in screwball comedy (past or present), it is always there as a *new* catalyst for eccentric behavior. But the use of fantasy in *What Women Want* simply reinforces an old romantic comedy status quo—the need for the male lead to grow up. Only after he becomes a mature adult can he qualify for (and appreciate) a meaningful relationship with a woman. Thus, Gibson goes from being a womanizing, overaged adolescent to a sensitive, caring partner for the love of his life (Helen Hunt).

While the focus films in this section were all major box-office hits, it might be enlightening to close out this examination of modern romantic comedies with a brief look at three entertaining but more commercially modest outings in the genre—*I.Q.* (1994), *The Truth about Cats & Dogs* (1996), and *If You Only Knew* (1999). Though box-office numbers eluded them, they were not without critical recognition. In fact, reviewers were often ecstatic about the movies, but it took audiences a while to find them. Not surprisingly, in each case the film documents all the traditional components of the genre. Without delineating each element, some romantic comedy highlights are examined.

Older witnesses for love are again present in abundance, particularly in *I.Q.* But the most movingly sentimental use of elderly romantic symbolism occurs at the close of *If You Only Knew*. As the focus young couple (Alison Eastwood and Johnathan Schaech) finally find each other and stroll away, the camera pans to an elderly couple and freeze frames on them kissing.

Each of these movies also briefly embraces the melodramatic overtones associated with broken relationships and/or unreturned love. The most poignant variation on this theme occurs in *The Truth about Cats & Dogs* and keys upon radio veterinarian Janeane Garofalo's ongoing disappointment with her personal appearance. Talk about a nearly universal romance-related concern! Who has not looked in the mirror at some point and been less than pleased? Maybe comedian Red Skelton put it best when, late in life, he observed, "I look in the mirror and I'm not my type anymore." Regardless, this concern over appearance is best articulated in *The Truth about Cats & Dogs* by, ironically, the beautiful model (Uma Thurman): "Did you ever look in the mirror so long that your face didn't make sense anymore? It just became shapes, not good or bad, just shapes?" Once again, the genre documents how people often contribute to their own romantic disappointments.

The happy resolutions here, however, as so often happens in the traditional romantic comedy, are based upon the persistence of the male suitor. The only thing atypical about this leading man slant is that Garofalo is the one who lied—substituting Thurman for herself when she is to meet a potential romantic interest, Ben Chaplin. (He has fallen in love with her voice and comic common sense after calling her radio talk show.)

The more typical romantic comedy situation, of course, involves courtship lies by the male that must be resolved, with examples of both in *I.Q.* and *If You Only Knew*. Tim Robbins's *I.Q.* mechanic pretends to be a scientific genius in order to get closer to Albert Einstein's brilliant niece (Meg Ryan). Through the assistance of the famous uncle (Walter Matthau), this initially works. But when the truth ultimately comes out, as it always does in this genre, there are the standard hurt feelings. In the final analysis, however, such love-related lying is seen as a natural outgrowth of the romantic comedy process.

In *If You Only Knew*, the male lie involves a young man (Johnathan Schaech) pretending to be gay. The girl of his dreams (Alison Eastwood) is advertising for a male roommate for her New York apartment. But because this is to be strictly a platonic security arrangement, her roomie must be gay. Out of both necessity (his apartment has burned) and the desire to be close to Eastwood, he accepts this falsehood, hopeful it will lead to romance. Naturally it does, but not before the genre's standard fallout, when the truth eventually surfaces.

New Twists in Modern Romantic Comedy

The birth of the modern cinema era (post-1960s) paralleled the end of the censorship code. Not surprisingly, this resulted in romantic comedy becoming more frank with its sexuality. This has sometimes resulted in a challenge for the genre. *Variety* critic Todd McCarthy put it best: "the screen's increased frankness makes adherence to the traditional standards [of romantic comedy] seem coy or naïve but foisting too much lewdness on old-fashioned conventions often produces coarse and unconvincing results."[17] This genre's modern era has still produced countless strong outings. While the genre's major modern auteur, Nora Ephron, remains conservative about adding sexuality to romantic comedy, even she recognizes the occasional need. This is Ephron's compromise from her *When Harry Met Sally . . .* script:

> Harry holds her. After a beat, Sally looks up at him, almost searching for something. She kisses him. A hungry, needy kiss. Harry is caught slightly off guard but returns the kiss. As they begin to make love—
>
> CUT TO:
>
> INTERIOR SALLY'S BEDROOM—LATER
> They've made love. Both of them lying in bed, Sally is in Harry's arms. Sally has a smile on her face. Harry stares straight ahead.[18]

This less-is-better approach is still what often serves as a modestly more sexually suggestive romantic comedy scenario. In fact, when

Ephron turned to directing *Sleepless in Seattle* and *You've Got Mail*, there was very little physical contact of any kind. *Sleepless* seldom even had Meg Ryan and Tom Hanks in the same city!

Modern romantic comedy, however, is still more likely to provide some sexual titillation. For instance, in *High Fidelity*, John Cusack and Iben Hjejle have a comically erotic love scene in the front seat of her car. But it is brief and with little real nudity. More suggestive is the same movie's comic orgy scene between Hjejle and Tim Robbins—as imagined by Cusack. Of course, the sexual tone is defused by Cusack's over-the-top imagination.

On the rare occasion when a romantic comedy love scene is played semi-straight, there is often a message involved. For instance, Bo Derek's incredible beauty makes her bedroom encounter with Dudley Moore in *10* (1979) very sensual. But after some amusing distractions, such as the recording of Ravel's *Bolero* skipping (it is the only song she makes love to), Moore stops their romantic dalliance. The problem is her character is both shallow and does not have a clue to the true nature of love and commitment. It is a noble "romantic" notion on his part (especially given the perfect "10" temptation that is Bo Derek). *10* writer/director Blake Edwards was probably inspired by a scene from Woody Allen's *Annie Hall* (1977), where love interest Diane Keaton is more interested in getting high prior to sex than in the actual act itself. Edwards seems to footnote this connection by having Derek offer Moore some marijuana prior to sex.

The Moore-Derek sex scene attains further clarity when one factors in an earlier love song–related comment by his composer character. Speaking to a bartender (Brian Dennehy) Moore comments on the sorry state of contemporary music, which he equates to a rock title not unlike the Beatles's "Why Don't We Do It In The Road?" Such homage to animalistic urges is little different from Derek's sex kitten nature—where's the love? Edwards might have added the following period joke to his screenplay: "What's the only good thing you can say about 'free love'?—The price is right." Of course, earlier in the movie Moore's character had succumbed to those same animalistic urges when he joined his neighbor's ongoing sexual orgy—which Edwards had filmed with a great deal of nudity and a cast of real-life pornographic actors.[19] Edwards usually plays the sexual card, regardless of the genre. After all, this is an artist who gave the normally most wholesome of actresses, Julie Andrews (his real-life wife), a topless scene in the black comedy *S.O.B.* (1981). Regardless, the often lustful *10* is ultimately the most moral of films.

Other examples of modern romantic comedy's more frank depiction of sexuality might range from the tender first time encounter of Johnny Depp and Mary Stewart Masterson in *Benny & Joon* (1993), to the erotic initial sexual act between Julia Roberts's hooker and Richard Gere's businessman in *Pretty Woman* (1990). *Variety* not only called the latter example the "sexiest routine" of *Pretty Woman* but also insightfully compared it to an equally steamy scene in the musically inclined drama *The Fabulous Baker Boys* (1989), given that Richard Gere is playing solo jazz piano late at night shortly before the tryst with Julia Roberts.[20] Bottom line, however, even though the genre now deals more realistically with the bedroom, actual depiction of the sexual act is still kept to a minimum. The genre continues to accent the *romantic* sensitive pathway to the bed over the sexual act itself. And if truth be told, the most controversially funny sex-related scene in modern romantic comedy history appeared miles away from the nearest bed—Meg Ryan's famous imitation of an orgasm in a restaurant routine from *When Harry Met Sally . . . .*

A second new age slant to romantic comedy involves addressing mental instability. Unlike screwball comedy's ongoing foundational use of affectionately "crazy" behavior, modern romantic comedy has, at times, embraced the subject on a more realistic level. Examples range from the minor neuroses of Jack Nicholson in *As Good As It Gets* (1997) to the potentially dysfunctional world of *Benny & Joon*, *Don Juan DeMarco* (1995), and *The Other Sister* (1999).

The beauty of Nicholson's problem is that he represents a sort of neurotic everyman, whose politically incorrect pronouncements often have a comic ring to them, á la Archie Bunker. Nicholson's character also reminds us, with his brief unscheduled visit to the overbooked psychiatrist, that many of us could (should?) be in therapy. But his disorders (largely obsessional compulsions) are made more palatable by playing the traditional game of making him a writer—artists are supposed to be "different."

The other examples cited are more problematic—situations that have required institutionalization and/or some sort of custodial home care. The best of the trio, *Benny & Joon*, again has the unstable character (a schizophrenic Masterson) portrayed as an artist, though her painting is more recreational than the profitable best-seller world of Nicholson's novelist. Her romantic partner (Depp) is a maverick mime who is probably no stranger to therapy himself, though this is never documented. Their romance blossoms after he begins to act as sort of a male nurse/companion to Joon while her brother Benny (Aidan Quinn) is at work. But again, eccentricity is equated with artistry because Depp's real gift is as a pantomimist cross between Buster Keaton and Charlie Chaplin. Critic Roger Ebert observed of Depp's inspired and essentially wordless performance:

> he simply behaves sometimes in the real world in the way Keaton and Chaplin behaved in their movie worlds . . . [Depp] takes a character that might have seemed unplayable on paper, and makes him into the kind of enchanter who might be able to heal Joon.[21]

Part of the bonus from this off-beat romantic comedy is that there are actually two love stories going on. Besides the delightfully kooky high-profile relationship of Depp and Masterson, Quinn has met a waitress (Julianne Moore) who finally pulls him out of his unhealthy preoccupation with both his sister's condition and his non-stop work schedule to pay for her care. Thus, the film sensitively documents how even the one "normal" character (Moore's waitress is a former "B" movie actress) has issues that need addressing and solving by way of love. But make no mistake—love is *not* used as some universal panacea for everyone's problems. Obviously, this is not a love story made in heaven, but as Ebert movingly states, the movie convincingly "suggests that love and magic can overcome madness, and for at least the length of the film I was prepared to accept that."[22] So was I.

The film's close is guardedly optimistic, but it is open-ended. Neither Depp and Masterson, nor Quinn and Moore, are yet an under-one-roof couple. Love is an important component in their joint march toward some sort of "increased normalcy" (whatever that might be), but the whole process will take time and the all important corollary to love—the ability to let go. (This need to trust and accept love is wonderfully equated with the film's use of the haunting ballad, "Have a Little Faith in Me.")

Don Juan DeMarco has several parallels with *Benny & Joon*, beginning with another mesmerizing performance by Johnny Depp. This time he is an impassioned young man who believes he is the world's greatest lover, which is not that far removed from his *Benny & Joon* obsession with Keaton and Chaplin. Also, like the latter film, *Don Juan DeMarco* is a dual-focus love story. Marlon Brando, as fascinating as ever, plays Depp's hospital psychotherapist. On the verge of retirement, Brando becomes entranced by his new patient. Depp's passion for the art of love rekindles his doctor's formerly dormant ardor for his wife (Faye Dunaway). An example of what eventually bowls over Brando, as well as any other character Depp's Don Juan encounters, is the almost over-the-top poetry he brings to his celebration of women. For instance, early in the picture he asks Brando: Haven't you known a woman

> who inspires you to love until your every sense is filled with her? You inhale her, you taste her. You see your unborn children in her eyes and know that you have at last found a home. Your life begins with her, and without her it must surely end.

Though in print it might seem to border on parody, Depp manages to sell it to Brando, and the audience.

Ultimately, as with *Benny & Joon*, the movie is about working toward a heightened normalcy that allows one to learn about life and *love* from the most unconventional of "teachers." And a pivotal lesson from Depp's Don Juan is the admission, "I am not limited by my eyesight." While the moral for romantic comedy might be the obvious "look for inner beauty," the meaning need not be limited to relationships. Depp's sensitive characters in both pictures seem to bring equal joy to everyone they encounter.

The weakest of these highlighted romantic comedies focusing on mental instability is director Garry Marshall's *The Other Sister*. Not coincidentally, Juliette Lewis's title character is the most mentally challenged of any figure thus far examined in the chapter. The film sentimentally chronicles the girl's attempt to break free of a smothering mother (Diane Keaton), a scenario not without parallels to Quinn's overly protective brother in *Benny & Joon*. In both cases, the break is made easier, at least for the girls, by a first boyfriend. For Lewis's character this involves a similarly mentally challenged figure (Giovanni Ribisi).

The Other Sister ultimately fails, however, because it pushes too hard for the mentally challenged title character to be the metaphorical teacher. It does not allow that phenomenon to occur naturally, as is the case with the other highlighted pictures. Moreover, *The Other Sister* awkwardly stacks the deck further in favor of the mentally challenged figure by making her mother the most abrasive of characters—alternating between domineering and hysterical. Maybe this *Other Sister* romance would have played more effectively if the focus couple had been cast with real mentally challenged actors, as was done during the television series *Life Goes On* (1989–1993). In this family drama the Down's syndrome son was played by a performer (Chris Burke) afflicted by the same congenital disorder. One of the series' most moving multiepisode stories involved Burke's romance with another Down's syndrome youngster. Still, one has to admire Marshall's *Other Sister* attempt to bring romantic comedy into a challenging new world. And as demonstrated with the other pictures, an entertaining case can be made for the power of love here, too.

Both Juliette Lewis in *The Other Sister* and Mary Stewart Masterson in *Benny & Joon* play strong heroines, despite being mentally or emotionally challenged, which brings one to a final new development for modern romantic comedy: the genre's leading ladies are more forceful. Thanks to the 1960s rebirth of the women's movement, which paralleled the start of cinema's modern era, the genre has more romantically active heroines. An example is Meg Ryan's *Sleepless in Seattle* character, who travels across the country to scout out this sensitive man (Tom Hanks) that so moved her on a call-in radio program.

Before examining this point further, it should be underlined that the standard romantic comedy formula, past and present, still generally dictates that the man ultimately makes the deciding (late in the movie) move, which culminates with the happy fadeout. As previous pages have documented, it is a genre convention that has remained constant through the years—often because the male has to grow up and/or make amends for some transgression. But within that ongoing framework, romantic comedy heroines have grown stronger in recent years.

An excellent example of this occurs with Helen Hunt's character in *As Good As It Gets*. She is a fiercely independent single parent mom scraping by as a New York City waitress. A relationship slowly develops between her and a neurotic regular customer (Jack Nicholson's novelist). His innate ability to say and/or do the wrong thing constantly infuriates her—which she is always quick to confront him about. But because of her, he is slowly finding his better side. This initially puzzles her and she, ironically, even gets in his face about a good deed. Nicholson's writer has assumed her sickly son's sizeable medical bills. Instead of a simple thank you she makes a lengthy crosstown commute in the middle of the night to deliver an insulting "don't expect any sexual favors" sort of a tirade. Clearly, being overly independent can be its own sort of problem. The bottom line here is Hunt's character makes no bones about getting in anyone's face, including benevolent best-selling novelists.

By the movie's close, however, when all the broken romantic comedy fences have to be mended for the required upbeat close, the genre's traditional formula kicks in. It is the man (Nicholson) going to Hunt to make things alright for love. This ending might have recycled an earlier Nicholson line—"You make me want to be a better man." That admission, or words to that effect, is essentially the classic closer "walk" that romantic comedy males walk throughout the genre's history.

One could convincingly argue that modern cinema's need for a strong romantic comedy heroine is why the third version (1994) of Leo McCarey's otherwise amazingly durable film *Love Affair* was a critical and commercial disappointment. The story's leading lady is probably too passive for today's audience, especially after her debilitating accident. A successful *modern* update would no doubt have her exploring spinal column injuries, á la Christopher Reeve, and taking part in the wheelchair Olympics.

The genre's strong contemporary heroine is best showcased in the collaborations between Nora Ephron and Meg Ryan. In *When Harry Met Sally . . .*, *Sleepless In Seattle*, and *You've Got Mail,* Ryan is essentially playing a variation of the very successful career woman Nora Ephron. Ephron implies the same connection herself in the introduction to her published screenplay for *When Harry Met Sally . . . .*[23] While not as directly autobiographical as Ephron's use of Ryan in the writer/director's disappointing seriocomedy *Hanging Up* (2000), in each of the aforementioned films the actress plays a strong professional woman—often with ties to writing. For instance, in *Sleepless* Ryan is a big city journalist; in *You've Got Mail* she is a New York City bookstore owner. Always likeable, she is also an argumentative control freak—initially at odds with her eventual love interest in two of the three films. But as with the earlier Helen Hunt example from *As Good As It Gets*, each of the Ephron-Ryan romantic comedy collaborations has the male lead ultimately being responsible for finally getting the couple together. Something new (a stronger female lead) is still married to that traditional formula.

Notes

1. Maria Montoya, "Bridget's Bloomin' Undies Bring Oversized Sales Surge," *USA Today*, May 30, 2001, p. 2-D.

2. Susan Wloszczyna, "Let Us Call Them 'Sweethearts,'" *USA Today*, July 12, 2001, p. 2-D.

3. Ty Burr (with Steve Daly), "America's Most Wanted" (cover story), *Entertainment Weekly*, July 20, 2001, p. 29.

4. Anthony Lane, "The Devil and Miss Jones," *The New Yorker*, April 16, 2001, p. 91.

5. David Ansen, "Off the Beaten Track," *Newsweek*, August 31, 1992, p. 58.

6. Ansen, "Off the Beaten Track," p. 58.

7. Joan Burke, "At the Movies," *Des Moines Register*, August 30, 1992.

8. Pauline Kael, "Spoofing *Cat Ballou*" (1965), in *Kiss Kiss Bang Bang* (Boston: Little, Brown, 1968), p. 28.

9. "Actress Finally Speaks about Notable Break-Up," *Muncie Star Press*, July 13, 2001, p. 2-A.

10. David Denby, "Star Athlete," *The New Yorker*, September 27, 1999, p. 104.

11. David Denby, "Crown Prince," *The New Yorker*, August 9, 1999, p. 82.

12. David Ansen, "Falling for Mr. Wrong," *Newsweek*, April 20, 1998, p. 63.

13. Roger Ebert (syndicated *Chicago Sun Times* reviewer), "'Sleepless' is warm, gentle romance," *Cedar Rapids Gazette*, June 25, 1993, p. 6-W.

14. Susan Wloszczyna, "'Sleepless': Ephron Makes 'em Like They Used To," *USA Today*, June 25, 1993, p. 1-D; Kitty Bean Yancey, "'Seattle' Director Seduces with Old-Fashioned Romance," *USA Today*, July 8, 1993, p. 12-D.

15. Michelle Kinsey, "You've Got Infidelity," *Muncie Star Press*, January 15, 1999, p. 1-D.

16. Kinsey, "You've Got Infidelity," p. 1-D.

17. Todd McCarthy, "Sundance" section, *Variety*, January 24, 1994.

18. Nora Ephron, *When Harry Met Sally . . .* (New York: Alfred A. Knopf, 1997), p. 75.

19. Jeff Lenburg, *Dudley Moore: An Informal Biography* (New York: Delilah, 1983), p. 99.

20. *Pretty Woman* review, *Variety*, March 21, 1990, p. 20.

21. Roger Ebert (syndicated *Chicago Sun Times* reviewer), "Love and Madness Meet in Charming 'Benny & Joon,'" *Cedar Rapids Gazette*, May 21, 1993, p. 7-W.

22. Ebert, "Love and Madness Meet," p. 7-W.

23. Ephron, *When Harry Met Sally . . .* , pp. vii-xvii.

CHAPTER SIX
EPILOGUE

How can I believe you? The car broke down. People stopped believing that one before cars started breaking down.

—Cary Grant to Irene Dunne, on
her alibi in *The Awful Truth* (1937)

Kittredge is no great tower of strength, you know, Tracy. He's just a tower.

—Grant, on Katharine Hepburn's
prospective groom (George Kittredge),
in *The Philadelphia Story* (1940)

Probably the most surprising thing about this chronicle of romantic and screwball comedy is the genre's consistency over time. While all genres tend to be in varying states of flux, as has been demonstrated in this text by the previous chapter, romantic and screwball comedy have not changed that radically from American cinema's golden age during the 1930s and 1940s. Indeed, seminal stars from these genres, such as Cary Grant and Katharine Hepburn, are bigger now than during their lifetimes.

What has been a more typical scenario break are times when one and/or the other of these comedy types has been outside the loop. For instance, the early 1950s was less than user friendly for both romantic and screwball comedy. The pivotal Cary Grant was so disgusted by this precarious-for-comedy turn of events that he briefly retired from the screen, observing: "It was the period of blue jeans, the dope addicts, the method [actor, á la Marlon Brando and James Dean], and nobody cared about comedy at all."[1] Luckily for everyone concerned, however, both Grant and these genres soon came back stronger than ever.

In differentiating between romantic and screwball comedy, the previous chapters have keyed upon five distinctive components for *each* of these genres. For screwball comedy this has meant the films of the genre can be examined for the basic characteristics of the pivotal antihero: abundant leisure time, childlike nature, male frustration (especially in relationship to women), a general propensity for physical comedy, and a proclivity for parody and satire. In contrast to this genre is romantic comedy's five-point configuration: accents sentiment over silliness, has a propensity for serious and/or melodramatic overtones, has more realistic characters (often employed), has traditional dating rituals (less controlling women), and has slower story pacing (especially near the end of the picture). At its most fundamental level, screwball comedy puts its emphasis on a *funny* spoofing of love, while the more traditional romantic ultimately *accents* love.

Change over time for these genres has been minimal both because each is an effective entertainment formula and because American film is still a relatively young art form—little more than a century old. An added element in the continued continuity of romantic and screwball comedy is a link to this same American cinema history. That is, modern (since 1960) examples of this study's two genres frequently anchor their stories in references to earlier movies. Often actual footage of the old picture is seen (such as a character watching a video or a late night movie on television), though the modern performer might also simply recreate a scene.

This classic film phenomenon was briefly alluded to earlier in the text with relationship to the pivotal use of *An Affair to Remember* (1957) in *Sleepless in Seattle* (1993) and *Charade* (1963) in *Pretty Woman* (1990). But these examples are merely the tip of the proverbial iceberg; such occurrences merit further attention, especially when the old film footnotes are from a genre that is different from the new movie. For instance, whereas the aforementioned citations from *Sleepless* and *Pretty Woman* represent romantic comedy clips being used in modern romantic comedy films, how does one assess Johnny Depp recycling clown comedy shtick by Charlie Chaplin and Harold Lloyd in *Benny & Joon* (1993)?

Each of these silent comedy recreations—the dancing dinner roll scene from Chaplin's *The Gold Rush* (1925) and Lloyd's thrill comedy portion of *Safety Last* (1923)—might not seem, to the uninitiated, as directly applicable to the new romantic comedy. But in both cases, the highlighted silent material is drawn from Chaplin and Lloyd scenes where these figures are giving their comic all to win the love of the leading lady. And this "all," with relationship to the building climbing portion of both *Benny & Joon* and *Safety Last*, literally means risking one's life for love. (Though Depp's *Benny & Joon* character is most often tied to Chaplin and Buster Keaton, the Lloyd element is very much there, too.)

Countless other classic film references abound in modern screwball and romantic comedy, from Howard Hawks restaging a major slapstick fishing scene from *Libeled Lady* (1936) for *Man's Favorite Sport?* (1964) to Garry Marshall using both footage of, and musical sound cues from, *The Graduate* (1967) in *The Other Sister* (1999). In *Irreconcilable Differences* (1984) a central character's career (Ryan O'Neal's film director) is even defined as problematic by his use (or misuse) of a classic screen property—an attempt at a musical version of *Gone with the Wind* (1939). And a special film reference for male viewers is how Tom Hanks's character in *You've Got Mail* (1998) uses *The Godfather* (1972) as sort of a new age font of crackerbarrel wisdom . . . by way of the Mafia. Thus, at one point Hanks asks himself rhetorically, "What should I take on vacation?" His *Godfather* answer comes back, "Leave the gun, take the cannoli." *The Godfather* becomes nearly as central to *You've Got Mail* as *An Affair to Remember* is to *Sleepless in Seattle.*

While a Mafia film and a romantic comedy are hardly of the same genre, the connection allows Hanks's character a degree of feint toughness to go with that wistfulness *New York Times* critic Janet Maslin likens to Jimmy Stewart shyness.[2] Moreover, it makes for an effective counterpoint to a Meg Ryan character who is so sensitive she is known to quote Joni Mitchell. Of course, one could comically argue that Hanks's use of *The Godfather* is merely a coping device for having a girlfriend (Parker Posey) at the film's beginning who is not unlike a New York variety of piranha. Even Hanks observes, "Patricia makes coffee nervous." But regardless of how one interprets it, Hanks's Mafia mantra is yet another example of film footnotes in the modern cinema genres of romantic and screwball comedy.

I am reminded of writer/director Lawrence Kasdan's populist *Grand Canyon* (1991) where he has an in-film producer (Steve Martin) observe, "You haven't seen enough movies. All of life's riddles are answered in the movies." Martin's character might just as well have been speaking about romantic and screwball comedy. As we become more and more a nation of video voyeurs, having new screen characters closely identify with beloved old screen characters (and scenes) helps us more readily relate to them all.

A variation of this is even occurring in film criticism, such as the aforementioned Janet Maslin comparison of Hanks to Stewart, or *Entertainment Weekly* critic Owen Gleiberman's tendency to liken Julia Roberts's 1999 *Runaway Bride* character to Carole Lombard.[3] But then, this is only natural when one considers directors encouraging such connections. For instance, Peter Bogdanovich had his *What's Up, Doc?* (1972) cast study *Bringing Up Baby* (1938), while *Irreconcilable Differences*'s Charles Shyer had his actors watching *His Girl Friday* (1940) and *The Lady Eve* (1941).[4] And of course, *Runaway Bride* director Garry Marshall had his cast aware of screwball comedy's army of "runaway brides," starting with Claudette Colbert in *It Happened One Night* (1934).

On a more personal note, as I work toward finishing the book in hand, I continue to be surprised over how past film critics and historians have used the genre designations of "romantic comedy" and "screwball comedy" interchangeably. Long ago (1977) comedy theorist Jim Leach penned a few lines that have had an ongoingly profound impact on me. With amusing insight on comedy he observed, "A genre which encompasses the visions of Jerry Lewis *and* Ernst Lubitsch is already in trouble."[5] Leach was encouraging a more ambitious look at *multiple* comedy genres, noting what most disciples of laughter have long believed: "If a genre is defined too loosely [as in the case of comedy], it ceases to be of any value as a critical tool."[6]

In the years since Leach made these prophetic (for me) observations, I have written a number of film comedy-related studies that attempt to map out the distinctive terrain of several genres of laughter. My first such exercise in this area was a text on screwball comedy.[7] While I have addressed numerous other topics since this 1986 book, my fascination with the genre and its first cousin, romantic comedy, has not waned. A further echoing of Jim Leach's concern about overly broad genres has encouraged me to rethink and expand here my earlier thoughts on screwball comedy, as well as make a case herein for a distinctively separate, but no less important, romantic comedy genre.

This text's new formulas for romantic and screwball comedy represent workable models for the foreseeable future, though a genre equation is always a work in progress, such as the seemingly recent viewer preference for stable romantic heroines over the screwball variety. If all of life's riddles are *not* solved in the movies, romantic and screwball comedies would still seem to offer disciples of love a veritable smorgasbord of answers. Personally, I would continue to opt for solutions in cinema because movies move us forever closer to Oscar Wilde's insightfully tongue-in-cheek observation: "Life imitates art far more than art imitates life."[8]

Notes

1. *Cary Grant: In the Spotlight* (New York: Gallery Press, 1980), p. 89.
2. Janet Maslin, *You've Got Mail* review, *New York Times*, December 18, 1998, p. 1-E.
3. Owen Gleiberman, "Veiled Intentions," *Entertainment Weekly*, August 6, 1999, p. 37.
4. Janet Maslin, "Generations Apart," *New York Times*, September 28, 1984, p. 10.
5. Jim Leach, "The Screwball Comedy," in *Film Genres and Criticism*, ed. Barry K. Grant (Metuchen, N.J.: Scarecrow Press, 1977), p. 75.
6. Leach, "The Screwball Comedy," p. 75.
7. Wes Gehring, *Screwball Comedy: A Genre of Madcap Romance* (Westport, Conn.: Greenwood Press, 1986).
8. Oscar Wilde, "The Decay of Lying" (1889), in *Criticism: The Major Texts*, ed. W. J. Bate (Chicago: Harcourt Brace Jovanovich, 1970), p. 642.

SELECTED FILMOGRAPHY

This two-part (screwball and romantic comedy) filmography includes pivotal movies both mentioned and examined in the text. The films appear in chronological order. (Movies released the same year are listed in the order they were reviewed by the *New York Times*.)

Screwball Comedy

1934 *It Happened One Night* (105 minutes).
Director: Frank Capra. Screenplay: Robert Riskin, from the Samuel Hopkins Adams story. Stars: Clark Gable, Claudette Colbert, Walter Connolly.

1934 *Twentieth Century* (91 minutes).
Director: Howard Hawks. Screenplay: Ben Hecht, Charles MacArthur, from their play. Stars: John Barrymore, Carole Lombard, Walter Connolly.

1935 *Ruggles of Red Gap* (91 minutes).
Director: Leo McCarey. Screenplay: Walter DeLeon, Harlan Thompson, and an uncredited McCarey, from the Harry Leon Wilson novel. Stars: Charles Laughton, Mary Boland, Charles Ruggles, ZaZu Pitts, Roland Young.

1935 *The Whole Town's Talking* (95 minutes).
Director: John Ford. Screenplay: Jo Swerling and Robert

Riskin, from the W. R. Burnett story. Stars: Edward G. Robinson, Ferguson Jones, Jean Arthur, Wallace Ford.

1936 *The Ex-Mrs. Bradford* (80 minutes).
Director: Stephen Roberts. Screenplay: Anthony Veiller, from a James Edward Grant story. Stars: William Powell, Jean Arthur, James Gleason, Eric Blore.

1936 *My Man Godfrey* (93 minutes).
Director: Gregory LaCava. Screenplay: Morrie Ryskind, Eric Hatch, from the Hatch novel. Stars: William Powell, Carole Lombard, Alice Brady, Gail Patrick, Jean Dixon, Eugene Pallette, Allan Mowbray, Mischa Auer.

1936 *Theodora Goes Wild* (94 minutes).
Director: Richard Boleslawski. Screenplay: Sidney Buchman, from a Mary McCarthy story. Stars: Irene Dunne, Melvyn Douglas, Thomas Mitchell.

1936 *Libeled Lady* (98 minutes).
Director: Jack Conway. Screenplay: Maurine Watkins, Howard Emmett Rogers, George Oppenheimer, from a Wallace Sullivan story. Stars: William Powell, Myrna Loy, Jean Harlow, Spencer Tracy, Walter Connolly.

1937 *Easy Living* (88 minutes).
Director: Mitchell Leisen. Screenplay: Preston Sturges, from a Vera Caspary story. Stars: Jean Arthur, Edward Arnold, Ray Milland.

1937 *Topper* (89 minutes).
Director: Norman Z. McLeod. Screenplay: Jack Jevne, Eric Hatch, Eddie Moran, from the Thorne Smith novel of the same name. Stars: Constance Bennett, Cary Grant, Roland Young, Billie Burke.

1937 *The Awful Truth* (89 minutes).
Director: Leo McCarey. Screenplay: Viña Delmar and an uncredited McCarey, loosely based upon the Arthur Richman play. Stars: Irene Dunne, Cary Grant, Ralph Bellamy.

1937 *Nothing Sacred* (75 minutes).
Director: William Wellman. Screenplay: Ben Hech, from the James H. Street story. Stars: Carole Lombard, Fredric March, Charles Winninger, Walter Connolly.

1937 *True Confession* (84 minutes).
Director: Wesley Ruggles. Screenplay: Claude Binyon, from the Louis Verneuil, Georges Berr play *Mon Crime*. Stars: Carole Lombard, Fred MacMurray, John Barrymore, Una Merkel.

1938 *Bringing Up Baby* (102 minutes).
Director: Howard Hawks. Screenplay: Dudley Nichols, from a Hagar Wilde story. Stars: Katharine Hepburn, Cary Grant, Charles Ruggles.

1938 *Bluebeard's Eighth Wife* (80 minutes).
Director: Ernst Lubitsch. Screenplay: Charles Brackett, Billy Wilder, from the Alfred Savior play. Stars: Claudette Colbert, Gary Cooper, Edward Everett Horton, David Niven.

1938 *Vivacious Lady* (90 minutes).
Director: George Stevens. Screenplay: P. J. Wolfson, Ernest Pagano, from the I. A. R. Wylie story. Cast: Ginger Rogers, Jimmy Stewart, James Ellison, Beulah Bondi, Charles Coburn.

1938 *Holiday* (94 minutes).
Director: George Cukor. Screenplay: Donald Ogden Stewart, Sidney Buchman. Stars: Katharine Hepburn, Cary Grant, Doris Nolan, Lew Ayres, Edward Everett Horton.

1938 *Mad Miss Manton* (80 minutes).
Director: Leigh Jason. Screenplay: Philip G. Epstein. Stars: Barbara Stanwyck, Henry Fonda.

1939 *Topper Takes a Trip* (80 minutes).
Director: Norman Z. McLeod. Screenplay: Eddie Moran, Jack Jevne, Corey Ford, from the Thorne Smith novel. Stars: Constance Bennett, Roland Young, Billie Burke.

1939 *Midnight* (92 minutes).
Director: Mitchell Leisen. Screenplay: Charles Brackett, Billy Wilder. Stars: Claudette Colbert, Don Ameche, John Barrymore, Francis Lederer, Mary Astor.

1940 *His Girl Friday* (92 minutes).
Director: Howard Hawks. Screenplay: Charles Lederer, from the Ben Hecht, Charles MacArthur play *The Front Page*. Stars: Cary Grant, Rosalind Russell, Ralph Bellamy.

1940 *Too Many Husbands* (80 minutes).
Director: Wesley Ruggles. Screenplay: Claude Binyon, from the W. Somerset Maugham play. Stars: Jean Arthur, Fred MacMurray, Melvyn Douglas, Harry Davenport.

1940 *My Favorite Wife* (88 minutes).
Director: Garson Kanin, with uncredited assistance from Leo McCarey. Screenplay: Bella Spewack, Samuel Spewack. Stars: Irene Dunne, Cary Grant, Randolph Scott, Gail Patrick.

1940 *Turnabout* (81 minutes).
Director: Hal Roach. Screenplay: Mickell Novak, Berne Giler, John McClain, from the Thorne Smith novel. Stars: Adolphe Menjou, Carole Landis, John Hubbard.

1941 *The Lady Eve* (97 minutes).
Director/Screenplay: Preston Sturges, from a Monakton Hoffe story. Stars: Barbara Stanwyck, Henry Fonda, Charles Coburn, Eugene Pallette, William Demarest, Eric Blore.

1941 *Topper Returns* (95 minutes).
Director: Roy Del Ruth. Screenplay: Jonathan Latimer, Gordon Douglas, based upon characters by Thorne Smith. Stars: Joan Blondell, Roland Young, Carole Landis, Billie Burke.

1941 *Here Comes Mr. Jordan* (93 minutes).
Director: Alexander Hall. Screenplay: Sidney Buchman, Seton I. Miller, from the Harry Segall play *Heaven Can Wait*. Stars: Robert Montgomery, Evelyn Keyes, Claude Rains, Rita Johnson, Edward Everett Horton, James Gleason.

1941 *Two-Faced Woman* (94 minutes).
Director: George Cukor. Screenplay: S. N. Behrman, Salka Viertel, George Oppenheimer, from the Ludwig Fulda play. Stars: Greta Garbo, Melvyn Douglas, Constance Bennett, Roland Young.

1941 *Ball of Fire* (111 minutes).
Director: Howard Hawks. Screenplay: Billy Wilder, Charles Brackett. Stars: Gary Cooper, Barbara Stanwyck.

1942 *To Be or Not to Be* (99 minutes).
Director: Ernst Lubitsch. Screenplay: Edwin Justus Mayer, from the Melchior Lengyel and Lubitsch story. Stars: Carole Lombard, Jack Benny, Robert Stack.

1942 *Take a Letter, Darling* (93 minutes).
Director: Mitchell Leisen. Screenplay: Claude Binyon, from a George Bech story. Stars: Rosalind Russell, Fred MacMurray, MacDonald Carey, Constance Moore, Robert Benchley.

1942 *Lady in a Jam* (81 minutes).
Director: Gregory LaCava. Screenplay: Eugene Thackrey, Frank Cockrell, Otho Lovering. Stars: Irene Dunne, Patric Knowles, Ralph Bellamy, Eugene Pallette.

1942 *The Major and the Minor* (100 minutes).
Director: Billy Wilder. Screenplay: Charles Brackett, Billy Wilder. Stars: Ginger Rogers, Ray Milland, Rita Johnson, Robert Benchley, Diana Lynn.

1942 *Once upon a Honeymoon* (115 minutes).
Director: Leo McCarey. Screenplay: Sheridan Gibney, from the Gibney, McCarey story. Stars: Cary Grant, Ginger Rogers, Walter Slezak.

1942 *I Married a Witch* (76 minutes).
Director: René Clair. Screenplay: Robert Pirosh, Marc Connelly, from the Thorne Smith novel *The Passionate Witch*—completed by Norman Matson. Stars: Fredric March, Veronica Lake, Robert Benchley, Susan Hayward, Cecil Kellaway.

1942 *The Palm Beach Story* (101 minutes).
Director/Screenplay: Preston Sturges. Stars: Claudette Colbert, Joel McCrea, Mary Astor, Rudy Vallee.

1944 *The Miracle of Morgan's Creek* (99 minutes).
Director/Screenplay: Preston Sturges. Stars: Eddie Bracken, Betty Hutton, Diana Lynn, William Demarest.

1944 *Arsenic and Old Lace* (118 minutes).
Director: Frank Capra. Screenplay: Julius J. Epstein, Philip G. Epstein, from the Joseph Kesselring play. Stars: Cary Grant, Raymond Massey, Priscilla Lane, Josephine Hull, Jean Adair, Jack Carson, Edward Everett Horton, Peter Lorre, James Gleason, John Alexander.

1947 *The Sin of Harold Diddlebock* (90 minutes, aka *Mad Wednesday*).
Director: Preston Sturges. Screenplay: Sturges, plus footage from Harold Lloyd's *The Freshman*. Stars: Lloyd, Frances Ramsden, Jimmy Conlin, Raymond Walburn, Edgar Kennedy.

1948 *Unfaithfully Yours* (105 minutes).
Director/Screenplay: Preston Sturges. Stars: Rex Harrison, Linda Darnell, Barbara Lawrence, Rudy Vallee.

1949 *I Was a Male War Bride* (105 minutes).
Director: Howard Hawks. Screenplay: Charles Lederer, Leonard Spigelgass, Hagar Wilde, from the Henri Rochard article. Stars: Cary Grant, Ann Sheridan.

1952 *Monkey Business* (97 minutes).
Director: Howard Hawks. Screenplay: Ben Hecht, I. A. Diamond, Charles Lederer. Stars: Cary Grant, Ginger Rogers, Charles Coburn, Marilyn Monroe.

1959 *Some Like It Hot* (120 minutes).
Director: Billy Wilder. Screenplay: Wilder, I. A. L. Diamond. Stars: Marilyn Monroe, Tony Curtis, Jack Lemmon, George Raft, Pat O'Brien, Joe E. Brown.

1964 *Man's Favorite Sport?* (120 minutes).
Director: Howard Hawks. Screenplay: John Fenton Murray, Steve McNeil. Stars: Rock Hudson, Paula Prentiss.

1972 *What's Up, Doc?* (94 minutes).
Director: Peter Bogdanovich. Screenplay: Buck Henry, Robert Benton, David Newman—loose remake of *Bringing Up Baby*. Stars: Barbra Streisand, Ryan O'Neal, Kenneth Mars, Madeline Kahn.

1972 *Harold and Maude* (90 minutes).
Director: Hal Ashby. Screenplay: Colin Higgins. Stars: Bud Cort, Ruth Gordon, Vivian Pickles.

1980 *Seems Like Old Times* (102 minutes).
Director: Jay Sandrich. Screenplay: Neil Simon. Stars: Goldie Hawn, Chevy Chase, Charles Grodin, Robert Guillaume.

1981 *Arthur* (96 minutes).
Director/Screenplay: Steve Gordon. Stars: Dudley Moore, Liza Minnelli, John Gielgud.

1982 *Victor/Victoria* (133 minutes).
Director/Screenplay: Blake Edwards, based on a 1933 Ufa film *Victor und Viktoria*. Stars: Julie Andrews, James Garner, Robert Preston, Lesley Ann Warren, Alex Karras.

1984 *Unfaithfully Yours* (97 minutes).
Director: Howard Zieff. Screenplay: Valerie Curtin, Barry Levinson, Robert Klane, from the Preston Sturges film. Stars: Dudley Moore, Nastassja Kinski, Armand Assante, Albert Brooks.

1984 *Irreconcilable Differences* (117 minutes).
Director: Charles Shyer. Screenplay: Nancy Meyers, Shyer. Stars: Ryan O'Neal, Shelley Long, Drew Barrymore.

1984 *All of Me* (93 minutes).
Director: Carl Reiner. Screenplay: Phil Alden Robinson, from the Ed Davis novel *Me Two*. Stars: Steve Martin, Lily Tomlin, Victoria Tennant.

1984 *Micki & Maude* (118 minutes).
Director/Screenplay: Blake Edwards. Stars: Dudley Moore, Amy Irving, Ann Reinking.

1987 *Blind Date* (93 minutes).
Director/Screenplay: Blake Edwards. Stars: Kim Basinger, Bruce Willis, John Larroquette.

1988 *A Fish Called Wanda* (108 minutes).
Director: Charles Crichton. Screenplay: John Cleese. Stars: John Cleese, Jamie Lee Curtis, Kevin Kline, Michael Palin.

1989 *Skin Deep* (101 minutes).
Director/Screenplay: Blake Edwards. Stars: John Ritter, Vincent Gardenia, Alyson Reed.

1991 *L.A. Story* (95 minutes).
Director: Mick Jackson. Screenplay: Steve Martin. Stars: Steve Martin, Victoria Tennant, Richard E. Grant, Marilu Henner, Sarah Jessica Parker.

1991 *Switch* (104 minutes).
Director/Screenplay: Blake Edwards. Stars: Ellen Barkin, Jimmy Smits, JoBeth Williams.

1992 *Housesitter* (100 minutes).
Director: Frank Oz. Screenplay: Mark Stein. Stars: Steve Martin, Goldie Hawn, Dana Delany, Julie Harris, Donald Moffat.

1992 *Honeymoon in Vegas* (95 minutes).
Director/Screenplay: Andrew Bergman. Stars: James Caan, Nicolas Cage, Sarah Jessica Parker.

1994 *Four Weddings and a Funeral* (116 minutes).
Director: Mike Newell. Screenplay: Richard Curtis. Stars: Hugh Grant, Andie MacDowell, Kristin Scott Thomas, Simon Callow.

1997 *My Best Friend's Wedding* (105 minutes).
Director: P. J. Hogan. Screenplay: Ronald Bass. Stars: Julia Roberts, Dermot Mulroney, Cameron Diaz, Rupert Everett.

1997 *In & Out* (90 minutes).
Director: Frank Oz. Screenplay: Paul Rudnick. Stars: Kevin Kline, Joan Cusack, Tom Selleck, Matt Dillon, Debbie Reynolds, Wilford Brimley, Bob Newhart.

1998 *The Object of My Affection* (110 minutes).
Director: Nicholas Hytner. Screenplay: Wendy Wasserstein, from the Stephen McCauley novel. Stars: Jennifer Aniston, Paul Rudd, Alan Alda, Nigel Hawthorne.

1999 *Analyze This* (103 minutes).
Director: Harold Ramis. Screenplay: Billy Crystal, Peter Tolan. Stars: Robert DeNiro, Billy Crystal, Lisa Kudrow.

1999 *Forces of Nature* (104 minutes).
Director: Bronwen Hughes. Screenplay: Marc Lawrence. Stars: Sandra Bullock, Ben Affleck, Maura Tierney.

1999 *Runaway Bride* (116 minutes).
Director: Garry Marshall. Screenplay: Josann McGibbon, Sara Parriott. Stars: Julia Roberts, Richard Gere, Joan Cusack, Hector Elizondo, Rita Wilson, Paul Dooley.

1999 *Mickey Blue Eyes* (103 minutes).
Director: Kelly Makin. Screenplay: Adam Scheinman, Robert Kuhn. Stars: Hugh Grant, James Caan, Jeanne Tripplehorn, Burt Young, James Fox.

1999 *Notting Hill* (123 minutes).
Director: Roger Michell. Screenplay: Richard Curtis. Stars: Julia Roberts, Hugh Grant, Hugh Bonnevillie.

2001 *Bridget Jones's Diary* (97 minutes).
Director/Screenplay: Sharon Maguire, from the Helen Fielding novel. Stars: Renée Zellweger, Hugh Grant, Colin Firth.

2001 *America's Sweethearts* (102 minutes).
Director: Joe Roth. Screenplay: Billy Crystal, Peter Tolan. Stars: Julia Roberts, Billy Crystal, Catherine Zeta-Jones, John Cusack, Stanley Tucci, Alan Arkin.

Romantic Comedy

1935 *Hands across the Table* (80 minutes).
Director: Mitchell Leisen. Screenplay: Norman Krasna, Vincent Lawrence, Herbert Fields, from a Viña Delmar story. Stars: Carole Lombard, Fred MacMurray, Ralph Bellamy.

1939 *Love Affair* (87 minutes).
Director: Leo McCarey. Screenplay: Delmer Daves, Donald Ogden Stewart, from a Mildred Cram, Leo McCarey story. Stars: Irene Dunne, Charles Boyer, Maria Duspenskaya.

1939 *Ninotchka* (110 minutes).
Director: Ernst Lubitsch. Screenplay: Charles Brackett, Billy Wilder, Walter Reisch, from a Melchior Lengyel story. Stars: Greta Garbo, Melvyn Douglas, Ina Claire, Bela Lugosi, Sig Rumam.

1940 *The Shop around the Corner* (97 minutes).
Director: Ernst Lubitsch. Screenplay: Samson Raphaelson, based on Nikolaus Laszlo's play *Perfumerie*. Stars: Margaret Sullavan, Jimmy Stewart, Frank Morgan.

1941 *The Philadelphia Story* (112 minutes).
Director: George Cukor. Screenplay: Donald Ogden Stewart, from the Philip Barry play. Stars: Cary Grant, Katharine Hepburn, Jimmy Stewart, Ruth Hussey, John Howard, Roland Young.

1942 *Woman of the Year* (112 minutes).
Director: George Stevens. Screenplay: Ring Lardner, Jr., Michael Kanin. Stars: Spencer Tracy, Katharine Hepburn, Fay Bainter, Reginald Owen, Minor Watson, William Bendix.

1943 *The More the Merrier* (104 minutes).
Director: George Stevens. Screenplay: Robert Russell, Frank Ross, Richard Flournoy, Lewis R. Foster. Stars: Jean Arthur, Joel McCrea, Charles Coburn.

1943 *Princess O'Rourke* (93 minutes).
Director/Screenplay: Norman Krasna. Stars: Olivia De Havilland, Robert Cummings, Charles Coburn, Jack Carson, Jane Wyman, Harry Davenport.

1944 *Standing Room Only* (83 minutes).
Director: Sidney Lanfield. Screenplay: Darrell Ware, Karl Tunberg, from an Al Martin story. Stars: Fred MacMurray, Paulette Goddard, Edward Arnold, Hillary Brooke, Roland Young.

1945 *Without Love* (111 minutes).
Director: Harold S. Bucquet. Screenplay: Donald Ogden Stewart, from the Philip Barry play. Stars: Spencer Tracy, Katharine Hepburn, Lucille Ball, Keenan Wynn.

1947 *The Bachelor and the Bobby-Soxer* (95 minutes).
Director: Irving Reis. Screenplay: Sidney Sheldon. Stars: Cary Grant, Myrna Loy, Shirley Temple, Rudy Vallee, Ray Collins, Harry Davenport.

1947 *The Bishop's Wife* (105 minutes).
Director: Henry Koster. Screenplay: Robert E. Sherwood, Leonardo Bercovici, from the Robert Nathan novella. Stars: Cary Grant, Loretta Young, David Niven, Monty Woolley, James Gleason.

1949 *Adam's Rib* (100 minutes).
Director: George Cukor. Screenplay: Garson Kanin, Ruth Gordon. Stars: Spencer Tracy, Katharine Hepburn, Judy Holliday, Tom Ewell, David Wayne, Jean Hagen.

1951 *The African Queen* (105 minutes).
Director: John Huston. Screenplay: James Agee, Huston, from the C. S. Forester novel. Stars: Humphrey Bogart, Katharine Hepburn, Robert Morley.

1952 *Pat and Mike* (95 minutes).
Director: George Cukor. Screenplay: Ruth Gordon, Garson Kanin. Stars: Spencer Tracy, Katharine Hepburn, Aldo Ray, William Ching.

1954 *Sabrina* (113 minutes).
Director: Billy Wilder. Screenplay: Billy Wilder, Samuel Taylor, Ernest Lehman, based on Taylor's play *Sabrina Fair*. Stars: Humphrey Bogart, Audrey Hepburn, William Holden.

1955 *To Catch a Thief* (103 minutes).
Director: Alfred Hitchcock. Screenplay: John Michael Hayes, from a David Dodge novel. Stars: Cary Grant, Grace Kelly.

1956 *The Iron Petticoat* (87 minutes).
Director: Ralph Thomas. Screenplay: Ben Hecht—asked to have name removed from credits. Stars: Bob Hope, Katharine Hepburn.

1957 *Desk Set* (103 minutes).
Director: Walter Lang. Screenplay: Phoebe Ephron, Henry Ephron, from the William Marchant play. Stars: Spencer Tracy, Katharine Hepburn, Gig Young, Joan Blondell, Dina Merrill.

1957 *An Affair to Remember* (114 minutes).
Director: Leo McCarey. Screenplay: Delmer Daves, Leo McCarey. Stars: Cary Grant, Deborah Kerr.

1957 *Love in the Afternoon* (130 minutes).
Director: Billy Wilder. Screenplay: Billy Wilder, I. A. L. Diamond, based on Claude Anet's novel *Ariane*. Stars: Gary Cooper, Audrey Hepburn, Maurice Chevalier.

1958 *Teacher's Pet* (120 minutes).
Director: George Seaton. Screenplay: Fay and Michael Kanin. Stars: Clark Gable, Gig Young, Mamie Van Doren, Nick Adams.

1958 *Indiscreet* (100 minutes).
Director: Stanley Donen. Screenplay: Norman Krasna, from his play *Kind Sir*. Stars: Cary Grant, Ingrid Bergman, Cecil Parker, Phyllis Calvert.

1958 *Houseboat* (112 minutes).
Director: Melville Shavelson. Screenplay: Melville Shavelson, Jack Rose. Stars: Cary Grant, Sophia Loren.

1959 *North by Northwest* (136 minutes).
Director: Alfred Hitchcock. Screenplay: Ernest Lehman. Stars: Cary Grant, Eva Marie Saint, James Mason, Jessie Royce Landis.

1959 *Pillow Talk* (110 minutes).
Director: Michael Gordon. Screenplay: Stanley Shapiro, Maurice Richlin. Stars: Rock Hudson, Doris Day, Tony Randall, Thelma Ritter.

1960 *It Started in Naples* (100 minutes).
Director/Screenplay: Melville Shavelson. Stars: Clark Gable, Sophia Loren, Vittorio De Sica.

1962 *That Touch of Mink* (99 minutes).
Director: Delbert Mann. Screenplay: Stanley Shapiro, Nate Monaster. Stars: Cary Grant, Doris Day, Gig Young, Audrey Meadows.

1963 *The Courtship of Eddie's Father* (118 minutes).
Director: Vincente Minnelli. Screenplay: John Gay, from the Mark Toby novel. Stars: Glenn Ford, Shirley Jones, Stella Stevens, Dina Merrill, Roberta Sherwood, Ronny Howard, Jerry Van Dyke.

1963 *The Thrill of It All* (107 minutes).
Director: Norman Jewison. Screenplay: Carl Reiner. Stars: Doris Day, James Garner, Arlene Francis.

1963 *Charade* (113 minutes).
Director: Stanley Donen. Screenplay: Peter Stone. Stars: Cary Grant, Audrey Hepburn, Walter Matthau, James Coburn, George Kennedy, Ned Glass.

1966 *The Glass Bottom Boat* (110 minutes).
Director: Frank Tashlin. Screenplay: Everett Freman.

Stars: Doris Day, Rod Taylor, Arthur Godfrey, John McGiver, Paul Lynde.

1967 *Barefoot in the Park* (105 minutes).
Director: Gene Saks. Screenplay: Neil Simon, from his play. Stars: Robert Redford, Jane Fonda, Charles Boyer.

1977 *Annie Hall* (93 minutes).
Director: Woody Allen. Screenplay: Allen, Marshall Brickman. Stars: Woody Allen, Diane Keaton, Tony Roberts, Carol Kane, Paul Simon, Shelley Duvall.

1978 *Heaven Can Wait* (100 minutes).
Director: Warren Beatty, Buck Henry. Screenplay: Elaine May, Warren Beatty. Stars: Beatty, Julie Christie, James Mason, Jack Warden, Charles Grodin, Dyan Cannon, Buck Henry.

1979 *Manhattan* (96 minutes).
Director: Woody Allen. Screenplay: Woody Allen, Marshall Brickman. Stars: Allen, Diane Keaton, Michael Murphy, Mariel Hemingway, Meryl Streep.

1979 *10* (122 minutes).
Director/Screenplay: Blake Edwards. Stars: Dudley Moore, Julie Andrews, Bo Derek.

1985 *The Sure Thing* (94 minutes).
Director: Rob Reiner. Screenplay: Steven L. Bloom, Jonathan Roberts. Stars: John Cusack, Daphne Zuniga, Anthony Edwards, Boyd Gaines, Tim Robbins.

1985 *Better Off Dead* (98 minutes).
Director/Screenplay: Savage Steve Holland. Stars: John Cusack, David Ogden Stiers, Kim Darby, Demian Slade.

1986 *Legal Eagles* (114 minutes).
Director: Ivan Reitman. Screenplay: Jim Cash, Jack Epps, Jr. Stars: Robert Redford, Debra Winger, Daryl Hannah, Brian Dennehy, Terence Stamp.

1987 *Roxanne* (107 minutes).
Director: Fred Schepisi. Screenplay: Steve Martin, update of

Cyrano de Bergerac. Stars: Steve Martin, Daryl Hannah, Rick Rossovich, Shelley Duvall.

1987 *Moonstruck* (102 minutes).
Director: Norman Jewison. Screenplay: John Patrick Shanley. Stars: Cher, Nicolas Cage, Vincent Gardenia, Olympia Dukakis, Danny Aiello.

1989 *When Harry Met Sally . . .* (95 minutes).
Director: Rob Reiner. Screenplay: Nora Ephron. Stars: Billy Crystal, Meg Ryan, Carrie Fisher, Bruno Kirby.

1990 *Pretty Woman* (117 minutes).
Director: Garry Marshall. Screenplay: J. F. Lawron. Stars: Richard Gere, Julia Roberts, Ralph Bellamy, Jason Alexander, Laura San Giacomo, Hector Elizondo.

1993 *Benny & Joon* (98 minutes).
Director: Jeremiah Chechik. Screenplay: Barry Berman. Stars: Johnny Depp, Mary Stuart Masterson, Aidan Quinn, Julianne Moore, Oliver Platt.

1993 *Sleepless in Seattle* (104 minutes).
Director: Nora Ephron. Screenplay: Nora Ephron, David S. Ward, Jeff Arch. Stars: Tom Hanks, Meg Ryan, Bill Pullman, Ross Malinger, Rosie O'Donnell, Gaby Hoffman, Victor Garber, Rita Wilson, Rob Reiner.

1994 *Love Affair* (108 minutes).
Director: Glenn Gordon Caron. Screenplay: Robert Towne, Warren Beatty, based on the 1939 Leo McCarey movie *Love Affair*. Stars: Warren Beatty, Annette Bening, Katharine Hepburn, Gary Shandling.

1994 *I.Q.* (95 minutes).
Director: Fred Schepisi. Screenplay: Andy Breckman, Michael Leeson. Stars: Tim Robbins, Meg Ryan, Walter Matthau, Lou Jacobi, Gene Saks.

1995 *Don Juan Demarco* (90 minutes).
Director/Screenplay: Jeremy Leven. Stars: Marlon Brando, Johnny Depp, Faye Dunaway.

1995 *The American President* (113 minutes).
Director: Rob Reiner. Screenplay: Aaron Sorkin. Stars: Michael Douglas, Annette Bening, Martin Sheen, Michael J. Fox.

1996 *If Lucy Fell* (94 minutes).
Director/Screenplay: Eric Schaeffer. Stars: Eric Schaeffer, Sarah Jessica Parker, Ben Stiller, Elle Macpherson, Dominic Chianese.

1996 *The Truth about Cats & Dogs* (97 minutes).
Director: Michael Lehmann. Screenplay: Audrey Wells. Stars: Uma Thurman, Janeane Garofalo, Ben Chaplin.

1996 *Jerry Maguire* (138 minutes).
Director/Screenplay: Cameron Crowe. Stars: Tom Cruise, Cuba Gooding Jr., Renée Zellweger, Kelly Preston.

1996 *One Fine Day* (108 minutes).
Director: Michael Hoffman. Screenplay: Terrel Seltzer, Ellen Simon. Stars: Michelle Pfeiffer, George Clooney, Mae Whitman, Alex D. Linz, Charles Durning.

1997 *Addicted to Love* (100 minutes).
Director: Griffin Dunne. Screenplay: Robert Gordon. Stars: Meg Ryan, Matthew Broderick, Kelly Preston.

1997 *As Good As It Gets* (138 minutes).
Director: James L. Brooks. Screenplay: James L. Brooks, Mark Andrus. Stars: Jack Nicholson, Helen Hunt, Greg Kinnear, Cuba Gooding Jr.

1998 *The Wedding Singer* (96 minutes).
Director: Frank Coraci. Screenplay: Tim Herlihy. Stars: Adam Sandler, Drew Barrymore.

1998 *You've Got Mail* (110 minutes).
Director: Nora Ephron. Screenplay: Nora Ephron, Delia Ephron, based upon Ernst Lubitsch's *The Shop around the Corner*. Stars: Tom Hanks, Meg Ryan, Parker Posey, Jean Stapleton, Greg Kinnear, Dabney Coleman.

1999 *The Other Sister* (129 minutes).
Director: Garry Marshall. Screenplay: Alexandra Rose, Blair Richwood. Stars: Juliette Lewis, Diane Keaton, Tom Skerritt, Giovanni Ribisi.

1999 *Never Been Kissed* (107 minutes).
Director: Raja Gosnell. Screenplay: Abby Kahn, Marc Silverstein. Stars: Drew Barrymore, David Arquette, Michael Vartan, Molly Shannon.

2000 *What Women Want* (126 minutes).
Director: Nancy Meyers. Screenplay: Josh Goldsmith, Cathy Yuspa. Stars: Mel Gibson, Helen Hunt, Alan Alda.

2000 *High Fidelity* (113 minutes).
Director: Stephen Frears. Screenplay: D. V. DeVincentis, Steve Pink, John Cusack, Scott Rosenberg, based on the Nick Hornby novel. Stars: John Cusack, Iben Hjejle, Todd Louiso, Jack Black, Lisa Bonet, Catherine Zeta-Jones, Joan Cusack, Tim Robbins.

2000 *If You Only Knew* (110 minutes).
Director: David Snedeker. Screenplay: Gary Goldstein. Stars: Alison Eastwood, Johnathan Schaech.

SELECTED ANNOTATED BIBLIOGRAPHY

With a few exceptions, this selected annotated bibliography is limited to book-length studies that devote all, or an appreciable amount of space, to screwball and/or romantic comedy. The accent is on comedy overviews rather than studies of individual artists. But examples of the latter approach are well documented in the numerous notes at the end of each chapter in this text. Please peruse these sites for literally *hundreds* of additional documents. However, *no* references were discovered that attempted to distinguish between romantic and screwball comedy.

Bergman, Andrew.
We're in the Money: Depression America and Its Films. New York: Harper & Row, 1972. (This valuable text was the basis of writer/director Bergman's Ph.D. dissertation. Unfortunately, it is the source of a misleading chapter connecting the post–*It Happened One Night* Capra to screwball comedy.)

Bernheimer, Kathryn.
The 50 Funniest Movies of All Time: A Critic's Ranking. Secaucus, N.J.: Carol Publishing, 1999. (Includes several informative chapters on individual films central to both screwball and romantic comedy.)

Bogdanovich, Peter.
Who the Devil Made It: Conversations with Legendary Film Directors. New York: Ballantine Books, 1997. (Film director/author Bogdanovich's most valuable book, with interviews pertinent to both screwball and romantic comedy.)

Byrge, Duane, and Robert Milton Miller.
The Screwball Comedy Films: A History and Filmography, 1934–1942. Jefferson, N.C.: McFarland, 1991. (A short but pivotal look at the genre—very well researched.)

Byron, Stuart, and Elisabeth Weis (eds).
The National Society of Film Critics on Movie Comedy. New York: Penguin Books, 1977. (An excellent anthology with numerous essays on individual films central to both romantic and screwball comedy.)

Cavell, Stanley.
Pursuits of Happiness: The Hollywood Comedy of Remarriage. Cambridge, Mass.: Harvard University Press, 1981. (Provocative look at screwball comedy, but his points sometimes seem forced.)

DiBattista, Maria.
Fast-Talking Dames. New Haven: Yale University Press, 2001. (Entertaining look at key comedy actresses of the 1930s and 1940s, but it avoids the issue of screwball versus romantic comedy.)

Durgnat, Raymond.
The Crazy Mirror: Hollywood Comedy and the American Image. New York: A Delta Book, 1972. (A pioneering look at American film comedy with several still pertinent chapters to romantic and screwball comedy.)

Gehring, Wes D.
Leo McCarey and the Comic Anti-Hero in American Film. New York: Arno Press, 1980. (The ties between McCarey and the antihero figure of American pop culture are extensively examined.)

Gehring, Wes D.
Screwball Comedy: Defining a Film Genre. Muncie: Ball State University Monograph Series, 1983. (This was the foundation for my later Greenwood Press book on the subject.)

Gehring, Wes D.
Screwball Comedy: A Genre of Madcap Romance. Westport, Conn.: Greenwood Press, 1986. (The genre is examined as an outgrowth of the comic antihero in American humor.)

Gehring, Wes D. (ed. and chief contributor).
Hardbook of American Film Genres. Westport, Conn.: Greenwood Press, 1988. (Individual chapters on screwball comedy, populism, and dark comedy first target several issues further addressed in this text.)

Gehring, Wes D.
Populism and the Capra Legacy. Westport, Conn.: Greenwood Press, 1995. (A book-length study of why the majority of Capra's celebrated work from the 1930s and 1940s should be placed under the populist banner, *not* screwball comedy.)

Gehring, Wes D.
Dark Comedy: Beyond Satire. Westport, Conn.: Greenwood Press, 1996. (Periodic examination of films that qualify as both dark *and* screwball comedies, such as *Harold and Maude*.)

Gehring, Wes D.
The World of Comedy. Davenport, Ia.: Robin-Vincent Publishing, 2001. (A general overview on genres of film comedy, including chapters on populism and screwball comedy.)

Grant, Barry K. (ed.).
Film Genre: Theory and Criticism. Metuchen, N.J.: Scarecrow Press, Inc., 1977. (The Jim Leach chapter on screwball comedy is pivotal to both a better understanding of the genre and why Capra should *not* be associated with the genre.)

Harvey, James.
Romantic Comedy in Hollywood: From Lubitsch to Sturges. 1987; rpt. New York: Da Capo Press, 1998. (This is a valuable reference text, but it makes *no* distinction between screwball and romantic comedy. It is also egocentric that in the 716 pages there are neither footnotes nor a bibliography.)

Haskell, Molly.
From Reverence to Rape: The Treatment of Women in the Movies. Chicago: University of Chicago Press, 1987. (A pioneering gender study with frequent ties to romantic and screwball comedy.)

Jenkins, Henry.
What Made Pistachio Nuts: Early Sound Comedy and the Vaudeville Aesthetic. New York: Columbia University Press, 1992. (Occasionally insightful observations on screwball comedy.)

Kael, Pauline.
When the Lights Go Down. New York: Holt, Rinehart and Winston, 1980. (Contains Kael's pivotal 1975 essay on Cary Grant, "The Man from Dream City.")

Kendall, Elizabeth.
The Runaway Bride: Hollywood Romantic Comedy of the 1930s. New York: Knopf, 1990. (A good read but it does *not* attempt to differentiate between romantic and screwball comedy.)

Mast, Gerald.
The Comic Mind: Comedy and the Movies. Indianapolis: Bobbs-Merrill, 1973. (A landmark film comedy study that addresses some screwball and romantic comedy topics.)

McCaffrey, Donald W.
The Golden Age of Sound Comedy: Comic Films and Comedians of the Thirties. New York: A. S. Barnes, 1973. (A pioneering look at all forms of 1930s screen comedy.)

Rosen, Marjorie.
Popcorn Venus: Women, Movies and the American Dream. New York: Avon Books, 1974. (Another early look at women in film that also examines numerous movies central to screwball and romantic comedy.)

Rowe, Kathleen.
The Unruly Woman: Gender and the Genres of Laughter. Austin: University of Texas Press, 1995. (A provocatively entertaining study that examines both television and movie comedy, and includes an impressive bibliography.)

Sennett, Ted.
Lunatics and Lovers. New Rochelle, N.Y.: Arlington House, 1971. (Pioneering work on screwball comedy but overly general in content. It works best as a reference instead of a theory text on genre.)

Sennett, Ted.
Laughing in the Dark: Movie Comedy from Groucho to Woody. New York: St. Martin's Press, 1992. (Sennett takes his comedy expertise to a broader canvas.)

Sikov, Ed.
SCREWBALL: Hollywood's Madcap Romantic Comedies. New York: Crown, 1989. (Though including a winning text, the numerous lush stills are the selling point for this book. But it does not distinguish between romantic and screwball comedy.)

Weales, Gerald.
Canned Goods As Caviar: American Film Comedy of the 1930s. Chicago: University of Chicago Press, 1985. (Like its inspired title, borrowed from director William Wellman, this wonderful text has several individual chapters devoted to key screwball comedies.)

INDEX

Adam's Rib, 79, *81*, 89, 94, 130–134, 137
Addicted to Love, 80, 88
An Affair to Remember, 22, 25, 71, 76, 83, 104–105, 115, 116, 168
Affleck, Ben, 160–161, 162
The African Queen, 98, 130, 134–35, 136, *137*, 138
Allen, Woody, 25, 78–79, 88, 114, 175
All of Me, 23, 42, 146, 153–154, 157, 171
An American President, 25
America's Sweethearts, 147, 151–152, 155, 163
Analyze This, 157–158
Andrews, Julie, 23, 46, 87, 166, 176
Annie Hall, 25, 79
Arsenic and Old Lace, 107
Arthur, 3, 23, 30, 38–39, 42, 148
Arthur, Jean, 12, 20, 41, 49, *51*, 52
As Good As It Gets, 25, 67, 73, 180–181, 182
Auer, Mischa, 52
The Awful Truth, 21, 60, 64, 85; Irene Dunne and, 12, 29, 53–54, *55*, 109, 117, 161; Cary Grant and, 35–36, *55*, 107, *109*, 123, 185; Leo McCarey and, 19, 30, 41, 56, 57, 61–62, 63, 100–101, 103, 104, 115, 156
Ayres, Lew, 38

Bachelor and the Bobby-Soxer, The, 72, 98, 112
Ball of Fire, 31, 33, 106
Barefoot in the Park, 24
Barry, Philip, 125, 130, 135
Barrymore, Drew, 68, 78, 159, 170–171
Barrymore, John, 7, 9, 11
Bazin, André, 133, 140
Beatty, Warren, 75
Bellamy, Ralph, 12, 52, 53, 54, 61–62, 64, 69, 100, 101
Benchley, Robert, 1, 18, 38
Bennett, Constance, *17*, 18, 107
Benny, Jack, 20
Benny & Joon, 75–76, 176, 177–179, 180, 187
Bergman, Andrew, 5, 158
Bergson, Henri, 32–34, 114–115

Better Off Dead, 76
Biberman, Abner, 61
The Bishop's Wife, 98, 111–112
Bluebeard's Eighth Wife, 37, 152
Bogart, Humphrey, 134–135, *136*, 137
Bogdanovich, Peter, 23, 31, 34, 46, 61, 103, 105, 159, 188
Boyer, Charles, 3, 19, 62–63, 69–70, *77*, 104
Bridget Jones's Diary, 146, 147, 151, 157
Bringing Up Baby, 2, 3, 15, 35, 42, 57, 94, 120, 188; Cary Grant and, 8, 21, 23, 31, 36, 37, 45, 56, 107, 165–166; Katharine Hepburn and, 1, 9, 48, 87, 93, 97, 120–121
Broderick, Matthew, 80, 88
Brooks, James L., 67
Bullock, Sandra, 24, 159–161, 162
Bunny, John, 59

Cage, Nicolas, 76, 78, 158–159
Capra, Frank, 5, 12, 60, 69, 82, 107
Catholic Legion of Decency, 6
Chaplin, Charlie, 6, 54, 57–58, 59, 177, 187
Charade, 111, 114, 115
Cher, 78
Chevalier, Maurice, 72
Cleese, John, 145, 146, 157
Clooney, George, 85
Cobb, Irvin S., *102*
Coburn, Charles, 20, 72, 73
Colbert, Claudette, 5, 7, *37*, 44, 45, *82*, 83, 152, 188
Cooper, Gary, 12, 31, 37, 152
The Courtship of Eddie's Father, 84
Cruise, Tom, 84, 88
Crystal, Billy, 3–4, 25, 67, 86, 93, 147, 155, 156
Cukor, George, 29, 105, *106*, 123, 127
Curtis, Richard, 146
Curtis, Tony, 21, 114
Cusack, Joan, 153, 166
Cusack, John, 75, 76, 78, 87–88, 151–152, 156, 163, 175

D'Arcy, Alexander, 53–54, 55, *58*
Day, Doris, 22, 24, 116, 117–118
Dean, Dizzy, 8
Depp, Johnny, 176, 177–179, 187
DeSica, Vittorio, 72
The Desk Set, 98, 130, 138, 139
Dixon, Jean, 38
Donen, Stanley, 100
Don Juan DeMarco, 176, 178–179
Douglas, Melvyn, 30, 36, 41, 44
Driver, Minnie, 72, 76
Duchovny, David, 72, 76, 88, 92
Duck Soup, 5, 15, 16
Dunne, Irene, 3, 10, 36, 39–41, 42, 44, 48, 50–51, 108, 115, 123, 124; *The Awful Truth* and, 12, 29, 43, 53–54, 55, 58, 61–62, 100–101, 105, *109*, 161, 185; *Love Affair* and, 19, 69–70, 74, 75, 77, 84

Easy Living, 29
Edwards, Blake, 23, 41–42, 46, 47, 54, 152, 166, 175

Elizondo, Hector, 73, 74
Ephron, Nora, 25, 67, 68, 72, 75, 139, 168–169, 174, 175, 181
Ewell, Tom, 79, 80, 133, 134
Ex-Mrs. Bradford, The, 14, 49, 50, *51*, 52

Fields, Sally, 24, 73
Fields, W. C., 5
Fish Called Wanda, A, 145, 157
Fonda, Henry, 31, 37, 44, 46, 50, 51, 60, 110, 148, *149*
Forces of Nature, 24, 159–162
Four's a Crowd, 53
Four Weddings and a Funeral, 146, 147, 150

Gable, Clark, 5, 7, 22, *82*, 83, 84, 151, 163
Garbo, Greta, 3, 44
Garner, James, 23, 24, 46, 73, 166
Garofalo, Janeane, 77, 173
Gere, Richard, 2, 74, 86, 91, 153, 164–165, 176
Gibson, Mel, 25, 85, 91, 93, 171–172
Gielgud, John, 23, 30, 38
Gilbert, Billy, 52
Gordon, Ruth, 132, 151
Gordon, Steve, 23
Grant, Cary, 19, 20, 23, 24, 33, 38, 42–43, 56–59, 84, 97–144, *106*, *113*, 149, 186; *The Awful Truth* and, 30, 53–54, *55*, 102–104, 107, *109*, 111, 118, 185; *Bringing Up Baby* and, 1, 8, 21, 31, 34, 37, 45, 57, 92, 93, *125*, 165–166; *His Girl Friday*, 52, 53, 61, 64, 107; *My Favorite Wife* and, 39–41, 42, 49, 50–51, 148; *The Philadelphia Story* and, 89, 92–93, *99*, 125–126, 185; *Topper* and, *17*, 18, 170, 171
Grant, Hugh, 85–86, 91, 146, 147, 149, 150, 163–164

Hagen, Jean, 134
Haliburton, Thomas Chandler, 47
Hands across the Table, 69, *70*, 80, 86
Hanks, Tom, 25, 73, 76, 85, 86, 90–91, 92, 114, 169, 187
Harlow, Jean, 6
Hatch, Eric, 48
Hawks, Howard, 7, 8, 10, 33, 100, 106–107, 116, 117, 187; *Bringing Up Baby* and, 23, 31, 45–46, 107; *I Was a Male War Bride* and, 20–21, 56–57; *Monkey Business* and, 20–21, 42–43, 61
Hawn, Goldie, 35, 54
Heaven Can Wait, 75
Hecht, Ben, 9, 63
Hepburn, Audrey, 3, 72, 76, 115
Hepburn, Katharine, 20, 38, 71, 84, 97–144, *99*, *106*; *Adam's Rib* and, 79–80, *81*, 94; *Bringing Up Baby* and, 1, 9, 34, 48, 56, 87, 92–93, 124, *125*, 131, 161, 165, 185
High Fidelity, 75, 78, 94
His Girl Friday, 8, 52, 53, 61, 64, 107, 188

Holiday, 29, 38, *106*, 120–121, *122*, 123, 124, 125, 154
Holliday, Judy, 79, 80, 133, 134
Honeymoon in Vegas, 157–159
Hooper, Johnson J., 47
Horton, Edward Everett, 38
Houseboat, 22, 84
House Sitter, 24, 146, 160
Hudson, Rock, 23, 45, 106
Hunt, Bonnie, 72
Hunt, Helen, 73, 91, 93, 172, 180–181, 182

If Lucy Fell, 72, 76–77, 79, 88
If You Only Knew, 172–174
I Married A Witch, 29, 49
In & Out, 164, 166
Indiscreet, 111, 117
I.Q., 73, 172, 173
Iron Petticoat, 98, 138
Irreconcilable Differences, 159, 163, 188
It Happened One Night, *xxii*, 5, 7, 11–12, 81, *82*, 87, 151, 163
It Started in Naples, 22, 72, 84
I Was a Male War Bride, 20, 43, 56, 59, 97

Jerry Maguire, 84, 88

Kael, Pauline, 108, 109, 110, 112, 161
Kahn, Madeline, 54, 68
Kanin, Garson, 103–104, 132, 140
Karras, Alex, 47, 166
Keaton, Buster, 6, 56–57, 177, 187
Keaton, Diane, 79, 175
Krasna, Norman, 73

LaCava, Gregory, 15, 16
The Lady Eve, 19, 31, 43–44, 50, 51, 52, 110, 148, *149*, 188
Lady in a Jam, 12, 21
Landis, Carole, 46, 50
L. A. Story, 154–155, 156
Laurel and Hardy, 6, 39, 52, 74, 103; Leo McCarey and, 4, 10, 11, 15–16, 41, 54, 55, 108
Legal Eagles, 24
Leisen, Mitchell, 29
Lloyd, Harold, 6, 56, 60, 187
Loggia, Robert, 72
Lombard, Carole, 7, *9*, 11, 20, 124, 147, 160, 188; *Hands across the Table* and, 69, *70*, 80, 86; *My Man Godfrey* and, 3, 8, 16, 34, 48, 155
Love Affair (1939), 2, 76, 89, 92, 93–94; Irene Dunne and, 3, *77*, 170; Leo McCarey and, 18–19, 69–70, 83, 104–105
Love Affair (1994), 2, 24, 71, 76
Love in the Afternoon, 22, 72
Loy, Myrna, *13*, 14, 72, 112, *113*
Lubitsch, Ernst, 1–2, 19–20, 22, 189

MacMurray, Fred, 20, 38, 41, 46, 49, 69, *70*
Mad Miss Manton, 49
Mad Wednesday. *See The Sin of Harold Diddlebook*

Major and the Minor, The, 33, 62–63
Man's Favorite Sport?, 23, 45, 106, 187
Marshall, Garry, 25, 153–162, 179–180, 187, 188
Martin, Dean, 75
Martin, Steve, 23, 42, 78, 146, 153–155, 156, 157, 171, 188
Marx Brothers, 5, 6, 8, 15, 16, 64–65, 74, 103, 128
Masterson, Mary Stuart, 76, 176, 177–179, 180
Matthau, Walter, 73, 173
McCarey, Leo, 19, 46, 47, 83–84, 85, *102*, 114, 123, 152; *The Awful Truth* and, 30–31, 35–36, 54–57, *58*, 62–63, 100–104, 105, 107, 109–111, 118, 156; Laurel and Hardy and, 4, 10, 11, 15–16, 41, 54, 55, 108; *Love Affair* and, 18, 69, 181; Marx Brother and, 5, 15–16; *My Favorite Wife* and, 38, 40–43, 63, 108, 156
McCrea, Joel, *37*, 45
Mickey Blue Eyes, 150, 157–158
Micki and Maude, 23, 41–42, 148
Midnight, 44
Milland, Ray, 33
Minnelli, Liza, 42, 148
The Miracle of Morgan's Creek, 19, 59, 60, 147
Mr. Deeds Goes to Town, 12, 60
Monkey Business, 20–21, 31, 61, 97, 110
Monroe, Marilyn, 21
Moonstruck, 76, 78
Moore, Dudley, 24, 42, 75, 87, 88, 148, 149, 150, 175–176; *Arthur* and, 23, 30, 38–39, 147
The More the Merrier, 20, 72
Murphy's Romance, 24, 73
My Best Friend's Wedding, 24, 159, 161–162, 166
My Favorite Wife, 30, 39–41, 44, 49, 50–51, 63, 108, 123, 148
My Man Godfrey, 2, 14–15, 21, 51, 52, 63; Carole Lombard and, 3, 8, *16*, 34, 48, 53, 155

Never Been Kissed, 68, 78
The Next Best Thing, 167
Nicholson, Jack, 176–177, 180–181
A Night at the Opera, 15
Ninotchka, 3, 10, 138
North by Northwest, 114, 115–116
Nothing Sacred, 3, 9
Notting Hill, 25, 85–86, 91, 146, 147, 148, 149, 155, 163, 164

The Object of My Affection, 167
O'Connor, Carroll, 72
Once Upon a Honeymoon, 19–20
O'Neal, Ryan, 31, 43, 46, 68, 105, 147, 187
One Fine Day, 85
The Other Sister, 176, 179–180, 187

Pallette, Eugene, 52
The Palm Beach Story, 1, 9, 12, 19, 21, 36, 44–45, 94

Pat and Mike, 22, 124, 130, 137, 138
Patrick, Gail, 39, 42, 51
Philadelphia Story, The, 20, 89, 92–93, 97, 98, *99*, 119, 125–126, 185
Pillow Talk, 24
Powell, William, *13*, 14, *16*, 34, *51*, 52, 53
Prentiss, Paula, 23, 45
Pretty Woman, 2, 25, 73–74, 86, 88, 91, 176
Princess O'Rourke, 73

Redford, Robert, 24, 25, 92, 114
Reiner, Rob, 25, 86, 87, 114
Renoir, Jean, 109–110
Return to Me, 72, 76, 88, 92
Ritz Brothers, 6–7
Roach, Hal, 46
Robbins, Tim, 73, 173, 175
Roberts, Julia, 2, 24, 25, 74, 149, 151–153, 156, 157–158, 159, 161–162, 163, 164–166
Rogers, Ginger, 19, 21, 33, 62
Rogers, Will, 64
Roosevelt, Franklin D., 5, 73
Roxanne, 78
Ruggles, Charles, 34, 35
Ruggles of Red Gap, 35
Runaway Bride, 25, 147, 151, 152–153, 156, 164–165, 188
Russell, Rosalind, 8, 10, 38, 52, 53
Ryan, Meg, 4, 25, 73, 80, 88, 90, 91, 92, 169, 173, 176, 180, 181
Ryskind, Morrie, 15, 16

Sabrina (1954), 3, 22, 76
Sandler, Adam, 75, 169–171
Schaeffer, Eric, 79, 88
Scott, Randolph, 44
Seems Like Old Times, 23, 35, 54
Shearer, Norma, 6
Shillaber, B. P., 47
The Shop around the Corner, 1, 68, 76, 80–81, 86, 89, *90*, 139
Simon, Neil, 23, 35
The Sin of Harold Diddlebock, 60
Six of a Kind, 41
Sleepless in Seattle, 68, 72, 74–75, 76, 84, 85, 86, 92, 94, 114, 168, 181, 187
Smith, H. Allen, 104
Smith, Thorne, 17, 46
Some Like It Hot, 21, 114, 158
Standing Room Only, 20
Stanwyck, Barbara, 37, 44, 49, 50, 51, 60, 148, *149*
Stevens, George, 10–11, 20, 46, 81, 100, 129–130
Stewart, Jimmy, 33, 86–87, 89, *90*, 91, 93, *99*, 125–126, 188
Streisand, Barbra, 2, 33–34, 43
Sturges, Preston, 1, 9, 19, 21, 23, 36, 43–44, 46, 59–60, 94, 147
Sullavan, Margaret, 1–2, 89, *90*
The Sure Thing, 87–88
Switch, 47

Take a Letter, Darling, 38, 46
Teacher's Pet, 22, 117–118
Temple, Shirley, 112, *113*
10, 87, 175–176

That Touch of Mink, 24, 117–118
Theodora Goes Wild, 3, 30, 35, 36, 44, 111
The Thin Man, *13*, 14, 35–36, 51–52
Thurber, James, 4, 18, 35, 46, 48, 115, 150–151, 156
To Catch a Thief, 114
Tomlin, Lily, 23, 42, 146, 154, 171
Too Many Husbands, 41, 49
Topper, *17*, 18, 30, 42, 49, 107, 146, 171, 172
Topper Returns, 49
Topper Takes a Trip, 49
Tracy, Spencer, 79–80, *81*, 84, 89, 94, 126–130, *131*, 132–134, 136–140
True Confession, 49, 63, 146, 147, 160
The Truth about Cats and Dogs, 77, 172, 173
Turnabout, 46, 49
Twentieth Century, 7, 11–12, 14, 47, 63

Unfaithfully Yours (1983), 23, 148

Victor/Victoria, 23, 46

Wayne, David, 80, 133, 134
The Wedding Singer, 75, 169–171
Wheeler and Woolsey, 6
Whitcher, Frances M., 47
Wilder, Billy, 10, 21, 22, 33, 49, 62, 158
Without Love, 20, 130, *131*, 135, 138, 139, 140
What's Up, Doc?, 2, 23, 31, 43, 46, 54, 68, 105, 147, 156
What Women Want, 25–26, 85, 91, 93, 171
When Harry Met Sally . . ., 4, 25, 67, 71–72, 86, 88, 93, 95, 139, 174–175
Woman of the Year, 20, 81, 84, 89, 126–130, 135

Young, Roland, *17*, 18
You've Got Mail, 1, 3, 68, 84, 86, 90, 91, 94, 139, 169–170, 181, 187

Zellweger, Renee, 84, 88, 146, 151

ABOUT THE AUTHOR

Wes D. Gehring is professor of film at Ball State University and an associate media editor of *USA Today Magazine.* He is the author of sixteen critically acclaimed books, including individual volumes on the comedy genres of populism, parody, personality comedian, dark comedy, and screwball comedy. His other books include biographies of Charlie Chaplin, the Marx Brothers, Laurel and Hardy, Robert Benchley, W. C. Fields, Red Skelton, and forthcoming volumes on Irene Dunne and Carole Lombard. His articles and poems have appeared in numerous journals.